NEW DIRECTIONS
IN SOCIOLOGICAL THEORY

318-1B- 187

NEW DIRECTIONS IN SOCIOLOGICAL THEORY

Paul Filmer

Michael Phillipson

David Silverman

David Walsh

COLLIER-MACMILLAN PUBLISHERS
A DIVISION OF
CROWELL, COLLIER AND MACMILLAN
PUBLISHERS LIMITED
LONDON

Collier-Macmillan Publishers
A Division of Crowell, Collier and Macmillan
Publishers Limited
London
First printing 1972
© Collier-Macmillan 1972

Printed in Great Britain by
C. Tinling & Co Ltd, Prescot and London

CONTENTS

PART TWO PHENOMENOLOGICAL ALTERNATIVES

Examines the main themes of phenomenology and their implications
for a sociology concerned with both form and content.
Ethnomethodology is introduced and the chapter concludes with a
discussion of the problem of validity and of the limitations of
sociology.

Characterizes "folk sociology" in terms of a reliance on commonsense
views of social order and examines an alternative view which sees
man as a practical theoretician and examines order as the outcome of
everyday interpretive work. The second part of the chapter illustrates
this theme with examples from conversational analysis and the study
of organizations.

Restates the previous analysis in more specifically methodological
terms by means of a distinction between the social world as a topic
for study and as a resource for explanations. Ethnomethodology is
discussed as a method of explanation focusing on the process of
interpretation.

Presents some major aspects of the ethnomethodological perspective
implied in the previous chapters. By reference to the work of
Garfinkel, the problematic and potentialities of ethnomethodology
are outlined and its points of contact with Lévi-Strauss's
structuralism and Chomskyan linguistics are discussed.

FOREWORD

This book consists of working papers which are the upshot of a series of seminars at Goldsmiths' College directed towards the highly unsatisfactory features of sociology as it has been traditionally conceived by its practitioners. From the outset, however, our intention has been to base a constructive pedagogy on the analysis that was formulated from our discontent. Moreover, we wanted this analysis to provide us with a basis for a positive and active sociological analysis, and the viability of traditional sociology to provide this was a central feature of our common concern.

While each of the papers, then, remains the individual responsibility of its author, they manifest a considerable degree of interrelationship in the sense that the book is a collaborative enterprise addressed to a radical reorientation of sociology. A primary feature of this reorientation is the adoption of a phenomenological perspective.

The authors wish to express their gratitude for the advice (not always followed) and encouragement of Aaron Cicourel, Maurice Roche, Alan Segal, and Roy Turner. They have also benefited considerably from their discussions with various colleagues and students, particularly Eddy Brunsden, Gordon Buchanan, Ken Cook, Joan Dulchin, Julia Hauxwell, Maryan Jeffery, Nell Keddie, Peter Lobel and Bill Richards. However, they wish to point out that they alone remain responsible for the contents and shortcomings of the book itself.

There's nowt so queer as folk.

OLD LANCASHIRE SAYING

Part I   An Analysis of Traditional Sociology

ONE

Introductory Comments

DAVID SILVERMAN

Any work entitled *New Directions in Sociological Theory* needs two kinds of initial justification. First, it must justify itself in a context in which, at least as far as British sociology is concerned, there has been far too much *talk* about theory and far too little *theorizing*. Second, it must establish a firm enough critique of what has gone before, to convince the reader that there is a case worth answering and that the "new directions" offered are genuinely new—in the sense of holding out the prospect of styles of theorizing which, rather than being half-baked "modifications" of existing positions, constitute alternative and convincing postures. Whether, indeed, another work which simply "talks" about theory (without reference to research materials) can be justified will depend upon how far our sense of the failings of contemporary sociology expresses (as we believe) a widely-held feeling of unease. It will also depend upon the extent to which the analysis of the data which the authors are currently gathering in a variety of studies can exemplify and support the arguments made in this book.[1]

This present work is an outcome of a series of seminars at Goldsmiths' College, which in turn were the outcome of the dissatisfaction of many staff and students with what we took to be the main features of contemporary British sociology. On the principle that it is better to test the water before diving into what may turn out to be a cold and unenjoyable bath, I offer at the outset of this chapter a brief list of these dissatisfactions so that the reader may judge whether

---

[1] These include studies of practical reasoning in an administrative organization, of natural language among opera buffs, and the acquisition of interpretive rules by young children. For an example, see Silverman and Jones (forthcoming).

he thinks the subsequent arguments worth following. In particular we seek to criticize:

(1) A view of theory as something constructed and negotiated from the armchair and presented to students as something quite separate from an understanding of the everyday world.

(2) A view of methodology as a set of techniques to be used to catch the unchanging properties of a "solid" factual world.

(3) A reliance on the unexplicated assumptions of commonsense knowledge expressed in a preparedness to impute "reasonable" motives to actors and to make phenomena non-problematic in terms of "what everybody knows".

(4) An absence of philosophical sophistication in focusing on "things" taken to be unquestionably obvious within a world through which our mind can roam at will.[2]

On a more positive note, one aim of this book is to introduce the reader to alternative views of the nature and tasks of contemporary sociology. Since the existing literature is scattered and generally taken to be difficult, a further aim is to make available in one volume an intelligible and coherent presentation of the field. The authors have no interest in communicating solely with themselves or with others who have been able to pick up the necessary jargon; their intention is to create an informed and, hopefully, enthusiastic audience and to stimulate others to debate and participate.[3]

This second aim is, I take it, all the more necessary given the apparent bewilderment sometimes produced by the more or less opaque character of much of the literature in the area. It is easy to abandon further interest when faced, for instance, with Garfinkel's definition of ethnomethodology as:

> the investigation of the rational properties of indexical expressions and other practical actions as contingent, ongoing accomplishments of artful practices of everyday life (1967, p. 11).

Yet the price of doing so is to lose the chance of coming to grips with what we take to be a fresh and challenging insight into the nature of social phenomena. There are, however, other ways in which this insight can be comprehended. I want to explore now what may be gained by examining the interpretations given to a French film of the early 1960s, *L'Année Dernière à Marienbad* (*Last Year in Marienbad*).

Scripted by the novelist Robbe-Grillet and directed by Resnais, the film was greeted by critical acclaim, often accompanied by a sense of confusion about how

---

[2] This issue of the very availability of the world is taken up later in this chapter.

[3] I am not unaware of the parallels between this situation and, on the one hand, politics (a mass party versus a small élite) and on the other, religion (a missionary church versus a self-enclosed sect). The issue revolves around whether "popularization" must result in the distortion of complex truths. The authors of this book happen to believe that sociologists have much to gain by stating their propositions wherever possible (and it generally *is* possible) in a relatively simple and comprehensible way.

to interpret the "meaning" of the events portrayed. We are shown the grounds and public rooms of what might be a palatial hotel. A man and a beautiful woman meet. The man attempts to convince the woman that they have met before (last year in Marienbad). He describes, in great detail, their meetings and the settings in which they occurred. The woman seems to lose some of her original conviction that she has never met the man. We are not informed of their relationship to the other characters present (who generally appear like ghosts in the background) nor, in particular, of the relationship between the woman and a mysterious second man (given to playing curious games with matches) who might, or might not, be her husband. Since this is all that the film reveals, it is hardly surprising that there are almost as many interpretations as there are critics. Apart from the (by now) trite comment that "it's all to do with the problem of communication", it has been suggested that we are witnesses to a confidence trick employed by a particularly smooth operator (the man) or, alternatively, that both leading characters are ghosts condemned to haunt the place for ever (hence the unreality of the other character). The interpretation that I want to suggest is no better (or worse) than the others and is equally a gloss, in so far as it involves glossing over what others might take to be key particulars in the film.

Robbe-Grillet has written the script, we know, as a "new novelist", influenced by phenomenology and concerned to explore the "reality" of everyday life.[4] In particular, the film implies the paradox that, while we cannot enter other people's minds, we are, nonetheless, able to impute meanings to their actions and succeed in creating a "routine", "predictable" world. The film illustrates then: (1) the concreteness of physical objects (the detail implied in Robbe-Grillet's novels and presented on the screen in terms of the elaborate descriptions, spoken by the man at the beginning and end of the film, of the corridors and rooms of the hotel); (2) the opacity of human motives (signified in a scene where the two main characters debate on the nature of the episode depicted by a sculpture—is it suggesting a situation of calm or of terror?) (3) that the sense of the concreteness of the reality of everyday life is not something given in its nature (for example, the sculpture can legitimately be taken to imply many contradictory things) but arises in the human construction of meaningful social universes. This is reflected in conversation which, by implying common, "routine" features of the social world, sustains our sense of its reality (in the film, the man, by concentrating on the routine circumstances of their supposed past meetings, creates a reality for the woman by means of his talk—she is almost convinced); (4) as *observers* too we necessarily have to make inferences about the social reality which we observe—we decide what is really happening (has happened). Since convincing evidence can be produced in support of different and sometimes opposed inferences, there is no one "right" account of a social phenomenon (in this case, a film). Indeed, after a period of time has elapsed and the events are reconsidered, both participants and observers may become convinced that some-

---

[4] This knowledge is irrelevant to the validity of my particular interpretation in the sense that what matters *socially* is the meaning imputed to the film by others rather than Robbe-Grillet's personal intentions.

thing entirely different was "really" happening and that their first account was "in error". (This is true of all socially produced phenomena but is particularly obvious if one looks at the changing critical standings of works of art); (5) the construction of "convincing" accounts is an interesting phenomenon in itself which should be examined, not to establish which account is "right" or to remedy "incorrect" accounts, but in order to establish what properties of the world are implied and taken for granted in what passes as a convincing account.[5]

II

While an analysis of *Marienbad* gives some indication of the focus of concern in this book, I now propose to outline a more formal statement of some unifying themes that will recur in the following pages. Although necessarily very general in nature since they reflect a consensus negotiated by four co-authors, they give a sense of coherence to the rest of the book.

SOCIOLOGY
Our commitment to sociology involves a rejection of sociologism and psychologism (the attempts to explain *all* phenomena in either sociological or psychological terms). Our focus is primarily on the shared world of social meanings through which *social* action (understood in Weber's sense as all action which takes account of the motives of others) is generated and interpreted. As sociologists, we are not concerned with analysing inner mental processes (although our own experience informs us that they occur); we seek to understand instead the rules used to locate meanings in the other's actions, expressions, gestures and thoughts.

PHENOMENOLOGY
One of the major strands of sociological thought has been positivist in the sense that it has minimized the differences between the social and physical worlds and sought to impose upon sociology a way of defining problems and of studying relationships which follows the canons of what its proponents take to be *the* "scientific method". As Walsh points out in Chapter 3, this view owes a great deal to the classical French sociologist Émile Durkheim, whose injunction to treat "social facts" as "things" has been embodied in sociological research in the form of prior hypotheses, operational definitions of variables and statistical tests of significance. This has the effect (intended, in Durkheim's case) of leaving out of consideration altogether (or simply treating as an intervening variable between structure and behaviour) the "internal logic" of the situation—the rules used by the participants themselves (including the observer through his own use of commonsense assumptions) to make available "facts" or "variables".

It is argued here that a science attains its status by adopting methods of

---

[5] A discussion of "accounting" and the generation of history by the construction of "plausible" accounts can be found in Cicourel (1968), Garfinkel (1967), Scott and Lyman (1968) and Sudnow (1968b).

[6] See Douglas (1967) and Cicourel (1968).

analysis which, while paying attention to the standards of rigour and scepticism, derive their rationale from the nature of the phenomena that are being investigated. As Northrop has put it:

a subject becomes scientific not by beginning with facts, with hypotheses, or with some pet theory brought in *a priori*, but by beginning with the peculiar character of its particular problems (1947, p. 274).

The "peculiar character" of social reality raises for us in its accomplished (that is, socially contrived) nature. Without entering into a complex argument, which is spelt out in later chapters,[7] it can readily be observed that the factual status of a physical or natural object or force (such as rain, gravity or electricity) is different in kind from the facticity or "thingness" of a social convention or institution (such as divorce, crime or "polite behaviour"). In particular, social phenomena are "real" because we organize our activities in such a way as to routinely confirm their real existence. But this is not to say that conscious intentions or internal states are at the heart of the matter. However I define my actions, if I am arrested for what is taken to be a criminal offence then I have to deal, as facts of my situation, with the socially organized activities of police, the courts and, perhaps, the prison system. Yet these institutions themselves are constituted as social facts by the routine forms of interpretation and action which those who operate them take to be "common", "proper" and "natural".

In posing questions about the fundamental character of the reality to which sociologists address themselves, we have been guided by what we take to be a phenomenological consciousness.[8] This has involved a series of inquiries that sciences generally take for granted or regard as not their proper concern. In particular, we seek to investigate the *nature* of social phenomena as a task prior to any attribution of causes and effects to phenomena. As already implied, we take the objective character of social reality to reside in socially organized acts of interpretation and maintain that social relations and institutions have no inherent meaning or nature. This follows Husserl, who writes:

A phenomenon is no "substantial" unity; it has no "real" properties, it knows no real parts, no real changes and no causality. . . . To attribute a nature to phenomena, to investigate their real component parts, their causal connections—that is pure absurdity, no better than if one wanted to ask about the causal properties, connections etc. of numbers (1965, pp. 106–7).

To give a simple illustration: according to this perspective, attempts to construct operational definitions of different forms of the family (for example, nuclear, extended) and then to establish social structural causes and effects of such forms are logically misguided. The problem for sociology arises in discovering what routines of interpretation and action constitute, for members, what *they* come to regard (for all practical purposes) as a "family" and as "typical" family life, and

---

[7] Especially Chapters 2 and 3.
[8] See especially Chapter 5.

how these interpretive schemes (background expectancies) rely on *their* sense of social structure.[9]

Our focus on phenomena themselves thus leads inevitably to questions about what *constitutes* them as phenomena. As will already be clear, our argument is that social phenomena are constituted (that is, made into objects, into "real" things) by the interpretive work of members. Deviance provides an example of the production of social order by interpretive work and this is illustrated in McHugh's programmatic statement:

> I have chosen to locate deviance in its items of production, not in its "causes" or "effects" in order to meet the sociological principle of describable social treatment. This principle stresses that it is the activity through which members deal with one another that maintains or changes society and its institutions by creating, filling, and emptying all the categories, organizations and units of society. It is to describe how the array called society is assembled out of what members *do,* not out of the causes and effects of what they do (1970, p. 155).

As an example of this analysis, one might examine members' search for knowledge in a case where a man is observed to throw a child from a window. Here one might ask "Is there a fire and no other way down, is the man in control of his faculties?" McHugh is then able to show that deviant acts are recognized on the basis of commonsense judgments about whether they "might not have been" because there were alternatives available (he terms this their "conventionality"), and whether they are performed by an actor who can be regarded as "knowing what he's doing" (their "theoreticity").

There is one further insight generated by a phenomenological consciousness. As Pollner (1970) has noted, the basis of science is the assumption of a world "out there" whose existence is independent of the processes through which it is studied and understood. The world, then, "presents itself as an essentially *preconstituted* field of objects which awaits explication" (p. 38). Phenomenology, on the other hand, implies the problematic character of this very availability of the world for analysis. More especially, it suggests that the constitution of the world by acts of interpretation applies equally to participant and observer (sociologist). The latter's version of commonsense reasoning ("analysis") and his glossing practices ("operational definitions") inevitably produce what Cicourel (forthcoming) has called "a self-validating circle" in so far as the gloss we use to describe the world necessarily confirms our view of it.

Yet this is not to deny that phenomenological analysis itself is caught in the same trap. Any analysis must assume an order: in its assumptions of a "real" world, analysis parallels everyday or "mundane" inquiry. As Pollner notes,

> All inquiry has a domain which is presumptively *independent* of its being taken up in concern. Indeed, without the presumption of an essentially objective world, inquiry loses its sense as inquiry. *All inquiry is mundane inquiry* (1970, p. 53).

---

[9] See Garfinkel's (1967) account of the disruption of "typical" family life by challenging those interpretive schemes. The term "member" is used to refer to a person who has mastery over natural language in a particular social setting—that is, someone who can "bring off" acceptable conversation.

"Radical inquiry" (to use Pollner's term), however, makes the availability of the world worthy of study as a phenomenon in its own right by an examination of the processes of commonsense reasoning employed by both participants and observers.[10] The distinction between "radical" and "mundane" inquiry arises not in their methods (or in the inquiries themselves) but in the order of problems that each considers. For:

> Radical inquiry does not concern itself with a world *per se* but with the facticity of a factual world, the objectivity of an objective world, and so on (ibid., p. 52).

Commonsense knowledge

It has been suggested that what is taken-for-granted about the world (for practical *and* scientific purposes) offers a source of data unrivalled in its richness and complexity. To take things for granted is to see them as "what everybody knows" them to be; taken-for-granted knowledge is thus necessarily "commonsense" knowledge in so far as its "obvious" nature can only be sustained in social settings depending on shared assumptions.[11]

The nature of commonsense knowledge was the central concern of Alfred Schutz, and all the authors of this book owe a special intellectual debt to his work.[12] Schutz argues that our knowledge of the world is organized in a series of typifications which structure our understanding of settings and actors by allowing us to infer the unknown parts of others' motives. According to our understanding of "what is really happening", we bring to bear what Schutz calls "cookbook knowledge", using tried recipes for success to achieve our purposes. Commonsense knowledge, then, defines our relevancies and our attribution of relevancies to others.

Schutz (1970) distinguishes three sets of relevancies that structure which objects and events strike us as interesting and important. "Topical" relevancies define what we take to be the issue at hand (such as friendly talk, deciding on an appointment to the staff, sentencing an offender) in any social setting. Typifications of the "topical" actors, symbols and objects arise within a scheme of "interpretational" relevancies, and one attributes meanings to the participants by referring to what seem to be the appropriate "motivational" relevancies. The "rightness" of these relevancies are routinely confirmed for us by the actions and words of others who (for all practical purposes) seem to be inhabiting the same subjective world. It follows that commonsense knowledge is both rational and moral. It is rational because it follows a commonly accepted logic and because it is nearly always "right"—in the sense that the view of the world which it produces is one which is confirmed by others. It is moral because failure to comply with

---

[10] Cicourel's (1968) study of juvenile justice illustrates a concern to make the "common sense" of the observer a research problem in its own right.

[11] To term knowledge "common sense" is to stress its socially sustained nature, not to deny the existence of "finite provinces of meaning" maintained in separate milieux.

[12] See Chapters 5 and 6.

"what everybody knows" (by an apparently "sane" man with other alternatives open to him) is routinely regarded as deviant and sanctionable, for to treat it otherwise would threaten the taken-for-granted status of the world (see the previous discussion of deviance).

Commonsense sociology

The role of commonsense knowledge in the construction of the social world implies that observation and analysis: (1) must ascertain the system of relevancies that members use to define social settings, actions and talk, and avoid the imputation of meaning by an observer; (2) should concern itself with what members take to be "routine", "obvious" and "uninteresting" in order to examine the manner in which socially organized activities constitute such a state. Yet few sociologists could successfully deny that the conventional sociological tradition is associated with both the imputation of meanings and a singling out of members' "problems" as the focus of interest. Where questionnaire items are used to elicit "attitudes" and quantitative scales established, one encounters "measurement by fiat" (Cicourel, 1964)—the imposition of the assumption of a direct equivalence between the sociologist's measuring instruments (such as attitude scales) and the realities to which they relate. Where a problem is defined in terms of sociological, rather than social, conceptions of what is problematic, nonetheless commonsense assumptions are normally made about the "routine", "obvious" and "uninteresting" features of the scene or case and concepts applied on this basis (for example, the conceptualization of behaviour not in accord with an organizational "rule" as "informal").[13] These similarities between the generation and maintenance of commonsense and sociological knowledge have led some writers to depict sociology as a "folk" science. What this term implies can be understood by considering a fable told by Pollner (1970).

Pollner tells of a sociologist from another planet who visits Earth with a research student. The professor asks his student to carry out fieldwork on the subject of Earth societies. After a relatively short while, the student returns. But instead of his own report, he has brought with him bound copies of all the existing sociology journals. "There was no need", he tells his master, "to explore any further. For there already exist these records compiled by Earthly sociologists. They tell us all we need to know." The professor reproves his student:" Can't you see", he exclaims, "that these records constitute data for analysis in the same way as do the societies themselves? For both rely on the tacit knowledge of their members and this knowledge defines the reality in ways that we must investigate."

The reliance of sociology, as a folk discipline, upon commonsense knowledge arises most clearly in its assumption of a preconstituted world available for study (sociology) or action (commonsense). This is reflected in the concentration of

---

[13] Cicourel (1970a) has suggested that the short-hand vocabulary of the social sciences bears important similarities to legal concepts. Like the latter: "They do not correspond to explicit sequences of events and social meanings, but the fit is managed through negotiated, socially organized activities" (pp. 6–7).

sociologists, following what they take to be the canons of scientific method, upon the causes and effects of phenomena and their ignorance (or, rather, reliance on commonsense knowledge) of the phenomena themselves. To the extent that social phenomena are examined, the sociologist tends to construct idealized accounts of their nature (such as attitude scales) but to avoid the rich experience of the participants (talk, gesture, intonation). Like the critics in their reception of *Marienbad*, the issue for him is what is "really" happening. He seeks to *remedy* the participants' understanding, as "one-sided" or "partial", and to construct an objective account of the event or situation. He specifically excludes from his analysis, by the way he sets up his problem, the manner in which social life as a whole proceeds on "partial" knowledge and how the process of giving "one-sided" accounts generates (for the participant and observer) what they take to be a "real" world.[14]

A basis for validity

The complexities of social phenomena that have been suggested so far demonstrate the difficulty of finding a basis for claiming any validity for our knowledge of the social construction of reality. The problem involved in laying claim to know what the other knows, which recurs as a theme in the following chapters (especially Chapters 5, 6 and 8) has been stated concisely by the cultural anthropologist, Goodenough:

> The great problem for a science of man is how to get from the objective world of materiality, with its infinite variability, to the subjective world of form as it exists in what, for lack of a better term, we must call the minds of our fellow men. We all of us succeed in doing so, somehow, or we wouldn't learn to understand each other. That language exists at all is evidence enough of this. But the processes by which we do it have eluded our grasp (1966, p. 39).

Ethnographers, it is true, have sought to describe cultures and to avoid analyses and explanations which might colour their descriptions. But this in no way overcomes their possible reliance on an outsider's view which imposes categories and concepts of "adequate" description upon the native culture.

Frake's (1966) study of the diagnosis of disease among the Subanun of Mindanao (Philippines) illustrates some of the problems of the ethnographer. Frake began by attempting a conventional ethnographic study of social structure but reports that he soon found this impossible without understanding native terminologies. Furthermore, this required knowledge of which statements were semantically as well as grammatically acceptable. At this point, he turned to a notion of ethnoscience—the folk rules and schemes of knowledge used by members to perceive, define, classify and explain social reality. The problem now became: what passes for knowledge and cognition among the Subanun (their "folk science") and, more specifically, what counts as illness and treatment

---

[14] As will be stressed later, even a phenomenological sociology can hardly be anything more than a "folk" discipline.

(their "ethnomedicine"). Frake's study of the ethnomedicine of the Subanun goes on to identify what symptoms define one as being sick, how diagnoses and prognoses are established by reference to folk taxonomies of disease, and what treatment is thought appropriate for each disease.[15]

While Frake defines his concerns in a sophisticated way, the problem still remains of how he can claim to know what are the rules of interpretation being used by the native in his label-assigning work. Frake himself suggests three methods—analytic, perceptual and explicit. The analytic method makes use of an outsider's means of coding recorded instances of a category; for instance, diagnosing an illness in Western terms and then comparing the Subanun diagnosis. Frake argues that this method is inappropriate because Western conceptions of science are too different to allow any meaningful comparison. Alternatively, one might examine the perceptual information which elicits the label from the native—when a disease is named, one observes the physical symptoms that the native is perceiving. Yet it is difficult to know precisely *what* information the native has in mind from the range available to him, and the perceptual cues the observer might notice could be a reflection of his own culture.

As a simple alternative, the explicit method only involves asking the native. Frake suggests that this method is more applicable since, while a Subanun experiences personally very few diseases, he must himself learn to diagnose diseases through verbal descriptions of their significant attributes. He argues that it is relatively easy for a Subanun to say what makes one disease different from another and, therefore, informants rarely disagree about the term itself—although they disagree frequently about its application to a particular case.

Frake's "explicit" method has a built-in means of validation, for the observer's propositions about what the natives "mean" are tested by reference to native opinion. Where the natives agree, then the observer is presumably "right".[16] The inherent difficulty with the method, as Frake himself implicitly recognizes, is that it tells you nothing about how meanings are assigned in the context of actual action scenes. Thus a dictionary knowledge of the meaning of terms would be of little help to a participant who wanted to know the appropriate term to be used to describe the conditions of, say, a dying patient apprehensive of his fate, in a situation where, indeed, it might be better not to use medical terms at all but simply to refer to his pleasant appearance, cheerful face and so on. Knowledge of the meaning of terms "in principle" but not of their application in socially defined situations could thus produce acute embarrassment when applied by the participant-observer.

While this suggests difficulties with "asking the native" as a method of validation, the argument implies that an observer's propositions can be supported to the extent that his descriptions of native imputations of meaning allow an outsider to "pass" among natives as, for all practical purposes, one of their own kind. To "know" a culture is, then, to have learned:

---

[15] See Psathas (1968) for a comparison of ethnoscience and ethnomethodology.

[16] Michael Phillipson, following Matza, examines this proposition in Chapter 5.

whatever it is one has to know or believe in order to operate in a manner acceptable to its members and to do so in any role that they accept for any one of themselves (Goodenough, 1966, p. 36).

The concern with the formal structure of practical actions by ethnomethodologists is designed to generate this type of knowledge by focusing on the background expectancies and the negotiations of meanings which allow members to "pull off" what they regard as acceptable and meaningful talk and action. In his own culture, the ethnomethodologist seeks to treat "obvious" and "uninteresting" interactions as anthropologically strange in order to examine the tacit knowledge that produces their commonplace character. Studies of the formal structuring of talk by Sacks and Turner and of the sense of social structure that underlies everyday definitions of organizational "problems", and attempts to resolve them (Cicourel, 1968; Sudnow, 1968; Silverman and Jones, forthcoming), have produced data whose validity can be examined by "feeding it back in" to actual social scenes within the culture.[17]

As has been already noted, however, the ethnomethodologist is equally as reliant on folk knowledge as the conventional sociologist.[18] The claims of both to knowledge of the social world and their attempts to validate these claims depend upon the unavoidable indexicality of their accounts (that is, they rely on the reader's tacit knowledge to fill in missing particulars) and reflexivity of their definitions of areas of interest (to define a field in a particular world is self-validating for it implies a preconstituted phenomenon available for study). This is explicitly recognized by Cicourel in his description of his research on deaf-sign language:

> In the research we seek a kind of *"indefinite triangulation"* procedure that would reveal the irreparable but practical nature of accounts used by subjects and researchers. I use the expression "indefinite triangulation" to suggest that every procedure that seems to "lock in" evidence (thus to claim a level of adequacy) can itself be subjected to the same sort of analysis that will in turn produce yet another indefinite arrangement of new particulars or a rearrangement of previously established particulars in "authoritative", "final", "formal" accounts. The "indefinite triangulation" notion attempts to make visible the practicality and inherent reflexivity of everyday accounts. The elaboration of circumstances and particulars of an occasion can be subjected to an indefinite re-elaboration of the "same" or "new" circumstances and particulars (forthcoming, p. 43).

Having given us a glimpse of the abyss, Cicourel implies the path away from it— what appears as a threat to the sociological enterprise becomes its central area of research interest. How accounts are constructed and read by providing for a factual world becomes a phenomenon worthy of study in its own right.[19] As he

---

[17] For a discussion of ethnomethodology, see Chapters 7, 8 and 9.

[18] Pollner's fable, referred to earlier, continues with the student recognizing that his own sociology, just as much as Earth-bound sociology, depends on tacit knowledge.

[19] For instance, Cicourel has asked a native signer to translate the meaning of the signing of another native signer and has compared this to the translation of another signer whose first language was oral language. Each of their accounts provided for different realities.

says in a discussion of linguistics (his remarks might equally well apply to conventional sociology):

> Linguists prefer to live with different kinds of conveniently constructed glosses, while the ethnomethodologist prefers to treat the *glossing* itself as an activity that *becomes the phenomenon of interest* while recognizing that no one can escape some level of glossing in order to claim knowledge about something (ibid., p. 17).

SUGGESTIONS FOR FURTHER READING

General introductions to phenomenological sociology are not readily available; indeed the lack of an entirely adequate text provides the rationale for the publication of this book.

For a collection of papers which includes much important recent material, see Douglas (1970), while papers by Cicourel and McHugh can be found in the cheaper but patchier Dreitzel (1970). Wagner (1971) is a highly useful (but expensive) introduction to the work of Schutz, together with well-organized selections from his writings.

The basic question raised by phenomenological sociology is whether the attempt to create "a sociology" in the manner of the natural sciences is not a mistaken enterprise altogether and whether, therefore, an alternative approach to the study of social phenomena would prove to be more fruitful; notwithstanding the prestige of methods of the natural sciences as a mode of cognition about the world.

Phenomenological sociology attempts to provide such an alternative by grounding itself on what it takes to be the particular characteristics of social phenomena, arguing that such characteristics require a methodology that is distinct from that of the natural sciences. In particular, it suggests a methodology which, whilst focusing on the meaningful character of social phenomena, does not degenerate into unexamined intuition.

TWO

Sociology and the Social World

DAVID WALSH

Given the prevailing orthodoxy of positivism in current sociological circles, the particular merit of the phenomenological movement among certain sociologists is to raise again a number of important questions about the nature of the sociological enterprise[1] itself. These questions are not entirely novel in the sense that some of them have provided a perennial accompaniment to sociological investigation from the very beginning. What is new is that they should have been raised at this moment by practising sociologists rather than by philosophers of the social sciences.[2]

The more recent activities of the majority of sociologists have been centered around the refinement of the particular methodological techniques of "scientific" sociology rather than with questioning the assumptions upon which such a sociology rests. One could, of course, answer that it is far more fruitful for sociologists to get on with the job of empirical analysis than with debating over what kind of sociology is the most appropriate. But the strength of such an argument would depend upon the quality of the output of "scientific" sociology and it is precisely this which has been the cause of concern of phenomenological sociologists. The dissatisfaction with traditional sociology, therefore, has emerged in the process of ongoing research activity and not out of some abstract speculation about how best to proceed. Phenomenological sociology, then, is a move to reconsider what the whole sociological enterprise is about, arguing that there is no longer a point in waiting for the next methodological corner to reveal "scientific" statements about social phenomena when the present path has come to look suspiciously like a blind alley.

---

[1] The particular sense in which this term is used is explained in the following pages.
[2] Numbered within the movement would be writers such as Cicourel, Garfinkel, McHugh, Luckmann, Pollner, Schutz, Sudnow, Winter, Zimmerman (see General Bibliography).

In contradistinction, positivism is that position in sociology which argues that sociology should attempt to constitute itself as a discipline in the manner of the natural sciences. Although there are varieties of positivism within sociology, all of them subscribe to the three basic premises on which the argument is grounded:

(1) That social phenomena are, for all analytical purposes, qualitatively the same as natural phenomena;

(2) That the techniques of analysis developed in the natural sciences are applicable to sociological investigation, and;

(3) That the aim of sociology is to produce a system of high-level, empirically grounded theoretical propositions which would provide the basis for predictive statements about social phenomena.

What follows, in the rest of this chapter, is a preliminary examination of these premises in an attempt to raise the crucial issues with regard to the generation of sociological explanation glossed over by positivistic sociology.

This chapter, then, constitutes a series of prefatory remarks to the more elaborate arguments introduced in the remainder of the book.

THE CHARACTERISTICS OF NATURAL AND SOCIAL PHENOMENA

The process of generating explanations is best understood as an activity which brings an organized conceptual framework (or paradigm to use Kuhn's[3] term) to bear on a given range of phenomena and a given order of problems with regard to such phenomena. A paradigm consists, then, of a system of theory, method and standards utilized by a discipline for purposes of explanation. What is particularly crucial about any paradigm is that the methodological rationale is grounded in metaphysical assumptions concerning the nature of the phenomena to which it is addressed—that is, it assumes the availability and preconstitution of the world of phenomena which is the subject of its investigations so that the substantive characteristics of that world are the correlates of the methodological procedures of the discipline. In this sense, a paradigm can be said to perform cognitive functions at three different levels. First, it suggests which entities nature does or does not possess. Second, it provides a map of nature. And third, it provides procedures by which the map of nature may be used to select what is relevant for further elaboration.

Positivistic sociology's attempt to use the natural-science paradigm necessarily involves, then, assuming that social phenomena posses the same characteristics as natural phenomena. It is incumbent, therefore, on positivistic sociology to demonstrate this similarity. What sociological phenomenology, on the other hand, argues is that positivistic sociology seriously mistakes the characteristics of the

---

[3] Kuhn (1970a). With reference to the natural sciences, Kuhn defines a paradigm as "universally recognized scientific achievements that for a time provide model problems and solutions to a community of practitioners".

social world in assuming their comparability to those of the natural world and hence that positivistic sociology must necessarily constitute a mistaken enterprise. What then are the characteristics of natural and social phenomena?

The first characteristic is that the natural world possesses no intrinsic meaning structure—that is, natural phenomena are intrinsically meaningless. Schutz puts this most clearly:

> It is up to the natural scientists to determine which sector of the universe of nature, which facts and which events therein, and which aspects of such facts and events are topically relevant to their specific purpose. These facts and events are neither pre-selected nor preinterpreted; they do not reveal intrinsic relevance structures. Relevance is not inherent in nature as such, it is the result of the selective and interpretive activity of man within nature or observing nature. The facts, data and events with which the natural scientist has to deal are just facts, data, and events within his observational field but this field does not "mean" anything to the molecules, atoms, and electrons therein (1962, p. 5).

The scientist is free, as observer, to construct paradigms of nature which explain its operations in a manner that is suitable to his cognitive concerns. What gives the natural sciences their cognitive strength, therefore, is not so much the rules of procedure that are used to investigate the natural world but rather the strong consensual agreement between scientists about the character of the world to which such rules are addressed and with reference to which these rules are appropriately organized. In other words, the natural sciences can be characterized in terms of the taken-for-granted paradigm shared by their practitioners.[4]

In contradistinction to the natural world, the social world is a world con-stituted by meaning—social phenomena are intrinsically meaningful. To quote Schutz again:

> For the sociologist, his observational field, the social world, is not essentially structure-less. It has a particular meaning and relevance structure for the human beings living, thinking and acting therein. They have preselected and preinterpreted this world by a series of commonsense constructs which determine their behaviour, define the goal of their actions, the means available for them—in brief, which help them find their bearings in their natural and socio-cultural environment and to come to terms with it (1964, pp. 5–6).

The social world, then, is an everyday world experienced and interpreted by its members as an organized universe of meaning in the form of a series of typifica-tions of the objects within it. These typifications take the form of commonsense interpretations of its operations that constitute a form of knowledge at hand, which, together with the personal experiences of the actor, constitute a taken-for-granted means of orientation towards this world. The process by which the social world is constructed, then, may be described as a process of first-order construction in terms of such social meanings.

The clear methodological implication that follows from the foregoing is

---

[4] "The paradigm is the taken-for-granted context within which one can locate facts and methods, and generate laws and theories" (Kuhn 1970a, p. 8).

that the sociologist, unlike the natural scientist, cannot determine from the outside which facts and events and which aspects of them are interpretationally relevant to his specific purposes. Sociological constructs, therefore, must necessarily take on the character of "constructs of the second degree, namely, constructs of constructs made by the actors on the social scene" (Schutz, 1967, p. 6). The key problem of such second-order construction revolves around distinguishing sociological explanations from commonsense explanations of the social world whilst retaining the systematic reference of the former to the latter. Essentially, then, the observer of the social world is placed in a different position with reference to his phenomena as compared with the observer of the natural world. In particular, observational activity on the part of the sociologist requires an understanding as opposed to a mere observation of the phenomena. The failure of positivistic sociology lies in its inability to grasp the meaningful constitution of the social world and the consequent reliance on a methodology inadequate for the exposition of that world.

It follows from the foregoing that the natural world can be characterized as an object world of material (sometimes tangible) sense data (facts) which are external to the observer and whose existence is independent of him. It follows that such phenomena may be examined externally in terms of the paradigmatically identified overt properties which are relevant to the scientist's task at hand. This is the crux of operations in the natural sciences, such as concept formation, theory testing and causal explanation, all of which directly refer to such identifiable overt properties.

Conversely the social world is a subject and not an object world. It does not constitute a reality sui generis divorced from the human beings who constitute its membership. Rather, the social world is the existential product of human activity and is sustained and changed by such activity. In so far as the social world is intersubjectively[5] produced by its members it becomes externalized vis-a-vis them—that is, it comes to possess a degree of objective facticity. In this sense, Durkheim is not entirely mistaken in arguing for the objective (factual) character of the social world but he fails to understand that the facticity of the social world resides in the manner by which its members apprehend it. It is not that a real objective factual social world exists out there to which the members of society are subject but that the actors in the process of apprehending this world (that is, explaining it, defining it, perceiving it) externalize and objectify it through the available mode by which apprehension can be articulated. Primarily this mode is that of natural language. Language, by virtue of the categories which it makes available for the interpretation of the appearances of the social world, objectifies and externalizes that world for its members. Sociology, therefore, requires a theory of language if it is to proceed to the analysis of social meanings.

---

[5] Intersubjectivity is a key term in the phenomenological explanation of the social world. Basically, intersubjectivity refers to the social processes by which an everyday commonsense world is constructed as a universe of meaning in the form of the reciprocal typifications of that world by its members. The term is discussed at greater length in the chapters by Phillipson and Silverman.

Clearly the conference of facticity on the social world that occurs as a result of the routine procedures employed by members to understand it does not make the social world an object world in the same sense as the natural world. The natural world does not depend upon human recognition for its existence even if the latter imputes a structure of meaning to that world which it does not intrinsically process. In contrast, a given social world would necessarily cease to exist if human recognition were withdrawn from it, since it has no existence apart from such recognition. In this sense, society is real (has objective facticity) because its members define it as real[6] and orientate themselves towards the reality so defined. Social facts are the practical accomplishment of members' routine practices for apprehending the social world and are regularly reaffirmed and sustained in the course of social interaction itself. It follows from this that the social world is also a world of multiple realities,[7] in the sense that members may focus on social situations in different ways and thereby read (account) what are ostensibly the same situations differently. One such reality would be the reality produced by the accounting procedures of positivistic sociology.

The social world, then, is a world constituted by the taken-for-granted meanings which its members use as a common scheme of reference by which appearances (events, actions, settings and so on) are interpreted and explained. Social structure, therefore, refers to the members' sense of social structure which is the product of the common scheme of reference that constitutes a set of socially standardized and standardizing, seen but unnoticed, background relevancies by which members make sense of their world. The important point is this: we cannot take for granted, as the natural scientist does, the availability of a preconstituted world of phenomena for investigation because the process by which a social world becomes available (i.e., is constituted) must itself be the problematic object of investigation. It follows, then, that the task of sociology is to examine the processes by which the social world is constructed. This, in turn, necessarily entails suspension of belief in the existence of that world as an objective reality.

The primary problem of positivistic sociology resides in its failure to suspend such a belief. In this sense, it remains firmly rooted within the natural attitude which, too, is engaged in the elucidation of the objective features of a taken-for-granted real social world. In so far as the order of problem addressed by the sociologist is the same as that of the ordinary members of society, sociology must be treated as another commonsense account of the social world. Just as ordinary members produce an objective reality as a practical accomplishment of the first-order procedures by which they interpret appearances, actions and situational factors as a document of an underlying pattern of meanings and relevancies, so the sociologist produces a similar reality by virtue of his documentary procedures. Furthermore, no special credence can be accorded to the reality produced by the

---

[6] It is this belief in the reality of the social world which characterizes what Schutz has called the "natural attitude" of the members towards that world.

[7] See Schutz (1962).

sociologist as compared with the realities produced by other members, since it has no existence outside of the interpretive processes by which it was constructed. Moreover, these processes of sociological construction constitute data available for analysis like the constructs of any other members.[8] In this sense, the accounts of positivistic sociology are a species of members' accounts and positivistic sociology, thereby, a species of "folk" sociology.

The discussion of the social construction of reality implies a radical distinction with regard to the orderly character of the social world as compared with the natural world. The explanations of the natural sciences are concerned with establishing order within the physical world in terms of an invariant sequence or concomitance of physical phenomena. As McIver (1942) points out, the natural scientist "tells us how things belong together and how they are bound together in specific processes of change". He does not proceed to ask why the natural world is characterized by invariance, as this is taken to be in the nature of things (a characteristic of the preconstituted world which he investigates) and hence there would be no point in asking such a question. It follows, therefore, that such order is a paradigmatically constructed order—that is, it is constructed in terms of the paradigm used by the scientist to examine the relationships between phenomena. The "nature of things", then, is what the paradigm takes it to be. An explanation in the sciences, therefore, is an account in which a sufficient order of regularity between events has been demonstrated. Scientific revolutions occur, as Kuhn points out, when new paradigms are created implying different orders of regularity.

In contradistinction, social order is the emergent product of human activity and the manner of its emergence, therefore, must become the central concern of sociological investigation. It could, of course, be argued that positivistic sociology also takes social order to be the central focus of its concerns, but the phenomenological criticism would be that it deals with it in an entirely unsatisfactory manner. Typically, positivism explains social order as being "out there" in an external social world produced by relationships between factors external to the members of that world, primarily through the agency of shared norms and values. But this not only leads to an illegitimate reification of society but more specifically avoids crucial issues about how a shared social world is possible at all. The result is that social order becomes a taken-for-granted background to the explanation of the social activity that occurs within its boundaries.[9] Even symbolic interactionism (which primarily focuses upon social meanings in terms of shared definitions of the situation) effectively ignores the processes by which shared meanings are accomplished. The unexplicated character of notions such as "shared norms and values" and "shared definitions of the situation" used by traditional sociologists

---

[8] More specifically, the accomplished character of sociological explanations requires, as a condition of their validation, the explication of the manner of their accomplishment: an explication of the background relevancies that underlie them.

[9] Chapters 3 and 4 explore this issue in more detail.

leads to the presupposition of the very processes that they seek to explain.[10]

Phenomenological sociology, on the other hand, is concerned precisely with the notion of sharing and the manner in which an orderly social world is established in terms of shared social meanings (or common understandings). Social order is the accomplishment of members' describing and accounting practices and has no existence independent of them.

> Structural arrangements provide boundary conditions by way of that which the actor takes for granted, typified conceptions that make up the actor's stock of knowledge, ecological settings, common linguistic usage, and biophysical conditions. The interaction remains structured by such boundary conditions but is also problematic during the course of action. But the actor's typified orientation to his environment minimizes the problematic possibilities of social encounters: the fundamental importance of common-sense ways of perceiving and interpreting the world is the taken-for-granted perspective which reduces surprise, assumes the world is as it appears today and that it will be the same tomorrow. The actor constructs his daily existence out of a set of tried-and-proved recipes (Cicourel, 1970a).

Moreover, what is involved in the notion of common understandings is effectively treated by phenomenological sociology. Here the major point made by such writers as Garfinkel, Cicourel and McHugh is that common understandings do not consist in measured accounts of shared agreement on substantive issues. No matter how specific the terms of a common understanding may be, they always possess a "wait-and-see" quality (what Garfinkel labels the "et cetera clause"[11]) which allows the contingent character of social interaction to be incorporated into them. Thus, common understandings are not formal rules in the sense of actuarial devices by which members predict one another's future activities but agreements that can be used to normalize whatever the actual activities turn out to be. Action is never just the product of formal rules; rules are enacted in social situations through a continuous interpretation of their meanings in the context of commonsense decision-making. What is important, therefore, is not formal rules but the procedures by which members demonstrate that activities are in accordance with a rule and thereby intelligible. Social meanings, then, and the social order which is produced by them, are the ongoing practical accomplishment of members achieved in situations of interaction.

The requirement, therefore, for a sociological analysis of the problematic character of social order is a suspension of the belief in the facticity of that order so as to concentrate on the routine practices and procedures of interpretation by which members accomplish it in interactional settings.

---

[10] Social order, then, is treated as a constituent of the preconstituted social world which the positivist sociologist is elucidating.

[11] The chapters by Silverman and Filmer consider in a more elaborated fashion, the notion of the "et cetera clause".

METHODOLOGICAL RATIONALITIES: THE MANAGEMENT OF EXPLANATION

Positivistic sociology has confused the rhetoric of scientific method with the actual practices by which scientific activity proceeds as the managed accomplishment of its practitioners. In particular, it ascribes inherent properties of objectivity to that method, thereby seriously mistaking the character of scientific explanations and the nature of their relationship to the phenomena which they address and upon which they are consequent.

Returning to Kuhn's concept of the scientific paradigm, he suggests that "it stands for the entire constellation of beliefs, values, techniques, and so on shared by the members of a given community" (1970a, p. 175). Not only does it prescribe, therefore, an appropriate set of methodological rules by which the scientist may pursue his explanatory activities; it also prescribes the nature of the universe to which such rules may be legitimately applied, and thereby supplies the criteria of truth and validity at the same time. The paradigm contains within it, then, answers to questions such as:

> What are the fundamental entities of which the universe is composed? How do these interact with each other and with the senses? What questions may legitimately be asked about such entities and what techniques employed in seeking solutions? (Kuhn, 1970a, pp. 4–5).

In this sense, the scientific paradigm is the common scheme of reference (to use Schutz's terms) or the set of background expectancies (to use Garfinkel's terms) that constitutes the taken-for-granted world of the scientist. Scientific explanations may be seen, therefore, as the managed outcome of the interpretive procedures of scientists organized in terms of the system of relevancies contained within the paradigm. Kuhn refers to such activity as "normal science".

In the process of explanation, the scientist translates the facts he investigates into the thought-constructs of his own discipline—that is, the thought-objects of commonsense perception are superceded by the thought-objects of science, so that they often shed many of those qualities that are capable of direct presentation in our consciousness. As Schutz puts it:

> scientific thinking involves constructs (i.e. sets of abstractions, generalizations, formalizations, idealizations) specific to the respective level of thought organization. Strictly speaking, there are no such things as facts, pure and simple. All facts are from the outset selected from a universal context by the activities of our mind. They are, therefore, always interpreted facts, either facts looked at as detached from their context by an artificial abstraction or facts considered in their particular setting. In either case, they carry along their interpretational inner and outer horizon (1962, p. 4).

The import of the last remark is particularly crucial with regard to the consequences attendant upon the substitution of a scientific language for a commonsense language since it implies that any language carries with it a specific conception of reality. The question then becomes that of deciding which of the possible languages and associated conceptions is deemed most appropriate for making sense of the world of phenomena under review. This, as Kuhn points out, is settled by the general theoretical assumptions about the nature of that world itself, and the order of relations between the phenomena within it that character-izes the particular paradigm used by the observer. In the case of the natural sciences, these assumptions take the natural world to be an object world of identifiable sense-data and the order of relations between them to be those of mechanical association.[12]

The language of science, therefore, is a language deemed appropriate to the presumed character of the world to which it is addressed. Because the world to which it is addressed is intrinsically meaningless, the scientist is free to slice it in any manner that suits his particular cognitive concerns as specified by the paradigm. It is this which explains the characteristic features of the formal rationalities in terms of which the language is constructed. The requirements of that language demand that scientific constructs be formulated so that they are both internally consistent and remain anchored in the sense data of the natural world, and can also be referred back to that world through sensory observation for purposes of verification. Moreover, such constructs should be defined so as to permit the possibility of measurement. A characteristic feature of the natural sciences has been their singular success at developing measurement techniques yielding numerical data as operational counterparts of the constructs of scientific models. They introduce a high degree of clarity into the concepts used in theoretical proposi-tions or in comprehensive theoretical systems, and allow for a greater degree of precision in the procedures of testing such theories. Now, as Cicourel (1964) points out, measurement presupposes a bounded network of shared meanings, and it is precisely these shared meanings which the scientific paradigm supplies. Moreover, this is possible because the world to which the paradigm is addressed is intrinsically meaningless, and thereby scientists are free to impose upon it meanings which are suitable to their concerns. The essential condition, then, is only that scientists should be in agreement with one another—and this is what the paradigm provides.

The validation of explanations in the natural sciences rests upon agreed procedures of verification centering around the operations of systematic observa-tion, replication and prediction. The data of the natural scientist are treated as a preconstituted object world, in which the particular conceptualization of the scientist determines its overt and manifest characteristics and the order of relations within it. The concepts and theories of the scientist operate as a system of hypotheses (sets of determinate statements) that are tested by deducing, from a set of general postulates and some set of specific assumptions, the logical consequences, and comparing these with records of observations regarded as the approximate empirical counterparts of the specific assumptions and specific

---

[12] There is, at present, considerable debate among scientists as to whether the associations between natural phenomena should be treated as relations of causality.

B

consequences. Ideally, such observation would proceed within experimental situations where it would be possible to isolate the phenomena under investigation, but alternative means of systematic observation may be devised where this is not possible. The central feature of observation is of course, then, replication— that is, theories and concepts must be so defined and hypotheses so framed as to make it possible for the observational process to be subject to continuous repetition.

The precise manner in which these agreed procedures of verification can be said to constitute a test of scientific explanations is at present the subject of heated debate. Popper (1959) has argued that validation proceeds in the natural sciences according to the principle of falsification. Proceeding from the rules of logic, he argues that an inductive argument of the form "if A then B, therefore B" is a logically inapplicable one whereas an argument of the form "if A then B, but not B, therefore not A" would be applicable. The denial of a consequence of a theory ipso facto denies the theory from which it originated. Theories can thus be falsified although they cannot be verified. A law (theory) which is incapable of falsification should not, therefore, be admitted into science at all. But, as Kuhn points out, such a principle of falsification

> requires that we produce the class of all logical consequences of the theory and then choose from among these, with the aid of background knowledge, the classes of all true and of all false consequences. . . . None of these tasks can be accomplished unless the theory is fully articulated logically and unless the terms through which it attaches to nature are sufficiently defined so as to determine their applicability in all possible cases (1970a, p. 16).

No theory could possibly meet such conditions and typically, the scientific paradigm is used to bridge the gap between the content of a theory and its application. Moreover, and as Popper himself points out (without accepting its consequences);

> in point of fact, no conclusive disproof of a theory can ever be produced, for it is always possible to say that experimental results are not reliable or that the discrepancies which are asserted to exist between the experimental results and the theory are only apparent and that they will disappear with the advance of our understanding (1959, p. 50).

Normal science,[13] then, uses systematic observation for purposes of confirmation by fitting data into the conceptual framework through which it is examined in a self-validating manner. The requirement that scientific theories be empirically verifiable, in the sense that they should contain general statements, concerning relationships between events, that assert either the conditions sufficient for the occurrence of certain types of events or the conditions both sufficient and necessary for the occurrence of certain types of events, implies an understanding that what is sufficient and necessary is determined by the system of relevancies of the

---

[13] Normal science refers to the everyday procedures of scientific activity conducted within the parameters of the prevailing paradigm shared by its practitioners.

scientific paradigm itself. In this sense prediction is, effectively, a self-fulfilling prophecy and not an independent test of any theory. "Confronted with the unexpected [the scientist] must always do more research to articulate the theory in that area that has just become problematic" (Kuhn, 1970a, p. 19). In this sense it is the scientist and not the theory who is tested by replication, and it is the scientist and not the theory who is at fault when discrepant findings arise.

What emerges, then, is the crucial nature of the common agreement between the community of scientists about the nature of scientific activity and its bearing upon the objectivity of scientific explanations. For Popper (1945), the consensual character of the scientific community determines the public nature of science which, in turn, guarantees that theories may be freely tested by members of the scientific community and hence the objectivity of scientific explanations assured. But, as Kuhn (1970a) demonstrates, scientific paradigms perform a normative as well as a cognitive function—they not only provide a map of nature but also provide directions for map-making. In consequence, science advances not cumulatively in terms of its everyday activities of replication and testing but through revolutions that involve a complete change of paradigm. In other words, when paradigms change there are usually significant shifts in the criteria determining the legitimacy of both problems and proposed solutions. The choice between competing paradigms cannot be settled in terms of the criteria of normal science (vide Popper), since these kinds of criteria remain securely tied to the particular paradigms from which they are derived. Rather, the choice must be made upon answers to questions such as: Which problem is it more significant to have solved? The point about such answers is that they are based upon values external to normal science. Moreover, the questions that produce them emerge only in those situations in which a particular paradigm is on the verge of total collapse.

More typical, then, of scientific activity are the practices of normal science, which are characterized by the consensual agreement among scientists about what procedures shall constitute scientific activity and hence which explanations will count as scientific explanations. Only those explanations that have been arrived at through the appropriate "scientific" procedures may be counted as "scientific" explanations. In this sense the procedures of normal science are self-validating. A scientific explanation is objective only in the sense that it grasps those aspects of reality that are relevant from the point of view of a body of accepted rules and procedures which constitute scientific method. This, in turn, implies that all such explanations (and this would be true of any explanation) are "glosses" (formalizations) that rely for their sense on a tacit understanding of the relevancies with reference to which they are constructed but which are never spelt out as part of the explanation—that is, the relevancies have to be filled in before the explanation makes sense. One may, therefore, suggest that such explanations are "indexical" by virtue of their contextual reliance on underlying relevancies that are glossed over in the explanation itself. Now, this is not a problem for natural scientists in so far as the world to which they address themselves is without intrinsic meaning, in which case they need only concern themselves with the adequacy of their explanations to their purposes at hand, not with the "ultimate truth" about that world. It only matters that they can reach agreement on what would be an adequate way of formulating the natural world.

It does matter very much, however, if the world to be investigated comes ready-sliced, so to speak, as is the case with the social world, and it is precisely in its failure to grasp this that positivistic sociology is at fault. The point about the social world is that it is constituted by the glossing practices of its members: it has been preselected and preinterpreted by its members in terms of a series of commonsense assumptions which constitute a taken-for-granted common scheme of reference (or background relevancies) by which the events, actions and appearances of that world are apprehended and regularly confirmed. In this manner factual reality is conferred upon the social world by the routine interpretive practices of its members. The implication of this is that every man is a practical theorist when it comes to investigating the social world, and not just the sociologist.

Now, what the positivist is unaware of as he sets about examining the social world is that he is engaged in constructing that world in a manner akin to lay members by virtue of the way in which his interpretive procedures rely upon taken-for-granted assumptions or background relevancies about the constitutive nature of that world. Moreover these assumptions are the same as those of lay members, namely that the social world exists as a real objective world. Where the positivist differs from the lay member, however, is in terms of his interpretive procedures, which are formulated in terms of the formal rationalities of the "scientific method". Primarily this involves the construction of models of social action which characterize such action in terms of a means-end relationship that is compatible with the principles of formal logic. Such models may then be used to interpret the actual actions of members within the real world in terms of the extent to which they deviate from the standards of formal rationality implied in the model. The rationale that lies behind the choice of such a "scientific" language is a belief, on the part of positivists, in the objective efficacy of such language in the elucidation of the "real" character of the social world.[14] Using this language, the sociologist proceeds to a documentary interpretation of that world[15] (to use Garfinkel's term)—that is, the sociologist interprets appearances, actions and situational factors as a reflection (document) of an underlying pattern of meanings and relevancies whereby the objective character of the social world is determined. This process of sociological documentation then sets the scene for a series of ironic comparisons on the part of sociologists between what the social world is really like and the ways in which its members misconceive its true character—the lay members of society are turned into "cultural dopes" manipulated by society.

What is missed, however, is an understanding by positivists of the manner in which these sociological accounting practices produce, in a self-validating manner,

---

[14] The foregoing discussion of scientific method demonstrates the mistaken character of this belief in the transcendental objectivity of formally rational procedures.

[15] Chapters 5 and 6 detail the specific procedures of positivistic method.

the world which is the subject of their investigations. That is by virtue of their reliance on the underlying system of relevancies in terms of which their accounts are constructed. As Cicourel (1964) points out, this self-validation is achieved by positivism in terms of the correspondences it assumes to hold between:

(1) The indicators used by the man in the street to identify meaningful objects and events, and the indicators used by the sociologist to identify meaningful objects and events.

(2) The actor's point of view and the observer's point of view (they share the same language and meanings to subsume observations and experiences).

(3) The normative rules governing the actor's perception and interpretation of his environment, and the theoretical and methodological rules governing the observer's perception and interpretation of the same environment of objects.

The techniques, then, by which the positivist collects his data are such as to leave the respondent with no other possibility but to respond in terms of the options which are made available to him by those techniques. Furthermore, the coding practices of positivists ensure that ambiguous responses can be fitted into the context of the observer's framework by an interpretation of them that complies with that framework. The whole process of testing, therefore, is a process by which data are fitted into an existing conceptual framework in terms of the system of relevancies which underlies it and is not, as positivists would claim, a process by which that framework is independently tested. In this sense, positivistic explanations are glosses managed in terms of the interpretive procedures of the sociologist.

Moreover, the glosses of positivistic sociology are actually commonsense glosses by virtue of the manner in which they take the objective character of the social world for granted. In this sense, they have an operational counterpart in the procedures of the lay members who also assume the existence of a real world as the background to the routine procedures by which they document the objects within it that are to be perceived, evaluated and described. Moreover these procedures, like those of the positivist, are self-validating and produce glosses like those of the positivist. Where such members' procedures differ from sociological procedures is in terms of the practical concerns from which they proceed. The attitude of the lay member towards the social world is a pragmatic attitude. He is concerned with mastering that part of the world which is relevant to the particular activities in which he is engaged. His interpretive procedures, therefore, take the form of recipes for achieving the aims of action. Successful understanding, therefore, is achieved when the member knows how things operate and can produce such operations with similar effects. In this sense, the interpretive procedures of the lay members of society may be described as a species of everyday rationality as opposed to the formal rationality of positivistic sociological procedures in that they allow the lay members to account and make sense of the social world for all practical purposes. The effect of such first-order procedures is, then, the same as that of sociological first-order procedures

—that is, they allow members (a category which would include sociologists) to produce and sustain a social world which is apprehended by virtue of those practices as an objective facticity. They are, therefore, no more nor less objective or subjective than the procedures of the sociologists, neither can the reality which is produced by them be described as either more or less objective than the reality produced by the sociologist.

The requirement, then, of a sociological understanding of the social world that is not just commonsensical is that it focus on a different order of problem from that of everyday commonsense understanding. Such would be achieved by examining the glossing practices of members (including those of sociologists) by which that world is constituted and made available. This, in turn, requires an analysis of the everyday rational accounting procedures of members. To substitute an alternative gloss of the social world in terms of formal rationality, as positivistic sociology does, not only mistakes the manner in which the social world is constituted but actually engages in the constitution of that world. By virtue of its reliance on the commonsense view of the social world as real, positivistic sociology is effectively engaged in an elaboration of this commonsense view and may be correctly described as a species of folk wisdom.[16]

CAUSALITY AND MEANING

The natural sciences operate, on the whole, with some operational concept of cause. Strictly speaking, the concept refers to the relationship between material events such that:

(1) Whatever event occurs has a cause.

(2) Where there is a difference in effect, there is a difference in the cause.

(3) Every cause is the effect of a prior cause, and every effect is the cause of a posterior, effect.[17]

The scientist uses the notion as an appropriate manner by which to establish the order in the physical world in terms of an invariant sequence or concomitance of physical events. However, the concept has always been subject to attack in the natural sciences. The major problem pointed to is that causality could only apply to situations where two events can be shown to be distinct from one another, and to occur in constant conjunction in a particular order over time. The primary difficulty is that if we say that A causes B under certain conditions, and that these conditions have causes, in the end we have to conclude that the cause of B is the whole antecedent universe. The cause of B becomes not one phenomenon A, but a vast array of phenomena not as separable factors but as a total conjuncture. Moreover, the conjunction is not just the cause of A but of all other events that

---

[16] The specific import of this last remark is that the sociologist's account of how things hang together in the social world is tacitly informed by his knowledge, as an ordinary member, of how things hang together in that world.

[17] McIver labels this conception "universal causality".

form, or emerge within, a previous state of the universe. Therefore, it is meaningless to say that *A* causes *B*; rather we should replace such statements by probabilistic ones that rest upon statistical notions of correlation between variables or of the concomitant variation of the variables of a system with respect to the relative constants of that system.

But, as Cohen points out, such statements do not dispense with the idea of causality.

> A scientific theory with this statistical form must assert that whenever one takes a large enough sample in which *X* occurs, it will be found that *Y* occurs 70 per cent of the time. Thus a scientific theory with a statistical form is also a universal proposition: it does not simply state the number of times out of one hundred on which it was found that *X* was the occurrence of *Y*; it states that invariably there will be a certain probability of *X* being the condition for the occurrence of *Y*. The invariance refers to the infinite possibility of selecting samples in which this type of relationship will occur (1968, p. 3).

Clearly, then, the operative natural-science paradigm investigates the interconnectedness of natural phenomena with some notion of causality. Moreover, the notion is an appropriate one for the purposes of science because it deals with a world of physical events.

Major problems arise, however, when the notion of causality is extended into the realm of social phenomena. The assimilation is achieved by positivistic sociology in terms of a treatment of social phenomena as facts which are an analytical counterpart to the facts of the natural world. It becomes appropriate, therefore, to treat the relationship between them as one of mechanical association as is the case, say, in Durkheim's account of the division of labour as the determinant of the emergence of organic solidarity.[1] But if, as phenomenological sociology suggests, the object of enquiry is meaningful or rule-governed activity, can the notion of causality still be applied to such? One possibility might be to extend the idea of cause to refer to the significance that members give to events and the meaning with which an act is invested by members; i.e. that we should treat the reasons which members give for their actions as the cause of those actions. But such a solution requires that the sociologists make a false distinction between reasons and actions. Actions belong, as McIntyre has suggested,

> to the realm of statements, concepts and beliefs; and the relation of belief to action is not external and contingent, but internal and conceptual" (1969, p. 52).

The connection, then, between beliefs and actions is one of logic and not one of cause. So, as McIntyre goes on to point out, the relationship between protestantism and the spirit of capitalism discerned by Weber could not have been one of causality, since he is actually talking about the logical influence of certain doctrines upon sets of activities.

> Weber in fact presents us with capitalist actions as the conclusion of a practical syllogism which has Protestant premises (op. cit., p. 55). What he specifically relates

---

[1] E. Durkheim: *The Division of Labour in Society* (1933).

causally to Protestantism is what he calls the spirit of capitalism, a concept by means of which capitalist attitudes appear to be contrasted with capitalist activities. In fact, of course, an attitude can never be identified except in terms of the activities in which it is manifested (op. cit., p. 54).

The sociological explanation of the rule-governed character of social action is not, then, a causal explanation but an explanation of how actions can be seen to fall under the social descriptions of them (social rules) available to the members of society. It attempts to elucidate the constitution of action by social rules by way of an examination of the logics utilized by the members of society when making sense of settings of social interactions. Social actions may be construed, thereby, as moves akin to moves in a language game.

However, an additional problem lies in the sociological treatment of motive as the property of persons (i.e. as an object residing within the mind of the person). We cannot gain entry into the minds of other persons to see what is taking place within them; we can only make inferences as to what is taking place. Now, as Blum and McHugh (forthcoming) point out, motives provide for such inferences, i.e. motives can be seen as socially organized treatments (social rules) for making sense of the actions of others by ascribing particular orientations to them.

> To provide a motive then, is to formulate a situation in such a way as to ascribe a motive to an actor as part of his commonsense knowledge, a motive to which he was orientated in producing the action. To give a motive is thus not to locate a cause of the action, but is for some observer to assert how a behaviour is socially intelligible by ascribing socially available actors' orientations (Blum and McHugh, op. cit.).

They go on to suggest that motive, as a member's method for deciding what alter "owns" provides a socially available rule by which members intelligibly relate biographies to events. Motives, then, are not the properties of members but socially organized treatments for the ascription of properties to members by other members. We should not, therefore, "search for motives in the objects of talk and treatment, but in talk and treatment itself" (Blum and McHugh, op. cit.).

Returning to the sociological account of motivated actions, it now becomes possible to see that the sociologist uses motives to do precisely the same kind of work in the analysis of social action that Blum and McHugh describe with reference to the use of motives by lay members in the everyday world. What is interesting, then, about the ascription of typical motives to societal members on the part of the sociologist, is how the rules of ascription are provided from within the paradigmatic framework by which he understands the social world. So, for example, the Marxist paradigm provides for an account of the social world whereby social action is seen to have its motive springs in material ends. In other words, it accounts the social world in such a manner that the characteristics of motivated acts are already presupposed as part of the account itself. In general, then, when the sociologist arrives at an explanation of actions in terms of typical motives, he is actually engaged in supplying these motives out of the framework which he employs to understand the world. But what is required for the analysis of motives as social practices is not the practices of sociologists but the practices of members, i.e. a description of "the socially organized conditions which produce the practical and ordinary use of motive in the mundane affairs of societal members" (Blum and McHugh, op. cit.).

Now if, as McHugh succinctly puts it, the task of sociology is to describe "how the array called society is assembled out of what members do, not out of the causes and effects of what they do" (1970, p. 155), what method would provide for such a description? The answer would seem to lie in a form of verstehen. Just as lay members construct the social world by way of the interpretive procedures by which they search and document that world, so the sociologist is required to proceed to an interpretation and documentation of these first-order procedures of lay members. The problem then arises of distinguishing between lay and sociological accounts. Such a distinction may be seen to proceed from the position of observer, as opposed to that of lay member. The observer is not a party to the social interaction of which he is the witness except in so far as the process of data collection is a collaborative enterprise between observer and observed.[18] His system of relevancies differs from that of lay members in that they revolve around the problematics which are the focus of his discipline. This frame of reference, which Schutz has labelled the "scientific attitude", supercedes the observer's biographical situation and the natural attitude which is associated with it, and thereby allows the observer's problem to determine what is relevant to its solution. In suspending the natural attitude, then, the observer suspends his belief in the reality of the everyday world in order to treat the processes of its constitution as the problematic focus of analysis. Only in this sense would it be possible to refer to what might be called the disinterestedness of the observer.

The ethnomethodologists have refined what is involved in adopting the observer's frame of reference by way of two injunctions. Firstly, the observer is enjoined to treat the procedures of the everyday world as anthropologically strange. Secondly, the observer is enjoined to explicate systematically the role played by mundane or commonsense reasoning as a resource in his own explanations of the everyday world. I will return to this point a little further on in the chapter. In terms of these injunctions ethnomethodologists have devised observational techniques such as those of participant observation[19] which make use of organizational records and tape-recorded interviews (e.g. A. Cicourel: *The Social Organisation of Juvenile Justice*, 1968) and the creation of experimental situations in which the everyday expectancies of lay members are disrupted (e.g. H. Garfinkel: *Studies in Ethnomethodology*, 1967 and P. McHugh: *Defining the Situation*, 1968). Also, increasing use has come to be made of the video-taping of social settings particularly in the work of Cicourel on the acquisition of

---

[18] The chapters by Phillipson examine the collaborative character of data collection in sociology.

[19] For a critique of the procedures of conventional participant observation see Chapter 7 (Silverman).

language by children.[20] The aim, then, of observation is to generate accounts of the properties of the everyday world by focusing upon the describing practices of lay members in actual settings of on-going interaction.

Now, insofar as the generation of observational accounts is itself a form of documentation, there are problematic features associated with their production. However, one problematic feature, viz. the traditional objection that verstehen results in a process of uncontrolled empathy on the part of the observer, can be dismissed immediately as by the point. Such an objection assumes that the task of sociology is that of eliciting the objective character of an underlying social world. Moreover, it assumes that the sociological explication of social meanings lies between the observation of overt behaviour on the one hand and solipsistic intuition on the other. But insofar as the social world is intrinsically meaningful for its members we cannot rely on overt behaviour to reveal such unless we assume a false identification of meaning with overt behaviour alone.[21] Nor does verstehen imply that the observer is required to intuit the meanings of lay members out of his own experiences of the same (which would lead to solipsism) but that he document the interpretive procedures of members as they go about their everyday affairs. The necessity of verstehen methods is, then, dictated by the inherent subjectivity of the social world itself and the consequent problem of providing for an account of it in terms of such.

The problem, then, is not that sociological accounts are produced by way of verstehen techniques but that they are accounts and as such, are subject to the limitations of all accounts, viz, they are situated within a context upon which they implicitly rely for their sense.[22] Cicourel (forthcoming) has usefully underscored the indexical (situated) features of accounts, features which sociological accounts share with all other accounts.

> (The) invariant properties of cognition and thought are plausible only within a world taken for granted and known through self-serving practical reasoning. Operating with this principle of practical reasoning, the observer seeks to create and sustain coherence by organising information into practical chunks and normatively acceptable categories.

All accounts of whatever kind, then, presuppose practical commonsense reasoning and rely on such as a *resource* for constructing meaningful and viable explanations, i.e. all accounts are necessarily contextual and hence indexical. The validity of phenomenological accounts cannot lie, therefore, in a claim to be context-free (i.e. free from the context of practical reasoning) and thereby objective but rather in the claim that they treat practical reasoning as the *topic* of investigation. It becomes incumbent upon the phenomenologist, then, to provide an account of his own accounting procedures (i.e. to show how his own account relies on practical reasoning) in order to reveal the manner in which

---

[20] The chapters by Silverman and Filmer provide an account of these observational techniques in operation.

[21] Chapter 3 provides an account of behaviouristic sociology.

[22] The situated character of accounts has already been pointed to in the preceding pages on the management of explanations.

it is situated.[23] It is in terms of this process that phenomenological accounts differ from positivistic accounts which remain rooted in the natural attitude and its unexplicated reliance upon a commonsense understanding of that world. Phenomenological accounts, therefore, necessarily rely on commonsense to elucidate the everyday world but, in the process of accounting, this reliance is systematically explicated.

Now if, as the foregoing suggests, it is possible to generate an infinite number of accounts of any social scene, is there a point at which, for all practical purposes, the sociologist might cut off this infinite regress of meaning in his own account? One solution to the problem has already been suggested, viz. that the sociologist is required to situate his own account. Another allied solution may be achieved in pragmatic terms whereby an adequate sociological account might be seen as one which was sufficiently detailed to provide a set of instructions which would enable a stranger to reproduce the scenes described in the account. Returning then to Goodenough's definition of culture (presented in the introduction to this book) as:

> whatever it is one has to know or believe in order to operate in a manner acceptable to its (society's) members and do so in any role they accept for any one of themselves,

an adequate sociological account would be one which provided the required knowledge to pass as a member of the given setting under examination.

In terms of this second solution, then, any sociological account must depend for its validity upon the criteria of adequacy advanced by Schutz. That is, it must be an account of members' actions in terms of social meanings (the criterion of subjective interpretation) and the meanings must be those actually used by members to categorize those activities and can be recognized by them as such (the criterion of subjective adequacy).

THEORY CONSTRUCTION

The characteristic of theories in the natural sciences is that they take the form of universal statements from which it is possible to deduce connections between types of events under specified empirical conditions.

Theory in the natural sciences takes a deductive form, i.e. theories are universal statements from which particular connections between types of events under specified empirical conditions may be logically deduced and tested according to agreed procedures of validation. Such theories prescribe, therefore, the nature of the world to which they are addressed in terms of the descriptions which they provide of both the events which are to be explained and the empirical conditions under which they are connected to one another. Moreover the deductive form of explanation requires that descriptions be formulated according

---

[23] Cicourel has suggested that the sociologist can reveal the situated character of his own account of a social scene by triangulating it with other accounts of the same scene provided by different members. Silverman discusses triangulation in Chapter 7.

to the logical requirements of deductive argument. Now this requirement can only be met if the descriptions which enter into an argument are treated as independent of the particular occasions of their usage, i.e. an assumption has to be made that descriptions are context-free, are not indexical. What is interesting, then, is how, in the natural sciences, the common paradigm shared by scientists provides for a treatment of descriptions in precisely this manner. This is not to suggest that scientific descriptions are, in any sense, independent of the social occasions of their usage, since scientific activity is an intersubjective (socially organized) activity like any of the other activities within the social world. Rather it is to suggest that the scientific paradigm affords socially available descriptions of the natural world which are regularly understood and sustained in the same terms by the practitioners of science. They assume then, that for all practical purposes, they are talking the same language as one another, and use this assumption to make sense of the scientific accounts with which they are provided by fellow scientists. The scientific paradigm, then, provides a shared taken-for-granted context of commonsense understandings which members of the scientific community can use as a common resource for the interpretation of scientific work. Moreover, the unproblematic character of such commonsense understandings is ensured by the fact that the natural world, being unpossessed of intrinsic meaning, is not free to act back upon the scientist.

However, if social interaction is itself constituted by the interpretive procedures of members, and if these procedures cannot be understood outside of the socially organized occasions of their use, then it is not possible for sociology to construct deductive theories of social interaction? The sociologist's own account is itself an interpretation which, in documenting the appearances, actions and situational factors of the social setting as evidence of an underlying pattern of meaning and relevancies, relies on just this underlying pattern of meanings and relevancies to make sense. The descriptions of the sociologist cannot, then, be treated as context-free and do not, therefore, allow of their formulation according to the logical requirements of deductive argument. The world to which he addresses himself cannot be treated by the sociologist as empty of meaning and open to whatever constructions sociology cares to put upon it. To do so in the form of deductive theorizing about that world is not only to fail to comprehend the manner in which it is constituted and made available by the interpretive procedures of its members but is also to engage in its actual constitution by way of a naïve reliance upon a commonsensical understanding of that world.

Sociological theory, then, must start from the bottom and build up.

> Because our statements about society and order ultimately rest upon the activities of members, we must make problematic the relationship between macroscopic properties such as "cultures" and the experiential properties by which they can be said to operate. To fully describe an institution as a locus of group rules, for example, requires some description of how the institution looks to those engaging in the action, because they will be acting according to how it looks to them, and in so doing the institution will be maintained and changed (McHugh, 1968, p. 9).

CONCLUSION

The paradigm employed by the natural sciences is singularly appropriate to the character of a world which is unpossessed of an intrinsic relevance structure and upon which, therefore, meaning may be conferred by the deductive analytical procedures of the community of scientists itself. To apply this paradigm to the entirely different social world which is constituted by an intrinsic relevance structure necessarily mistakes both the character of that world and the character of the scientific paradigm itself. The aim of sociological phenomenology is, therefore, to suggest an alternative way of doing sociology to that of positivism and, moreover, an alternative which locates its foundations in the character of the social world.

SUGGESTIONS FOR FURTHER READING

BLUM, A., McHUGH, P. (1971) "The Social Ascription of Motives", *American Sociological Review*, Vol. 36, No. 1.

CICOUREL, A. (1964) *Method and Measurement in Sociology*, Free Press, New York.

GARFINKEL, H. (1967) *Studies in Ethnomethodology*, Prentice-Hall, Englewood Cliffs, New Jersey.

KUHN, T. (1970 rev.) *The Structure of Scientific Revolutions*, University of Chicago Press, Chicago.

LAKOTOS, I., MUSGRAVE, A. (eds.) (1971) *Criticism and the Growth of Knowledge*, Cambridge University Press, London.

McIVER, R. (1942) *Social Causation*, Ginn, New York.

POPPER, K. (1959) *The Logic of Scientific Discovery*, Routledge and Kegan Paul, London.

SCHUTZ, A. (1962) *Collected Papers*, Vol. I, Nijhoff, The Hague.

SCHUTZ, A. (1964) *Collected Papers*, Vol. II, Nijhoff, The Hague.

In Chapter Two, it was suggested that the interpretive procedures by which the positivistic sociologist produces and sustains a sense of social reality are effectively no different from those employed by ordinary members of society to achieve the same. Both sets of procedures produce explanations that are self-validating glosses of that reality by virtue of the reliance of such procedures on taken-for-granted assumptions about the reality which the reader is required to fill in before he can make sense of the explanations provided. Moreover, both sociological and lay explanations are commonsense glosses because they assume the pre-constituted character of that reality as an objective reality—that is, they are rooted in the natural attitude. There are no grounds, therefore, for treating one as superior to the other as an account of social reality.

Chapter Three is concerned with a documentation of the commonsensical character of positivistic sociology.

THREE

Varieties of Positivism

DAVID WALSH

DURKHEIM AND SOCIAL FACTS

All varieties of positivism in sociology have been influenced by Durkheim's polemical attempt to establish a scientifically grounded sociology in *The Rules of Sociological Method* (1938), summed up in his famous dictum to treat social facts as things.[1] Basically, he argues that whenever men come to interact together, they produce an emergent level of reality which is distinct from that of the individuals, and which is external to such individuals and exercises control over their actions. This reality sui generis consists of two kinds of phenomena. "First: ways of acting, thinking, and feeling, external to the individual, and endowed with a power of coercion, by reason of which they control him. . . . They consist of representations and of actions. . . . Since their source is not in the individual, their substratum can be no other than society, either the political society as a whole or some one of the partial groups it includes, such as religious denominations, political, literary, and occupational associations, etc. (this is the level of social organization). The second group of phenomena are: other facts without such crystallized form which have the same objectivity and the same ascendancy over the individual. These are called "social currents". Thus the great movements of enthusiasm, indignation and pity in a crowd do not originate in any one of the particular individual consciousnesses" (1938, pp. 3–4). This world of reality is, then, the objective word of social facts. But what is missing in Durkheim's account is some actual analysis of the processes by which the structure of social interaction produces an emergent social reality. That is, questions such as how an emergent social world is accomplished through shared gestures, signs and language, and the processes by which the shared character of such comes to be recognized

---

[1] "Social phenomena are things and ought to be treated as things" (Durkheim, 1938, p. 27).

by the members of society, are ignored in the Durkheimian account of social reality.

In effect, then, Durkheim assumes as the background to his sociological investigations the taken-for-granted commonsense view of the social world as an objective reality. The manner in which a social world becomes available as a phenomenon for investigation through the routine interpretive practices of its members is not, itself, treated as a problematic feature of that world. Sociology is to address itself to an already preconstituted world of social facts in order to determine the relationships between such facts—"the determining cause of a social fact should be sought among the social facts preceding it and not among the states of individual consciousness" (1938, pp. 110–11). Durkheim then proceeds to an elaboration of the appropriate procedure of sociology which is basically that classificatory typologies of social facts may be drawn up in terms of the overt characteristics of such facts. These typologies are then employed to establish causal and functional relationships between the social facts, using the technique of statistical correlation in the form of deductive comparisons.

What is particularly problematic about Durkheim's own work is that he continually vacillates over the nature of the social reality to which he addresses himself. At one point, the world of social reality is effectively treated as the realm of social facts; at another point, social facts turn out to be not the social reality but rather an external manifestation of it. In this second account, social reality is an internal reality; what Durkheim calls the collective consciousness of society. The problem here is that the relationship between the social facts and the reality of which they are a manifestation (indices) is never precisely established, so this internal reality takes on a certain disembodied quality. Moreover, in his later work, Durkheim moves increasingly away from social facts to social consciousness per se (see, for example, *The Elementary Forms of Religious Life*). Probably this is best explained in terms of his particular concern with the establishment of a scientifically grounded morality. Attempts to establish such a morality would founder in so far as the external characteristics of moral systems would become the focus of analysis, and such an analysis could only reveal the existence of cultural relativism in the moral sphere. Therefore, Durkheim, in the search for an objective morality is forced into an internal analysis of social life in order to establish the priority of the moral claims of society.[2]

BEHAVIOURISM

Sociological behaviourism takes its stand on the most literal interpretation of the two dicta advanced by Durkheim—namely, to treat social facts as things and to examine their relationships in terms of their observable properties. What is argued is that scientific observation and analysis is possible only with regard to overt behaviour operationally defined—that is, we can only analyse the behaviour

---

[2] I am indebted to Peter Lobel of North-Western Polytechnic for this point. I hasten to add that there is little else with which he would agree in this chapter.

of an object of (1) specified characteristics reacting to (2) a stimulus of specified characteristics within (3) a specified field of force. All social phenomena are reducible to the facts of overt behaviour which is then to be understood as the product of stimulus-response situations. The chief theoretical proponent of such a view, George Lundberg (1964) makes the corollaries of such a position clear:

(1) All phenomena are equally tangible, observable, and measurable.[3]

(2) Symbols are groups of words designating people's responses to other conditioning to respond in a given way.

(3) All subjective actions, such as "mind", "feeling", "motives", are meaningful for the scientist in so far as they are operationalized in terms of overt characteristics; if not, they are unverifiable.

The social world, then, may be characterized as an external object-world. This world consists of "the responses of the organisms-in-environment. . . . This includes the postulate of the external world and variations both in it and in the responders to it" (1964, p. 5). Those responses are brought about by the conditioning influences of the social environment, which constitutes a system of action, and take the form of "habit-systems". We may examine the operation of conditioning influences on behaviour through formulating hypotheses and testing them by "orderly assembling of data that will establish more firmly, modify, or refute the hypotheses. A hypothesis which is corroborated by repeated observations made by all qualified observers is thereupon called a principle or a law." (*ibid.*, p. 2)

Homans (1961) has developed a similar perspective in terms of social behaviour as an exchange process. He focuses on two levels of behaviour referred to as sub-institutional (dyadic face-to-face relationships) and institutional. The former constitute the basis of the latter. His argument is that subinstitutional relationships may be examined as relationships involving profits and costs to the individuals involved in them. Such are the stimuli to which the individual responds. The basic proposition is that the individual will develop positive sentiments towards the other individual in the relationship, except where his costs are higher than his profits for doing so. He elaborates further that (1) if individual *A* acting in a particular stimulus situation has been rewarded, the more similar a second stimulus is to the first, the more likely is the recurrence of the activity that was rewarded and (2) the more often within a given period of time *A* rewards the activity of *B*, the more often will *B* produce that activity. What is not made clear is the processes by which stimuli are recognized by the actor and integrated into the exchange. Moreover, the concept of exchange is so widely defined as to include virtually any and every action in what amounts to a tautological manner. Homans argues that such processes underlie institutional behaviour, the

---

[3] "What we have to work with as immediate data are our knowledge of sensory experience, i.e. inferences (symbolic representations), from sensation. . . . Thus, the social world can be conceptualized on the basis of inference from our subjective sense-data" (1964, p. 43).

only differences being that (1) in a complex organization, activities are maintained by contrived rewards, such as social approval, rather than by primary rewards and that (2) the process of exchange of rewarding activities becomes more indirect. Increasingly, reliance must be placed on stated norms. Hence complex organizations constitute systems organized through the institutionalization of a common normative structure—that is, one in a state of equilibrium. What remains unexamined are the problematic issues involved in the notion of a common normative structure and its relationship to dyadic interrelations, nor does he satisfactorily resolve the meaning of the concept of equilibrium.

In general then, Homans's account of social behaviour is unsatisfactory in many respects. As Cicourel points out:

> It is not clear how the actor utilizes "external" symbols (including structural information about occupation, age, wealth) when engaged in direct exchanges with others. Nor does Homans clarify how the actor infers "what is going on" over the course of inter-action (1970a, p. 18).

The particular problems of social behaviourism may be laid at the door of its reductionist conceptual framework which translates meaningful social activity into an object-world of overt behaviour. The question is then: How much sense can be made of social life in these terms? Presumably, the behavioural paradigm might make sense if a parallelism could be demonstrated between mental events (meanings) and material events such that it was possible to specify for every mental event, without using mentalistic terms, a behavioural state that corresponds to it. The meaning of the actor would then consist of his behavioural activity. But this would still leave over a series of highly problematic issues such as:

(1) How would one adequately account for the presence and efficacy of mind in the social world?

(2) How would one deal with the same overt behaviour that may have entirely different meanings to the actors?

(3) How would one examine negative actions (intentional refraining from action which escapes sensory observation)?

(4) How would one deal with non-face-to-face relations which operate on the basis of assumed meanings which are difficult to capture by sensory observations?

(5) The observer's own knowledge.

The attempt to encapsulate the social world in terms of the overt behaviour of its members misses the precise character of that world, namely its intrinsic meaningfulness.

Moreover, the richness of social life is hardly reducible to the straight-jacket of recurrent stimulus-response patterns. The evidence available from the works of sociologists and social psychologists, such as Mead, Garfinkel and Cicourel, points to the fact that the process of intercommunication between individuals, which lies at the heart of social relationships, is not merely one of stimulus and response but involves perceptual judgments on the part of the actors which, in turn, are the product of the organizing activity of consciousness. Social action is inexplicable without some concept of meaning which, in turn, depends upon some explanation of the emergence of mind.[4] Human activity and social processes cannot be reduced to behavioural categories examinable in terms of the concatenation of external forces that are observable, quantifiable and calculable without a consequent trivialization taking place.

VARIABLE ANALYSIS[5]

The nature of the analysis

Unlike behaviourism, variable analysis does not necessarily deny the meaningful character of social phenomena but attempts to reduce social life to variables and their relationships. Meaning is treated as an intervening variable. Such variables are structural and organizational categories of social life, identified as realities in terms of objective indices through the use of sociological concepts and models and of which social action is taken to be the product. The variables are seen as regularized patterns of interaction (such constitutes the definition of social structure in this approach). A recent paper has attempted to spell out more precisely these categories of social phenomena (variables) to which the sociologist is to address himself. It distinguishes between three such categories:

> *Category I:* Sociologists study phenomena which exist independently of the conceptions men have of them, e.g. age structure.

> *Category II:* Sociologists examine many phenomena which exist independently of the will of the individual though not independently of all or any conception men have of them. Class is one case in point, language another. Durkheim calls them social facts. It is important to realize that though social facts are realities which do not exist independently of any human conception of them, not all their characteristics are necessarily contained in these conceptions. Nor need the actors whose regularized action constitutes the social fact be aware of its relations to other aspects of the social structure, as is the case with many functional relations, e.g. suicide rates.

> *Category III:* Sociologists study social acts, i.e. behaviour meaningful to the actors concerned and considered from their viewpoint. It is assumed when studying action that actors exercise choice, if only between acting and doing nothing, or at least that it is possible to exercise choice. Categories I and II are not necessarily mutually exclusive. Social facts comprise social acts, or expectations of them, but the reverse need not be true (Bryant 1970, pp. 95–7).

I leave aside, for the moment, the remarkably ambiguous and contradictory manner in which social meaning is employed in this categorization of social phenomena to highlight its general point, namely that variables are to be identified externally using objective indices to determine their real existence.

---

[4] The requirement here turns, in part, on a satisfactory account of the "self".
[5] The term is taken from Blumer (1967).

Actors' meanings are not ignored, then; rather they are turned into variables themselves such as cultural prescriptions, role expectations, norms, values, interests and so on, which can, themselves, be identified in terms of objective indices. Such variables are given independent status vis-a-vis the actor, in the sense that he is conceived of as the passive vehicle of their operations. This is achieved by treating these variables as either internalized by the actor or as enforced by external mechanisms of social control, in a way that emphasizes their determinant character with regard to social action. By focusing on such stabilized social meanings as intervening variables, rather than upon how the actor operates such meanings, explanation can proceed by way of analysing action as the product of the mechanical association of variables within an external social world. Meaning, therefore, becomes a taken-for-granted element in the analysis itself. But, as Cicourel (1964) has pointed out, social meanings cannot be taken for granted in this manner. Norms and values are, at the very most, only formally stated or written rules. To explain how they operate with reference to social action, it is necessary that we examine the actors' differential perception and knowledge of them. What becomes crucial, therefore, is how the actor manages the discrepancies between formal rules, his expectations of what is expected or appropriate, and the practical and enforced character of both stated and unstated rules. Social meanings are thereby the problematic focus of concern.

Explanation in variable analysis proceeds by way of an attempt to establish causal connections between the specified variables on the assumption that:

> when we investigate stable social relations . . . or social relations in as much as they are stable, then there is often no need to go through the action scheme. . . . We can take it for granted, in which case "social fact" includes the idea of structured "social acts" (Bryant, 1970, p. 101).[6]

The procedure is usually one of establishing statistical correlations between variables and following up those relationships that are statistically significant (frequently comparative analysis will be brought into play at this point). Such correlations are used as a basis for the imputation of causal connections.

The important feature of such causal imputation lies in the observers' determination of what correlations are sociologically relevant because it is this which determines the explanatory outcome. Not every statistically significant correlation between the variables will be treated by the observer as sociologically relevant.[7]

It is at this point that the role played by theory in variable analysis takes on a degree of clarity. It is not just that the relationship between theory and research is vague and ill-defined that constitutes a problematic feature of such theory but that it implicitly relies on the observer's own everyday sense of social structure by virtue of the manner in which it takes the existence of an objective social

---

[6] What is particularly interesting about this statement is its commonsense assumption of a stable social order as the unproblematic background to social action. But how, one could meaningfully ask, is social order accomplished?

[7] See Chapter 5.

reality for granted. The process of data collection, then, is structured by the conceptual framework in such a way as to make it a self-validating exercise with regard to that framework[8]—that is, the data are made to fit the framework. The sociological demonstration of how things hang together, therefore, implicitly reflects the observer's everyday sense of how things hang together and is validated on this basis. It is no surprise, then, that replication is a problematic feature of variable analysis since conflicting accounts of supposedly the same phenomena revolve, not around data, but around competing conceptualizations of it. Thus, the deductive activity that characterizes much sociological theorizing is of a common-sense kind even in its most systematic formulations.

But the explicit formulated quality of such deductive theorizing distinguishes it from other forms of variable analysis which might be described as mindless and militant empiricism. By mindless empiricism, I refer to the kind of sociology in which no explicit theorizing takes place at all. Instead, we are treated to a series of unconnected findings about disparate subjects—I have in mind, here, the immense flow of methodologically "correct" trivia to which most sociological journals bear witness. Militant empiricism could be described as the kind of sociology that specifically eschews theory in favour of what it calls a practical concern with the facts. A most interesting example of such sociology is what has come to be known as the British Empirical Tradition (at least by the British). Its characteristic feature is the substitution of the practical concerns of governmental or non-governmental agencies and/or the moral concerns of the liberal establishment for sociological theory. The latter, no doubt, explains the particular frequency of the studies dedicated to the analysis of the incidence and causes of poverty in British Society.[9] The effect is to confuse social with sociological problems and to enshrine a self-consciously articulated commonsense (moral) view of sociology as a problem-solving discipline. The result, not surprisingly, is the production of a remarkably unselfconscious, naïve and sterile sociology.

These critical remarks may be given greater substance, however, by the examination of examples of variable analysis.

Examples of variable analysis

SUICIDE

Returning to Bryant's typology; he suggests we may distinguish social phenomena which exist independently of the will of the individual though not independently of all or any conception of them (Category II). Suicide rates were given as an example of such phenomena and it is useful here to consider Durkheim's work on the subject which is often taken to be a classic example of scientific procedure in sociology.

---

[8] The same, of course, is true in the natural sciences but there it is of little consequence because (1) the data are intrinsically meaningless and (2) there is consensual agreement between scientists with regard to the appropriate conceptual framework relevant to their concerns.

[9] This is not to deny that poverty may be a phenomenon of interest to sociologists.

Durkheim argues that certain morphological factors cause certain degrees and patterns of social interaction which, in turn, produce certain degrees of social integration. Social integration, as a state of society, is defined in *Suicide* (1952) in terms of the individual's tie to society. The argument here is that the tie is the cause of given degrees of egoism, altruism and anomie, and that the balance of the degrees of egoism, altruism and anomie is the cause of the suicide rate in a given society. The central point made by Durkheim is that the meaning of the statistical associations between the variables cannot be determined by finding out how the individuals see them but, rather, juridical norms may be treated as indicators and measures of fundamental meanings because they alone are objective facts. For Durkheim, then, suicide rates are a social fact to be examined in terms of associated social facts and not in terms of the social meanings of the members of society.

The result is unsatisfactory for a variety of reasons. Despite the claims by Durkheim that subjective meanings are to be ruled out of his account of suicide, it becomes clear that his analysis is permeated at every level by meanings supplied to make sense of his data. Moreover, these meanings are not, themselves, part of the data under investigation (which would be a requirement of his methodological rationale) but are, rather, drawn from his own commonsense understanding of everyday social experiences. Basically, the introduction of commonsense understandings into the analysis occurs because Durkheim, having rejected the meanings of the actors as part of the explanation, is left with a problem of closing the gap between unchanging juridical norms on the one hand and fluctuating suicide rates (from one group to another) on the other. J. Douglas (1967) has examined in some detail the manner in which Durkheim's commonsense understanding invades and vitiates the analysis.

First, although Durkheim is supposedly concerned with an account of suicide only in terms of overt behaviour, the social meanings of the statistical associations are of critical importance for his theoretical explanation—for example, the high degree of education and low suicide rate among Jews as compared with the high degree of education and high suicide rate among Protestants is explained in terms of the different significance that education has for Jews. Second, the social meanings of the statistics are supplied whole by Durkheim after it becomes clear that the statistics do not support the theory. This can be illustrated by returning to the example just quoted. Here Durkheim is attempting to demonstrate the existence of a relationship between education and the suicide rate, arguing that a high degree of education is associated with a high suicide rate. The problem is that this does not fit Jews, which forces him to supply an explanation of this discrepancy in terms of an imported meaning (the different significance of education for Jews) which makes sense of this discrepancy but which is not, itself, part of the data. The important question then becomes that of establishing where Durkheim derives these imported meanings from, since they are not derived from the data. The answer is that the meanings of the relationships between the data on external associations and suicide rates tends to be established by Durkheim in terms of his own commonsense knowledge of social action in

European societies. So, for example, the argument advanced by Durkheim that common morality reproves suicide is nothing more than a taken-for-granted assumption on his part that common morality corresponds to his morality since he offers absolutely no evidence from the data to support it. Or, again, in explaining the different relations between non-marriage, marriage and suicide rates for men and women, he invokes differences between the masculine and feminine mind and social position in the form of a commonsense interpretation that conveniently fits his theory but is not demonstrated by any evidence.[10] What these examples point up is that Durkheim's analysis is not conducted, in fact, in terms of external social forces as the independent determinants of social action. Rather, he proceeds to an argument that implies that social meanings cause social action and, hence, suicide. The problem is that he never treats the actual structures of social meaning employed by the actors but merely takes them for granted by substituting his own commonsense meanings for theirs.

A second major problem of *Suicide* is the nature of the statistical data on which the analysis relies and which is never questioned. The relevant point here is that these data have not been gathered by the sociologist but are official data.[11] Now the characteristic feature of official statistics is that they reflect the practical concerns and meanings of the agencies which collect them. The data are biased in terms of the requirements of practical decision-making of such agencies and, as such, are quite unreliable. Douglas has suggested that we may distinguish a number of major ways in which such unreliability is manifest. First, there is often more than one set of official statistics that may be used for analysis—for example, in France, both the Ministry of the Interior and the Department of Criminal Justice collect statistics on suicide and there are major discrepancies between them. How is one to choose between them? Second, there are clear sub-cultural differences in attempts to hide suicide which will be reflected in the official statistics (for example, among Catholics as compared with Protestants). The extent to which such attempts to hide suicide are successful may depend on how strongly integrated are such sub-cultural groups. With regard to this point, Douglas suggests that:

---

[10] "When a widow is seen to endure her condition better than a widower and desires marriage less passionately . . . it is said that a woman's affective faculties, being very intense, are easily employed outside the domestic circle, while her devotion is indispensable to man to help him to endure life. Actually, if this is her privilege, it is because her sensibility is rudimentary rather than highly developed. As she lives outside of community existence more than man, she is less penetrated by it; society is less necessary to her because she is less impregnated with sociability. She has few needs in this direction and satisfies them easily. With a few devotional practices and some animals to care for, the old unmarried woman's life is full. If she remains faithfully attached to religious traditions and thus finds ready protection against suicide, it is because these very simple forms satisfy all her needs. Man, on the contrary is hard beset in this respect. As his thoughts and activity develop, they increasingly overflow these antiquated forms. But then he needs others. Because he is a more complex social being, he can maintain his equilibrium only by finding more points of support outside himself, and it is because his moral balance depends on a large number of conditions that it is more easily disturbed" (Durkheim, 1952, pp. 215–16).

[11] The reliance on official statistics is not just a characteristic of Durkheim's work but of most other studies of suicide conducted within a similar framework.

the more integrated the deceased individual is into his local community and with its officials, the more the doctors, coroners, or other officials responsible for deciding what the cause of death is will be favourably influenced, consciously or sub-consciously, by the preference of the deceased and his significant other (1967, p. 213).

Third, there are significant variations in the social imputations of motives in terms of which suicide is defined as such. Finally, there are more extensive and professional statistics for certain populations than others. Official suicide statistics are, then, problematic by virtue of the social meanings that surround them.

What emerges, therefore, as a requirement of the analysis of suicide is the necessity of investigating the social meanings by which acts are defined as such, since it is this process of definition which brings suicide into existence as a social phenomenon. Here Douglas has sought to demonstrate how suicide is constituted by the meaningful categorizations of officials charged with the investigation of certain kinds of acts. As a central feature of such categorization is the common-sensical imputations of intention to die as the most crucial element in defining suicide. Characteristically such an imputation is the outcome of a process of negotiation.

> The imputation of the official category of the "cause of death" is very likely the outcome of a complex interaction process involving the physical scene, the sequence of events, the significant others of the deceased, various officials (such as doctors, police), the public and the official who must impute the category (ibid., pp. 189–90).

Official suicide statistics are the organizational record of this process of documentation. Suicide, then, as a phenomenon available for investigation is highly problematic by virtue of its constitution by such interpretive procedures.

The answer to the problem does not lie in collecting more precise statistics to get at some "real" rate of suicide as though this had some concrete existence in an external social world and was the product of a number of interrelated structural variables. Rather we need to examine the social meanings of suicide and the routine practices by which such meanings are enforced.

> How many "suicides" there are in a given group at a given time is dependent on the concrete argument processes used. A sociologist might arbitrarily choose one dimension of meaning of "suicide" and attempt to construct a "real rate" for this dimension. However, such a procedure would probably be irrelevant in explaining such meaningful action as suicide. Moreover, how could one ever avoid the prior social screening process, which is subject to all of the essentially problematic meanings that result from an argument process? And, even if one could do this, how could one construct a "real rate" of "intention", so necessary in almost all formal and commonsense definitions of suicide and so essentially problematic itself? (ibid., p. 231).

The problems presented by Durkheim's account of suicide stem essentially from his sociologistic account of society, in which phenomena such as suicide rates, social integration, social order and so on, are conceptualized as realities "out there" in an external social world operating independently of human meaning and activity. Consequently he misses the precise character of such phenomena, which is the manner in which they are constituted by social meanings. In particular, he misses the manner in which suicide is constituted as a social act by a commonsense definition in terms of intentional death, which is, in turn, the basis of the official categorization of such acts. The result is that, in order to make sense of suicide rates, Durkheim continually bends the data to fit his preconceived conceptualization and associated theories by supplying interpretations of the data that suit the latter. In this sense, his analysis frequently rests upon unexplicated, speculative and untested commonsense assumptions about social reality. One is left with the impression, as Douglas (1970a) remarks in a different context, that Durkheim knows the general structure of reality and now needs only to confirm it. But it is precisely this which is open to question not only as regards the work of Durkheim but also as regards positivistic sociology in general.

CRIME

Attempts to explain the causes of crime possibly provide an even more pertinent example of the problematic features of variable analysis than Durkheim's analysis of suicide. The characteristic feature of such criminological studies consists in procedures which correlate criminal behaviour with varieties of social structural variables, such as education, class position, family background, poverty and so on, in an attempt to locate the determinants of such behaviour. Typically these variables are identified in terms of objective indices constructed by the observer. Actors' meanings are taken for granted or ignored as part of the explanation.[12] The aim of such studies is usually the practical one of prediction. This focus on prediction would seem to be best explained in terms of the social-problem orientation as opposed to the sociological-problem orientation of criminology. In effect, this means that the practical concerns of the agencies of law and order in society, which revolve around problems of the detection and prevention of crime and delinquency, are treated by criminologists as the central problematic of their investigations. This consequent confusion of social with sociological problems operates to the detriment of sociology.

What status can we accord to the concepts of crime and the criminal as categories of social action and social actor provided by this kind of analysis? The answer is problematic for a variety of reasons. First, crime is a legal category of action. Within such terms then, the only manner in which crimes (as social acts) could be said to be alike is that they are all violations of the law, in which case the only cause of crime, in this sense, is the law itself. What is a crime in one society is no crime in another society and what is a crime at one time in a particular society is not a crime at another. Second, the only common characteristics shared by official criminals is they have been caught breaking the law. Finally, official criminal statistics, like official suicide statistics, refer, in effect, to official detection and public reporting rates and, as such, are both organizationally generated and reflect organizational meanings. In so far as criminologists rely on officially produced statistics to compute the real rate of crime and then use them

---

[12] See, for example, Mannheim and Wilkins (1956).

to arrive at explanations of the causes of these rates, they merely compound the various problems involved by taking over organizational definitions of appearances. Crime (and the criminal), then, are not "objective" categories of action (and actor) the causes of which can be examined, but commonsense social meanings used by the members of society to label certain kinds of actions and actors as being of a given kind. Sociological analysis, therefore, should focus upon the processes by which acts are labelled to arrive at a meaningful examination of "criminal" activity.

Many of these criticisms of the traditional approach of criminology have been made by sociologists other than the phenomenologically oriented. For example, the work of leading interactionists, such as Becker, Cohen, Erikson, Lemert and Matza, has been primarily concerned with reorienting sociology away from a concern with crime to a concern with social deviance in precisely these critical terms. Moreover, in advocating that social deviance and not crime should constitute the focus of sociological investigation, they have stressed the importance of social meanings with reference to deviant activity. Under the heading of "labelling theory", this perspective examines the manner in which groups create deviance by making rules, the infraction of which constitutes social deviance. Social deviance, then, is not a quality of the act but a consequence of the application of rules and sanctions to an offender. The social deviant is the person who has been labelled as such. One may then look at the degree of deviance and the manner of its production by focusing upon ongoing processes of action and reaction through which individual behaviour and outlooks develop. The self-conceptions of the deviating individual are considered in relationship to the processes of labelling produced by the audience that confers social deviance (either the wider society or the more specific agents of social control). The argument, then, is that social deviance is, to a large extent, an ascribed status—it reflects what other people do as much as what the deviating actor himself does.[13]

What remains problematic about labelling theory, however, is the manner in which it examines social meanings and the processes of labelling. First, although proponents of labelling theory suggest that "social deviance" is a highly ambiguous category of social action, they fail to spell out the precise connotations of their own usage both as an observer's category and as an actor's category of action.[14] Second, the actual relationship between the commonsense labelling activities of the members of society and the observer's conceptualization of these processes of labelling remains unexplicated—how is the sociologist's conceptual framework generated with reference to these processes? Finally, and in relation to

---

[13] For a discussion of labelling theory, see Phillipson (1971b).

[14] "It is also a fact of social life and not just a product of sociology's confusion, that there are obscure borderlands between deviance and conformity; people themselves are sometimes unsure of themselves and sometimes cannot agree on what is deviant" (A. Cohen, 1966, p. 12). "The subject itself does not seem to have any natural boundaries" (Erikson, 1966, p. 5). "All is not well with deviation as currently conceived, and that its adoption into the official lexicon of our discipline may be premature" (Lemert, 1964, p. 57). See Phillipson and Roche (1971).

this last point, labelling theory continues to be firmly anchored in the depiction of the real world that underlies appearances even though it shifts its concerns away from positivistic categories of behaviour to meaningful categories of action. Thus, the examination of everyday deviant activity in terms of shared symbols and meanings remains wedded to an account of what the social world is really like. It differs from positivism in conceiving of that world and the socially deviant acts within it as having a shifting precarious and negotiated character. However, it still treats of that world as "real" and "out there". Socially deviant acts, then, are part of that world and are available for examination as such. In this sense, analysis may proceed to attempts to measure the actual rates of social deviance within society. It is at this point that such theory parts company with sociological phenomenology, which would deny the existence of the social world independently of the social meanings that its members use to account it and, hence, constitute it. In this sense, sociological accounts addressed to the elucidation of the under-lying reality of the social world remain a species of members' explanations rooted in the commonsense attitude which takes that world for granted—they remain first order accounts.

The import of this last remark is that the sociological analysis of social deviance must necessarily examine the commonsense procedures of typification by which members of the everyday world identify and make sense of social acts as deviant acts. With reference to this, McHugh has suggested that the commonsense identification of deviant acts rests upon two taken-for-granted assumptions (background relevances), namely, that the act took place within a situation of choice and that the actor knew what alternatives were open to him.

> That is to say that members, judgers, assessors, and labellers have a notion of the behavioural possibilities in any scene and, beyond that, a notion of the actor as an agent of his own behaviour. It makes a difference to them whether an act had to occur or not and whether an actor knows what he is doing or not, and it is upon these two commonsense considerations that the social designations of responsibility, conformity, and deviance depend in any given state of affairs. These considerations, thus, are commonsense rules for deciding what is deviant and what is not, for distinguishing between various kinds of deviance (1970, p. 152).

From this it becomes clear that the acts *per se* are uninteresting since social deviance refers to the ways in which acts are received and accounted. The empirical observation of social deviance, therefore, should be the empirical observation of the processes of accounting social deviance and the commonsense criteria of social deviance that are used by lay members to identify and document deviant acts in the ongoing processes of practical decision-making that take place within the context of social interaction.

This latter point is of particular importance because the identification and documentation of social deviance as a reality by the members of society is not just the unproblematic outcome of a simple application of interpretive criteria (rules). It is, rather, the outcome of processes of negotiation between members as they conduct their routine everyday activities. The negotiated character of social deviance as a social reality has been amply demonstrated by Cicourel in *The Social Organization of Juvenile Justice* (1968). In this study, Cicourel focuses upon the practical decision-making activities of agencies formally charged with the task of handling juvenile delinquency as they go about their routine tasks. He shows how social deviance is organizationally generated by such agencies in terms of these activities. Conversations between the delinquent, his parents, the policeman who arrested him, the lawyer and the judge are pieced together and the sum total of such conversations represents the organizational documentation that a delinquent act has or has not occurred.

Additional work by Sudnow (1968b) has produced similar findings. He focuses upon the commonsense practices developed by public defenders in United States courts for dealing with the routine problems of dispatching cases through the courts with the minimum trouble and delay. Primarily the problem is dealt with by persuading the defendant to plead "guilty". This is achieved in a bargaining process between the defendant and the public defender whereby the former is offered the possibility of a lighter sentence if he will facilitate the course of justice by pleading guilty to a lesser offence. The bargaining process takes place within the context of a commonsense understanding shared by the defendant and the public defender of what would constitute a normal crime of the kind for which the defendant is being prosecuted. This understanding of the normal is, in turn, grounded in the public defender's previous experiences of cases of "this kind". The plea of guilty, therefore, involves something altogether different from merely being the unproblematic outcome of charges pressed by the police in situations where they are certain that a crime was committed by the defendant. Moreover, the crime which gets recorded in the official statistics is related to the acts of the defendant only through this process of interpretation; in effect, it constitutes them as phenomena.

The general point, then, which emerges is that all organizations (including the agencies of law and order in society) develop routine practices and procedures for handling clients and documenting their activities.[15] Organizational statistics (which would include official criminal statistics) are nothing more than a record of such documentation. Social deviance, therefore, is the outcome of complex processes of commonsense typification by which acts are labelled as such (particularly by official organizations). The kind of sociology which treats social deviance as being a quality of acts and proceeds to count such acts statistically in order to relate them to structural categories, remains firmly rooted within the commonsense view of the social world as a real world. These commonsense assumptions, then, constitute the implicit basis of its frame of reference. In this sense, such sociology is really a species of folk wisdom which does little more than elaborate the commonsense attitude towards social deviance. Conversely, what requires examination, if sociology is to distinguish itself from folk wisdom,

---

[15] In a different context, Sudnow has examined the social organization of death in a hospital setting. He shows that death and dying are "the set of practices enforced when staff employ those terms in the course of their work on the hospital ward" (1968a, p. 8).

are the actual processes of commonsense typification themselves, since it is they that constitute social deviance as a social phenomenon.

DEMOGRAPHY

If we now turn to the examination of phenomena defined by Bryant as phenomena that exist independently of the conceptions men have of them (category I), it remains true that these, too, are data which cannot be divorced in any useful sociological sense from social meanings. Typically, the kind of phenomena dealt with by demography (age structure, family size, migration, population size) are presented as though they were hard objective data. However, analysis suggests that an interpretation of the social meanings within which they are embedded is a requirement of their explication.

For our purposes, it is particularly useful to focus on family size. The family is conceived, by demographers, as a structural entity integrated into a larger organized set of structural conditions (such as the kinship system, the occupational system and the pattern of economic development) and, is generally seen in terms of the requirements of these larger conditions. The decisions which occur within the family with regard to size are then assumed to be responses to such conditions. In particular, the process of industrialization is identified by demographers as a process involving the progressive rationalization of the social structure which articulates itself to the family in terms of a series of demands involving formally rational choices (such as between having more children or giving more freedom to the wife, or between having more children or spending more money on fewer children, or between having more children or increasing the family's standard of living in general). However,

> we cannot take it for granted that the focal point of family life revolves around not being able to conceive, a desire for male offsprings, having "too many" children, still-birth, and the like although these issues certainly intrude upon some part of a family's existence (Cicourel, 1967, p. 59).

Nor can we assume that the processes of practical decision-making within a family setting that give rise to the number of children within that family represent some determined response to larger structural requirements in the manner suggested. The social processes internal to the family that produce differential births are the outcome of complex procedures of practical decision-making. A requirement for the analysis of differential births, therefore, is an examination of "how families emerge through marriages of some type, sustain themselves over time, or dissolve and/or become reconstituted in different arrangements" (ibid., p. 62). Values about family size refer to the everyday rules invoked by actors and require analysis in terms of those rules. Family size, then, like any other demographic data, is problematically related to the practices of everyday decision-making on the part of social actors.

Hawthorne in a recent paper on fertility (1968), argued more extensively in a later book) has recognized some of these problems. He attacks demography, both for its lack of a sound theoretical structure and its failure to examine the causal importance to fertility of people's intentions. He argues for an analysis that will combine the two, suggesting that one might usefully use a model of fertility which conceptualizes societies (social systems) as regulating themselves so as to achieve an optimum level of population size. To avoid the inherent reification implied in the notion of social system, he further suggests that the intentions of a social system be understood as no more than the sum of individual intention or as the majority intention. With this in mind, he suggests that any theory of fertility will have at least three sorts of explanations in mind:

> causal, tracing connections between structure and fertility intentions; teleological, tracing them between the intentions and fertility behaviour; and functional, a species of causal relationship, tracing connections between the fertility behaviour and its effects on the population itself (1968, pp. 68–9).

But the problems with such an account are still (1) the deterministic connotations of social structure introduced by the notion of cause, and (2) the ambiguous character of "equilibrium" and "optimum population size". These problems remain despite the recognition of the importance of actors' intentions.

However, the general problem pointed to by Hawthorn remains a valid one, namely, that an effective analysis of demographic data cannot proceed without a solid theory of basic social processes. This in turn would require the analysis of "how persons perceive and interpret their environments so that cultural definitions continually alter the meanings placed upon even the most clear-cut and unambiguous matters" (Cicourel, 1964, p. 130).

> In seeking rational sets of conditions in his data, the demographer even when recognizing that cultural patterns shape the progressive rationalization of society, continually imputes rationality to the actors . . . obviously a classification is required which would show the extent to which the rationalization of society, urbanization and secular ways of thinking are transformations of strict rationality in the scientific sense. This entails showing how cultural definitions and action patterns based on commonsense conceptions of kinship, primary relations, religions beliefs, and the "good life", and so on, alter strict rationality (ibid., pp. 130–1).

The explanations of demographic data, in terms of the thesis of rationalization, are impositions of the observer's meanings upon the data. Success is related to the survey techniques used by demographers.

> The individual responds to that conception of the world with whatever alternatives the researcher presents him and hence to a conception of himself and his way of life that enables the researcher to decide what and where the individual stands in the general scheme of things that links kinship with economic development and population growth (Cicourel, 1967, p. 61).

A related point is made by Hawthorne, in his critique of survey methods in demographic analysis, when he attacks the naïve inductivist manner in which surveys are used to look for, rather than test, hypotheses.[16] The point, then, about the imposition of meaning by demographers is that not only is it unfounded but that it is also self-validating.

The alternative to standard demography, therefore, would be examination of the data in terms of an understanding of the commonsense meanings that actors employ in their everyday activities. The rationale that lies behind such an approach is one which argues that the data are, themselves, nothing more than the outcome of such activity.

CRITICAL SUMMARY OF VARIABLE ANALYSIS

Two interrelated general points of criticism can be directed towards variable analysis.

First, the general critique developed with reference to variable analysis in this chapter has sought to demonstrate that the social world is constructed by its members in terms of their accounting procedures for explaining it. In the process of accounting, members rely on tacit commonsense assumptions about the nature of the objects and events within the social world and, in these terms, confer objective facticity upon that world—that is, they turn the social world of which they are part into an objective reality for themselves. The social construction of reality is, therefore, a process of first-order construction. Now it follows that positivistic sociological explanations are also a species of first-order construct in so far as they attempt to elucidate the nature of the social world in terms of its objective dimensions. Moreover, such explanations are glosses like the explanations of lay members of society in the sense that they make tacit use of assumptions about the objects and events within the social world. The difference is that analysis is conducted in terms of the commonsense of "scientific" discourse which revolves around the principles of formal logic or rationality. The point, however, is that such explanations, like the explanations of other members of society, structure reality in certain preconceived ways. The sociologist who engages, therefore, in such explanations is engaged, like lay members, in the construction of the social world and not in the explication of its construction. What characterizes positivistic sociology is its inability to grasp this crucial fact so that it remains ignorant of the manner in which its research procedures (like the everyday procedures of the members of society) produce the reality to which it addresses itself. Instead, it treats its frame of reference and questions as somehow tapping the objective reality which underlies appearances.

What requires analysis, however, are the processes by which social reality is constructed. Such a requirement does not dictate that sociological constructs should be the same as members' constructs; rather they should constitute a

---

[16] Hawthorn argues that although in practice such methods substitute simple correlations for causal relations, the former are taken as being cases of the latter. Moreover, the various correlations are treated in an unconnected manner *vis-à-vis* one another. Finally, the actual selection of variables for investigation is often more or less unguided by any particular rationale other than ease of handling and commonsense assumptions of what may be important.

species of documentary constructs that systematically relate to the social meanings employed by actors in their everyday activities. This process of documentary construction can be achieved if the sociologist suspends the commonsense belief in the reality of the social world in order to examine the processes by which it is constructed. In this sense, sociological accounts are erected in terms of the sociologist's system of relevancies which should centre around the treatment of the commonsense world as a topic of investigation. The sociologist thereby removes himself from the position of simple lay member of that world to observer of it. This does not, of course, make the explanation he produces any less of a gloss (all explanations necessarily rely on tacit underlying assumptions) but does allow the glossing practice itself to be an object of examination, and not an unexamined resource for the explanation. The weakness of positivistic sociology rests, in the last analysis, on its failure to move from the position of everyday member to that of observer, a failure which is entailed in the acceptance of the commonsense view of the social world as an objective reality bolstered by a naïve belief in the efficacy and objectivity of its own procedures. To this extent, positivistic sociology is engaged in the process of underscoring and elaborating the commonsense view of the world itself.

The second point is that in so far as variable analysis addresses the relationship of social meanings to social action at all, it fundamentally misconceives the character of that relationship by treating social meanings as an intervening variable between other social conditions and the social act.[17] Not only is the social world constituted by social meanings but such meanings are not unitary and distinct variables but rather intricate and inner-moving. Even where social life is rationalized through an organized structure of social meanings, the interpretations that actors place upon such meanings as they address objects, events and situations requires examination. It is, therefore, the dynamic and self-organizing character of social meanings to which the sociologist must address himself. Social meanings, then, are only to be understood within the context of their management in settings of social interaction.

It follows that sociology requires an examination of the commonsense world of daily life rather than a settlement of it by theoretical representation or a taken-for-granted assumption of it as the background to social activity. Instead of assuming the social standardization of meanings in terms of objective categories, such as role prescriptions, norms and values, the sociologist should examine how action allows the actor to discover, create and sustain this standardization. This, in turn, requires a reversal of the traditional sociological account of the relationship between social action and social structure which treats the former as determined by .the latter – social structure cannot refer to anything more than members' everyday sense of social structure since it has no identity which is independent of that sense.[18]

---

[17] For further comments, see Chapter 5.
[18] See Cicourel (1970b).

In conclusion, then, positivism seriously mistakes the character of the social world in assuming the common identity of natural and social phenomena. The methodological problems it sees as associated with such a common identification and which it treats as the teething problems of a young science, possessing relatively unsophisticated techniques (for example, the complexity of social phenomena, defining sociological variables, constructing models and measuring variables, constructing objective criteria of validity), are both misunderstood and are irrelevant. The task of sociology is not that of how best to refine its techniques for capturing the elusive reality of a taken-for-granted social world, because such an approach remains firmly anchored in a naïve commonsense view of that world. Moreover the interpretive procedures by which the positivist sociologist examines the social world are procedures of first-order construction that actually determine the reality of that world. To add the sophisticated rider to first-order sociological accounts that the social world is more complicated than it might seem to its lay members (who are, in this sense, cultural dopes) does no more than elaborate the commonsense view of that world. If a distinctively sociological frame of reference is to be developed, it must take as its topic the structure of the commonsense world itself: it must examine the everyday procedures used by the members of society to construct a social world. This would necessarily involve abandoning the present infatuation with the methodology of the natural sciences in favour of the development of a methodology appropriate to the analysis of world building as a social process. This is not to presume, of course, that the accounts produced in this manner could avoid a reliance on commonsense assumptions to make sense themselves but that such assumptions would be explicated in the process of accounting and not be taken-for-granted as part of the account.

SUGGESTIONS FOR FURTHER READING

BRYANT, C. (1970) "In Defence of Sociology", *British Journal of Sociology*, Vol. 21, No. 1.

CICOUREL, A. (1967) "Fertility, Family Planning and the Social Organization of Family Life", *Journal of Social Issues*, Vol. 23, No. 4.

CICOUREL A. (1968) *The Social Organization of Juvenile Justice,* Wiley, New York.

DOUGLAS, J. (1967) *The Social Meanings of Suicide*, Princeton University Press, Princeton.

DREITZEL, H. P. (ed.) (1970) *Recent Sociology No. 2*, Macmillan, New York.

HAWTHORN, G. (1968) "Explaining Human Fertility", *Sociology*, Vol. 2, No. 1; *The Sociology of Fertility*, Collier-Macmillan, London.

LUNDBERG, G. (1964 rev.) *The Foundations of Sociology*, David McKays, New York.

McHUGH, P. (1968) *Defining the Situation*, Bobbs-Merrill, Indianapolis.

PHILLIPSON, M. (1971) *Sociological Aspects of Crime and Delinquency*, Routledge and Kegan Paul, London.

SUDNOW, D. (1968) "Normal Crimes", in Rubington and Weinburg (eds.) *Deviance: An Interactionist Perspective.*

Functionalism switches the focus of sociological explanations towards the analysis of the social world as a system of interconnected social phenomena organized through the agency of a common normative framework. Not only does it retain many of the problematic features pointed to in the previous chapter, therefore, but it now introduces the additional problem of the reification of society which is implied in the concept of system. Moreover, the central notion of a common normative framework fails to come to grips with the character of social meaning in relationship to social action.

FOUR

Functionalism and Systems Theory

DAVID WALSH

FUNCTIONALISM

Functionalism differs in analytical approach from variable analysis by choosing to focus on the reciprocal relationships between structural and organizational variables within the context of an organized framework. Merton defines its central orientation as expressed "in the practice of interpreting data by establishing their consequences for the larger structures in which they are incorporated" (1957, p. 46). Functionalism, then, proposes a model of society conceptualized as a system of social relationships and clusters of such relationships (institutions). The characteristic feature of the system is the manner in which it is organized into an ordered and self-maintaining entity by a common pattern of norms and values, which ensures both the reciprocal interdependence of its parts and the consequent integration of the whole. Action is a product of system properties.

Using a biological analogy, functionalism hypothesizes that the operations of the social system may be likened to the operations of an organism operating within an environment. Just as the physical environment within which an organism operates places requirements upon that organism whose fulfilment is the necessary condition for the survival of that organism, so the environmental context within which the social system operates places similar demands upon it. Moreover, the organizational structure of the social system (like that of an organism) may be represented as an adaptive response to these environmental demands. The parts of the social system may be said to be functional, therefore, in the sense that they contribute to the survival of the system by virtue of the operations which they perform vis-à-vis the required conditions of its existence. Change of the social system (like that of an organism) is a process of evolution whereby the system becomes better adapted to an existing environment or adapts to a changing environment. Some allowance is made for the possibilities of arrested development or even regress of the social system but the process of social change is basically one of increasing differentiation and integration of the system.

TALCOTT PARSONS

Although the work of anthropologists and sociologists such as Spencer, Malinowski, Radcliffe-Brown and, in particular, Durkheim represent classic formulations of the functionalist model of the social system, there are a variety of reasons for choosing the work of Parsons to the exclusion of these others. First, Parsons's model of the social system is probably the most elaborate formulation that has been produced to date within the functionalist framework. Second, Parsons has been a major directing influence on the work of American functionalists in the last thirty or so years and much of the work produced by such sociologists has, to a great extent, tended to be an elaboration of its initial formulations. Third, in so far as Parsons has claimed to incorporate what is usually considered to be the antithetical action frame of reference into his model, this allows of a useful exploration of the potential tension between the ideas of "action" and "system". Finally, the model of the social system proposed by Parsons incorporates ideas taken from earlier writers: moreover, Durkheim is discussed extensively elsewhere in this book.

Parsons claims that his model of the social system locates, as its central concern, the problem of social order. Yet, surprisingly in this respect, he chooses to define the social system in terms of order.

> The most general and fundamental property of a system is the interdependence of parts or variables. Interdependence consists in the existence of determinate relationships among the parts or variables as contrasted with the randomness of variability. In other words, interdependence is order in the relationship among the components which enter into the system (Parsons and Shils, 1951, p. 107).[1]

Order, in turn, is the product of two processes stemming from the common normative pattern which organizes the interdependence of the parts of the system, namely (1) a tendency of the social system to self-maintenance (equilibrium) and (2) a tendency of the social system to maintain certain boundaries relative to an environment (homeostasis). Now the presupposition, on the part of Parsons, of the orderly character of systems in terms of common norms and values actually settles, in terms of theoretical representation, the problem to which the model is supposedly addressed, namely the problem of social order. Consequently, social order becomes the taken-for-granted background to the explanation of system processes in general and social action in particular.

The central feature of the model, then, is an analysis of the operations of the system in the environment. The environment, which itself is a series of systems, articulates to the social system in terms of the functional prerequisites for the

---

[1] In so far as the social system is both defined and explained in terms of social order, there is an inevitable tautological quality in the reasoning processes involved at this point.

survival and equilibrium of that system. In turn the organization of activities within the system represents the structured response of the system to these requirements. Parsons, therefore, is concerned with the areas of interchange between the social system and other systems. These other systems he labels the physical system, the cultural system and the personality system. The primary reality of the physical system is the scarcity of resources which gives rise to the functional prerequisite of *adaptation*. The adaptive problem is that of rationally organizing the object world (through the allocation of personnel and resources) such as to attain the ends of the system. This prerequisite is met by the activity of the economy. The primary reality of the cultural system is the problem of the co-existence of men and, more particularly, the legitimation of the system's normative order.[2] This gives rise to two prerequisites, *goal attainment* and *integration*.

The problem of *goal attainment* is that of ensuring that the action system moves steadily towards its goals and is met by the activities of the polity. The problem of integration is that of maintaining cooperation between the inter-related units in the face of the emotional strains produced by both the processes of goal-attainment and the manner in which the products of cooperation are shared (the problem of social solidarity). This problem is met by the activities of religion or by some functional alternative (such as secular ideologies) which legitimate the social order. The primary reality of the personality system is the unsocialized individual, which gives rise to the prerequisite of *latency*. The latency problem is that of making sure the units have the required motivation to move the system towards its goals by participating in the appropriate activities. This problem is met by the family which: (1) undertakes the process of primary socialization (building the requirements of the social system into the structure of individual personalities), and (2) provides emotional support for its members.[3] The four prerequisites interlock with one another such that adaptation and goal-attainment constitute the "task area" of "instrumental activity" and integration and latency the "social emotional area" of "expressive activity". The two problems, then, faced by the social system, and in terms of which it must organize its activities, are those of creating technically effective methods by which the ends approved by the cooperators may be achieved and of maintaining efficient cooperation between them.

Parsons claims that the social system is a system of action but one can ask: In what sense? Primarily, the answer is, in two senses: first, the social system is an emergent product of any processes of social interaction and second, the vehicle of the operation of the system's activities is the actor as role performer. The action structure of the social system is, therefore, a reciprocal role structure. Starting from the assumption that all action is goal directed and relational (to both innate needs and acquired orientations), Parsons suggests the emergent

---

[2] Again the focus on the legitimation of an existent order rather than on the emergence of that order is illustrative of Parson's taken-for-granted treatment of the problem of order.

[3] Parsons seems remarkably complacent about the extent to which the family may be anything but an emotional refuge for its members.

character of the social system in terms of a paradigmatic account of interaction between ego and alter. Whenever alter and ego interact, such interaction means that ego in pursuing goals must take account of alter and vice versa. When both take account of one another, there must arise common expectations with regard to one another's actions that structure the interaction. The more recurrent the interaction, the more such expectations become mutual and standardized; in other words, a norm of interaction emerges which structures the definition of the situation of interaction for the actors.

> An established state of a social system is a process of complementary interaction in which each conforms with the expectations of the other(s) in such a way that alter's reactions to ego's actions are positive sanctions which serve to reinforce his given need dispositions and thus fulfil his given expectation (Parsons and Shils, 1951, pp. 204–5).

What is not clear in this account is how actors come to recognize what constitutes an expectation, how they recognize each other's expectations, how they evaluate and relate these expectations, how they relate expectations to the features of the social settings in which they arise, how they recognize the features of the social setting, and how they deal with perceived discrepancies in both settings and expectations. In fact, Parsons's account of social interaction assumes the existence of a background of socially standardized meanings shared by ego and alter in such a manner as to both allow them to recognize what is happening in the situation and to orient themselves accordingly. But this is precisely the problematic feature of social interaction.

With regard to the orientational aspect of social interaction, Parsons suggests that this is structured by the necessary requirements of interaction *per se*. The actors must resolve certain fundamental dilemmas about how to orient themselves to one another before interaction can proceed. The emergent definition of the situation that arises in the situation can be seen, therefore, as the product of their specific resolution. Parsons distinguishes six dichotomous pairs of orientational dilemmas which he labels the pattern variables (they are: (1) universalism versus particularism, (2) specificity versus diffuseness, (3) achievement versus ascription, (4) affective neutrality versus affectivity, (5) self-orientation versus collectivity-orientation, and (6) long-run versus short-run). Parsons is not suggesting that the individual personally resolves these dilemmas but that the social system, by virtue of its institutionalized value preferences, has resolved them for him. In turn, the systemic resolution of these dilemmas represents a response to the functional prerequisites. What remains problematic in Parsons's discussion of the pattern variable are the manner of their derivation and their relationship to the meanings employed by actors in actual social settings. They seem to represent little more than deductive preferences on his part.[4]

Drawing on this discussion of the ego-alter paradigm and the pattern variables, Parsons assembles his model of the social system as follows. Social interaction on an extensive scale gives rise to an emergent network of social

---

[4] The commonsensical character of these preferences is discussed at a later point in the chapter.

relationships (the social system), organized (homeostasis) and integrated (equilibrium) in terms of a common value orientation (the centralized value system) such as to standardize the particular activities (roles) within it and to maintain itself in the face of the conditions of its emergence (adaptation). The social system, then, constitutes a system of social action in what can only be called a most abstract sense as Parsons himself recognizes.

> Since the social system is made up of the interaction of human individuals, each member is both actor (having goals, ideas, attitudes, etc.) and object of orientation for both other actors and himself. The interaction system, then, is an analytical aspect abstractable from the total action processes of its participants. . . . A society is a type of social system, in a universe of social systems, which attains the highest level of self-sufficiency as a system in relation to its environment. . . . This view contrasts sharply with our notion of society as being composed of concrete human individuals (Parsons, 1966, pp. 8–9).

The reification of the social system is complete then, in the Parsonian model, since "concrete human individuals" have been excluded from it.

By incorporating social meanings into his model in the form of standardized norms and values and action in the form of structured roles, Parsons is free to treat action as determined by the characteristics of the social system *per se*. The actor is articulated to the social system through processes of socialization and social control. The former is treated by Parsons in terms of the internalization of roles by the actor—that is, the internalization of the appropriate normatively oriented expectations attached to locations within the organizational structure of the system. At the level of the personality system, this represents an identification with such expectations in the form of need dispositions to conform to the socially prescribed pattern of behaviour. However, the complexity of social settings and disjunctions within the personality system may disrupt the process of internalization in such a manner as to encourage deviant orientations on the part of the actor. Such deviance is brought under control by mechanisms of social control. Thus the processes of socialization and social control "work hand in hand with mechanisms of defence and adjustment in the personality system to motivate actors to conform within the given system of expectations, counteract deviance and other strains in the system to bring it back to a given state and maintain the initial equilibrium" (Buckley, 1967, p. 25).

Action, therefore, is an appendage of the social systems in a number of senses. First, roles are structured activities determined by the functional requirements of system as a whole. Second, roles are received and internalized by the actor. Third, social action and interaction is the product of role playing. Finally, the whole operation is policed by mechanisms of social control that check deviance and ensure conformity with common norms and values. Ironically, then, Parsons provides, not an account of action (which presupposes some idea of self-conscious activity),[5] but an account of behaviour or conduct. This somewhat nullifies his claim to have produced a model of the social system which

---

[5] See Chapter 9.

incorporates the action frame of reference within it. Moreover, the focus on common norms and values, and the consequent reciprocity of roles that characterizes the structure of the system, settles, in theoretical terms, rather than resolves the problem of social order.

Critique of the functionalist system model

CONTINGENCY AND REIFICATION

The system model places a primary emphasis on the character of social life as emergent network of orderly closed relationships. However, the extent to which social relationships may be treated as closed in this manner is entirely problematic. Moreover, the form which such closure might entail is equally problematic. The requirement of analysis, therefore, is an examination of the emergence of social order in relation to the contingencies of everyday social life. This requirement turns on our examination of order as the routine accomplishment of the everyday interpretive procedures of the members of the social world within the context of social interactions. Blumer succinctly characterizes the social world as a world organized in terms of social interaction: "Organization is the socially constructed framework inside of which social action takes place and is not the determinant of that action" (1962, p. 189).[6] Moreover, the structural features of social organization "are the product of the activity of acting units and not of forces which leave such acting units out of account" (Ibid., p. 189). What system theorists identify as structural features of the social system, namely, norms, values, culture, roles and so on, are structural conditions of activity by virtue of their recognition and definition as such by actors; in other words, social structure necessarily refers to the actors' sense of social structure, assembled through a common scheme of reference. With these strictures in mind, we can return to the central features of the functionalist account of the social system.

The most important notion with regard to social action is that of "role". If the social system is a normatively oriented system of action organized in response to the necessary requirements for its survival, then "role" may be conceived of as a standardized item of behaviour[7] located within that organized framework of action. Attached to such roles, therefore, are appropriate normative expectations which govern the required behaviour of performers in given social settings. These expectations are, in turn, linked to the centralized prescriptive framework of the social system in a manner which ensures the consensual complementarity of roles and role expectations. Roles, then, are received by the actor from the social system and internalized by him in conformity with the expectations attached to them. Social action is, thereby, the outcome of internalized role expectations. Parsons sets up his account of this process in the following terms.

---

[6] He fails to provide, however, a satisfactory account of the manner in which an orderly social world emerges out of interaction.

[7] Inevitable destinies, to use Berger and Pullberg's term (1966).

Roles and role playing represent a situation of double contingency for the actor. On the one hand, the actor orients himself to the expectations of other actors and, on the other hand, the actor orients himself to other actors' expectations of himself. The two sets of expectations interlock to produce a pattern of socially standardized behaviour on the part of the actors that is in accord with such expectations. The actor has, therefore, a vested interest in maintaining the stability of the whole operation. However, a number of problematic features emerge in this account.

One problem concerns the question of deviance. What happens if the actor deviates from the prescribed expectations and how would such deviance come about? Parsons addresses the first part of this question in terms of secondary mechanisms of social control (primarily other actors) which come into play to coerce the deviant back into line. The second he addresses in terms of the possibility of faulty processes of socialization whereby the actor has failed to internalize (or failed to adequately internalize) the required role expectations. Such failure may be located in terms of disjunctions within the personality system of the actor himself, which is hardly a satisfactory sociological account of deviance. More sociologically, he suggests that deviance may be traced to the presence of conflicting and competing values within the social system so that different actors may internalize different norms and values. The latter case describes a situation whereby the actor acts in conformity to the prescriptions of the subgroup (subsystem) to which he belongs but is deviant with respect to the social system in general. But this merely compounds the problematic character of Parsons's whole account of deviance, moving the problem of deviance to the higher level of subsystem deviance for which an explanation must necessarily be provided. Moreover, what now are we to make of the argument that society is a system integrated by centralized values that regulate its activities and define its boundaries? What now is the normal standard of behaviour against which deviance can be measured? Clearly the position advanced by Parsons is unable to provide a satisfactory account of the phenomenon of deviance at all since his model virtually presupposes its absence.

A second problem of the model is its presupposition of role consensus—that there are clearly defined expectations attached to particular locations within the social system. This is problematic by virtue of the available evidence concerning everyday role performance which points to the varied interpretations that actors place on roles and which, itself, requires investigation. Moreover, Parsons chooses to ignore the various problems associated with the recognition and learning of roles in relationship both to the contingent settings within which they are acquired and the agents from whom they are acquired, so, for example, in his examination of the American middle-class nuclear family, he prescriptively represents the process of socialization as the internalization, on the part of the child, of the achievement and universalistic values appropriate to the performance of roles required by the needs of the industrial system that virtually writes off as deviant what he takes to be the ascriptive and particularistic components of working-class socialization. What is assumed, rather than explained, is the congruence between the middle-class family and the requirements of the industrial system[8] and the consequent lack of congruence between the working-class family and the industrial system. Moreover, all of the key terms of this account remain unexplicated in a taken-for-granted manner.

In general, then, what is lacking in Parsons's model is a satisfactory account of how actors come to recognize roles and perform them accordingly. Like all functionalists, he treats norms and values as formal rules of interaction which measure fixed amounts of consensual agreement between actors upon substantive issues. But this idea of concensual agreement assumes precisely that which is to be explained. At the very most, norms and values represent only idealized and generalized rules, expectations, and definitions of the situation (that is, social meanings). What is problematic is the manner of their enactment. How do actors depict rules and invest them with meaning; in other words, how do actors recognize rules? How do actors recognize which rules apply in what situation? How do actors recognize when an action conforms to a rule? How do actors deal with discrepancies between rules or between rules and the unstated conditions of their operations? None of these questions is either handled or can be handled by an approach that focuses upon the determinate character of social rules within the context of a social system and yet they are crucial to an understanding of the character of social action and social order. Rather, the systems framework treats social order as the taken-for-granted background to social action in terms of institutionalized norms and values and their internalization by actors.

It is at this point that the contribution of phenomenological sociology can be interposed, for it provides an alternative approach to the problematic features of action and order. This is done in terms of the intersubjective known and taken-for-granted world of commonsense meanings which constitute the socially standardized and standardizing expectancies by which the members of society make sense of this world. These expectancies provide the background to the interpretive procedures by which members assemble the appearances of the social world into an organized and orderly framework on the basis of "what everybody knows". Such expectancies are not to be understood as formal meanings imposed on social settings of interaction but are, rather, given the contingent character of such settings, subject to continuous reinterpretation through the practices of everyday decision-making on the part of interactants within the context of such settings (the "et cetera" clause). It is, therefore, the practical and enforced[9] character of social meanings which 'allows them to operate as a

---

[8] Goode (1963) has noted many of the problems in this assumption of congruence.

[9] Schutz has suggested that enforcement may relate to the extent to which behavioural patterns interlock and become standardized and institutionalized in the form of socially approved laws, mores, folkways and habits. A parallel idea has been suggested by P. Cohen (1968) in terms of the extent to which social relations are involute—that is, the extent to which interaction is always with the same others in every activity. For example, fundamentalist sects may successfully create a counter-reality to that of the external world by isolating their members from that world and tying them into a network of involute relationships internal to the sect. Berger (1968) has made a similar point with reference to the professions.

common scheme of reference. Social order, then, is an order negotiated in terms of a self-organizing framework of meaning (self-organizing, that is, in terms of the interpretive activities of the members of society). In order to investigate notions such as "role" and "social structure", therefore, we need to examine members' everyday categorizations of how things hang together in terms of their implicit assumptions about what everybody knows (that is, the members' sense of roles and social structure) since these terms have no sense outside of their ordinary usage by members. Attempts by sociologists to suggest that their own usage of these terms implies something different from members' ordinary usage, disguises the necessary reliance these attempts place on the same common-sense assumptions as those of the ordinary members of society.[10] Moreover, because the categorization of appearances (social meanings) is expressed in terms of language, we require a theory of language in which the rules of language are seen as generated in interactional settings.[11]

A further requirement would be an alternative formulation of the "self" from that provided by the system framework in terms of a passive determinism. Such an account might very well be provided by a phenomenological reworking of the work of Mead extending his discussion of "taking the role of the other" in terms of the idea of "intersubjectivity" and extending the discussion of the "I" which is where Mead's conceptual framework is at its weakest. I live within a stream of consciousness. Whereas I can grasp the "other" in his immediate present as I interact simultaneously with him, I can never grasp my own immediate presence except through reflection; in other words, I depend on others in the "we-relationship" for the confirmation of my being-in-the-world. The possibility of the actualization of "self-in-the-world" depends, therefore, on the inter-subjective experience of "self" and "other" in the "we-relationship".

> Being conscious of oneself, moreover, is the reflective awareness that one is the intentional source of encounter; in brief, self-consciousness (or distance from oneself as acting, thinking, feeling and so on) is dependent upon the symbolization through which the process of consciousness can be given to itself (Winter, 1966, pp. 104–5).

Hence the "we-relationship" can be understood as the social matrix of symbolization because the self gains distance through the response of the other to its gestures and disclosures. Thus the "self" receives, from the other, the meaning of gesture and symbol through which its own consciousness can become an object of reflective awareness. The "self" discovers its intentional self directed towards the "other" actualized as a biography—that is, in terms of lived past experiences organized reflectively (and hence made meaningful) in terms of intention. The important point, then, is that, whereas the emergence of the

---

[10] For example, sociological role categories such as "mother", "father", "son", "daughter", "husband" and "wife" make sense as role categories only because they are everyday role categories with whose ordinary usage we are familiar as members of society. Such familiarity allows the reader to fill in the missing relevancies in the sociological account of roles.

[11] This is precisely the objection to conventional work in the sociology of language. See Silverman's chapters for an analysis of ordinary language with respect to social life.

"I" is dependent upon the intersubjective experience of "self" and "other", it is not determined by the "other".

It follows from this that the world of human activity is a world of differentiated perspectives and this, in turn, has consequences for the problem of interpreting action. The understanding of an act requires the placement of it within the meaning-context to which it belongs. This, in turn, involves distinguishing between the action as it takes place and the completed act, a distinction which only the actor, himself, is in a position to accomplish. By implication, then, the meaning of an act to the actor is the product of (1) the actor's experiences of consciousness while the action is in progress, (2) the future experiences which are the actor's intended action, and (3) the past experiences which are the actor's completed acts. A meaningful lived experience is one selected out from the others by the actor in terms of intention and is meaningful because of this selection (meaning is the product of the reflexive act). Moreover, the meaning of an act is private to the actor (indexical) by virtue of such selection. It follows, then, that the particular meanings of particular acts to the actor are unavailable for analysis as we cannot enter into his private world of internal consciousness.

However, if the specific meaning of an act to the actor is not available for analysis, it is available for interpretation on the part of other actors as the ongoing intersubjective accomplishment of social interaction. The unity of "self" and "other" (the social world), then, is actualized in the form of an intersubjective world of commonsense meaning through the generation of shared gestures, signs and language such that social life is interpreted by way of objectified and reflected expectations. Primarily, the ability to generate an emergent commonsensical structure of meaning is achieved through the reciprocity of perspectives whereby (1) the actor assumes that he would see the world in some way as the actor whose actions he is interpreting, if he were that actor, and (2) the actor assumes that, for all practical purposes, the sector of the world in which both he and the actor whose meaning he is interpreting is the same for both of them. Thus, the intersubjective commonsense world of everyday life remains a paramount reality from which different modes of orientation take their departure and with which they must come to terms. However, in so far as the specific meaning of the social world to the particular actor is a corollary of the intentions with which he addresses himself to that world, it cannot, itself, be objectified. The "I", therefore, is subject to the social world within which it operates (and upon which it provides a perspective)—not in the sense of being subsumed under the structures of that world, but in the sense of being subsumed under the possibilities made open to it by the structures of that world. The social world defines the situation of the "I" but does not define the "I". The task of sociology, therefore, cannot be to determine the character of the internal meanings that actors give to their acts but rather to explore the parameters within which "I" and the social world operate in terms of an analysis of the routine procedures whereby the members of that world interpret and construct the appearances, acts and events within it.

METHODOLOGY

The substantive comments advanced in the last few pages have a more specifically methodological parallel. A number of interrelated problems stand out in this respect which centre around the character of the model proposed by functionalism and the deductive theoretical activity which underpins it.

The term "model" may be used in either of two senses. According to P. Cohen,

> In the first sense, it refers to the use of analogies which facilitate explanation by suggesting certain similarities between unknown or unobservable processes and others which are better known. In the second sense, the term refers to a set of assumptions which are used to circumscribe and isolate a number of interrelated processes which can then be treated as autonomous areas of reality (1968, p. 15).

In the functionalist systems framework, the two are combined since the assumptions about operative social processes are worked through in terms of an organic analogy. However, to return to the term "model" itself, a major point is that the application of models to the social world must rest on a demonstrable degree of isomorphism between the elements in the model and the elements in the reality to which it is to be applied. Without such demonstrable isomorphism, the subsequent analysis continually risks the fallacy of misplaced concreteness in so far as the model is itself, treated as the reality and not an abstract construction of it.

Now, the feature of the functionalist model is that it continuously results in misplaced concreteness by reason of the manner in which it treats the social system as a natural system like that of an organism. It could, of course, be objected that functionalists are not actually claiming that societies are organisms but only that there are some kinds of approximate similarities between the two which allow of a heuristically valuable analysis of the former in terms of an analogy with the latter. However, this is belied by the actual analysis that is performed, which relies on a virtually literal application of biological terms to social processes. What else can be made, for example, of analysis directed towards the needs of the social system or the equilibrating activities of the units of the social system?

The appropriateness of such a characterization of social processes would not, itself, be in doubt, if the precise sociological meanings of the concepts derived from biology (where their meanings are not in doubt) could be distinguished in some kind of empirical terms, but this is precisely what is not available in the functionalist model. So, for example, explanations of social processes under the heading of the functional prerequisites of survival, adaptation, normal and abnormal, growth and evolution, natural selection and so on, remain empty of the required content that would make them meaningful. The general framework of the analogy, then, is grounded in an extremely doubtful manner. As Buckley points out, the properties of organisms are quite clearly characterized in the biological sciences.

> (a) In an organismic system we do have a relatively fixed structure that is normal for a species at a given time.

(b) This normal biological structure provides us with quite definite criteria against which to assess deviant or malfunctional structures and processes.

(c) As such tendencies towards deviance from the normal structure arise . . . automatic mechanisms of control come into play and conserve the normal structure.

(d) When these fail the organism disintegrates (dies) and fuses into the environment (1967, pp. 30–1).

The requirement, then, of the application of such an analogy is the demonstration that the social system has a fixed normal structure which, when it changes beyond certain limits, results in the extinction of the system. However, as can be empirically attested to, societies are characterized by continuous change of their structure, and the rates of change vary quite considerably between societies. Moreover, what sense is to be made of the idea of necessary prerequisites for survival and normal internal structures for their satisfaction, when societies, even in similar environments, manifest considerable differences between one another?

The failure, then, of the organic model to spell out the precise character of the terms that it operates with and the lack of isomorphisms between the model and society results in a somewhat empty general programme of near-tautological dimensions. Either it is argued that, without the presence of a particular item in the system, the system would fail to survive (without explaining what this would mean in empirical terms) or, alternatively, we are told that without a particular item, the system would be different (without a characterization of what this difference would consist in). Moreover, the whole model presupposes that there is both a finite number of parts to society and deter-minate relationships between them which the sociologist can assemble from the outset in deductive terms. But societies are the arbitrary constructs of their members and identifiable only in terms of the manner of their construction.

This brings into focus the whole deductive character of functionalist theoretical procedures which requires some examination itself. One immediate question concerns the grounds out of which the deductive speculation is actually generated. Clearly, it is not the data, *per se*, which give rise to theory in this particular approach since the data are examined only after the main outlines of the system and its characteristics have already been settled in advance by the sociologist. We must, therefore, look elsewhere for its sources. In particular, I would suggest that a suitable direction in which we could look would be one which focused on the unexplicated commonsense assumption[12] about the social world that functionalist systems theory trades upon. At every turn, the framework is invaded by notions about the objective presence of the social world and its structural features (roles, values and so on) which rely on the sociologist's sense of such notions as an ordinary member of society.[13] This is particularly apparent in the quite ethnocentric portrayal of the features of the social system in American terms by Parsons. For example, he argues for "democratic associa-

---

[12] Mills (1959) has wittily attested to the commonsense character of much of Parsons framework.
[13] I have pointed to this characteristic feature in more detail elsewhere in this book.

tion" as a necessary structural requirement for complex social systems to reach the highest levels of adaptation. Or again, the whole concept of social evolution is coloured by ethnocentric notions of a progressive change in the direction of the arrangements of western societies, apart from the strong moral overtones that the idea of progress, itself, carries.

The characteristic feature, then, of this kind of theoretical activity is the incorporation of commonsense assumptions into a set of high-level formal deductive propositions concerning a reified social system which disguises the character of such assumptions. Questions are then posed and answered at an equally abstract level within the context of the logic of these assumptions. The role of data, therefore, is little more than that of illustrative material to be fitted into the appropriate theoretical categories. Nor is it possible that it could be otherwise since the whole model takes for granted what it is supposedly required to explain, namely, social order and social change. As Cohen points out: "functionalism does not provide an explanation of its own assumptions; that is, functionalist ideas do not explain why it is that functional interrelationships exist in all social life, and why the degree of functional interdependence in societies or in sectors of societies itself varies" (1968, p. 66). This in turn demands, as Cohen himself acknowledges, an analysis of processes of action and interaction.

The demand can be met by the phenomenological analysis of the everyday processes by which a known and taken-for-granted social world is constructed by its members in terms of commonsense interpretations of that world. In so far as these interpretive procedures may be described as rules by which members make that world rational and accountable for all practical purposes, analysis should be primarily concerned with how members manage the discrepancies between the formal rules, their expectations of what is expected or appropriate and the practical and enforced character of both stated and unstated rules. Cicourel and Garfinkel suggest that the analogue of social interaction as a game provides a means by which such analysis can be accomplished, by virtue of the way in which it allows the observer to explicate what the basic rules are that will be considered normal (for those players who seek to abide by the rules) and the manner in which such rules make the features of social settings accountable to their members.

The game model is erected with reference to five kinds of rules:

1. A set of boundary conditions within which the player exercises choice.
2. The specification of an assumption on the part of the player of a norm of reciprocity with respect to the alternatives which are binding on each other.
3. The specification of an assumption by the players that whatever they expect of each other is perceived and interpreted in the same way.
4. Rules of preferred play (the discretion provided the player with respect to compliance on this part).
5. Game-furnished conditions (the general conditions of the game, such as information available to players).

The first three of such rules we may label "constitutive expectancies". "Constitutive expectancies" may be assigned to a particular set of possible events and not to others, in which case they may be said to provide a "constitutive accent" for this set of events.

Following the use of such a model, the observer is in a position to investigate processes such as the different kinds of rules honoured by the actor in his perceived environment; proper, improper and strange play; the properties which promote the stability of social interaction; how situations are defined and change over time; and how actors infer each other's role of the other, and according to what rules and how they shape their self-roles accordingly. Moreover, the focus upon how members use norms to define perceivedly normal events directs our attention to questions such as the typicality of everyday events; how past and future events are compared by actors; how the actor assigns causal significance to events; how such events are fitted into typical means-ends relationships; the way in which events are deemed necessary to the moral order. Although, as Cicourel points out, the limitations of such a model are clearly recognizable (social norms do not have the bounded conditions of game models and the rules of everyday life are non-calculable because of the discrepancy between their ideal description and their practical and enforced character), it still allows the identification of the finite provinces of meaning produced by definitions of the situation and the manner in which members make sense of their experiences in the course of social interaction.

Cicourel (1968) and Garfinkel (1967) have used such a model to examine the manner in which social organizations generate routine practices for handling clients. But as these studies are examined elsewhere, I prefer to illustrate the use of this model in terms of Scott's analysis of horse-racing. Scott suggests that horse-race meetings constitutes a routine setting in terms of a self-organizing structure of information. The routine practices of the members of that setting (punters, jockeys, trainers, bookies, track officials) centre around attempts to conceal and uncover certain strategic information—that is, information strategic for the practical adequacy of their activities.[14] Primarily these practices seek to remedy the ambiguity and incompleteness of the information required to translate the means-ends relationships involved in the members' actions into relationships of suitably efficient rationality. So, for example, the punter develops routine devices for eliciting the kind of information (the previous "form" of the horses entered in the race, the particular condition of the horses on the day of the race, the "form" of the jockeys riding the race, whether a trainer has entered a horse in a race in order to win it or only to exercise it, and so on, which reduces the "risky" activity of betting to a normal routine accountable activity that is, to a rational activity). Other members proceed in similarly routine ways. Thus, horse-racing may be described as a game characterized by a set of rules that provides a framework of possible action. Within this framework, we can treat happenings as game-generated events and players as game-generated identities.

---

[14] Scott (1968).

Players adopt certain strategies to deal with certain recurrent problems according to their interests. This, in turn, produces standardized orientations with reference to action. The result is that players who align their activities in terms of such orientations are identified and typed by other players and interaction is aligned in terms of such typification. In this manner an ordered social setting is produced by the accounting practices of its members.

The particular advantage of such a model is that it meets the requirement of isomorphism by the manner in which it is systematically related to the empirical data with reference to which it is generated (namely, the actual everyday activities of the members of society as they construct a social world). It eschews, therefore, the procedures of formal rationality both for the purposes of its construction[15] and the purposes of its validation[16] and avoids the unnecessary reification of society implied in the notion of "social system". Moreover, unlike the models of functionalist systems theory, it is not addressed to the construction of the social world in "objective" terms but to an elucidation of processes by which it is constructed as an objective world for and by its members.

THE MARXIST MODEL OF THE SOCIAL SYSTEM

An alternative systemic perspective to that of functionalism is provided by certain kinds of Marxism[17] and might usefully be considered at this point. They propose a model of the social system as a system of social relationships organized around an economic infrastructure in terms of power and coercion. Primarily, the model is directed towards the dynamics of system change in terms of the social processes by which structural contradictions within the economic infrastructure give rise to manifest social conflict. A distinction is made, thereby, between the institutional relationships of the system (hypothesized as the objective conditions of social life) and the social activity to which they give rise.[18] Such institutional relationships are distinguished as the forces of production, the relations of production (the organized social relationships that correspond to the forces of production) and the legal and political superstructure.

The relations of production, in the first instance, are the division of labour which arises out of the instruments of production and varies accordingly the property relationships which are a normative expression of them and constitute the basis of the class structure. The class position of an individual, therefore, is a function of his placing within the productive process and remains, thereby, independent of that individual. Marx refers to this as "class in itself". As such, it constitutes the objective conditions for the emergence of consciousness of position in the social scheme of things on the part of the individual. Marx refers

---

[15] See the previous discussion of formal and everyday rationality.

[16] See the previous discussion of subjective interpretation.

[17] The work of Marx himself, is somewhat ambiguous in this respect but tends to take on an increasingly systemic reference. Lefebvre (1968) has located this ambiguity in the polymathic character of Marx's writings.

[18] See Lockwood (1964).

to this as class "for itself". For the systemic Marxist, then, social action stems from the objective position of the actor within the class structure as mediated by his conscious awareness of that position. It may be characterized as a species of instrumental rationality whereby the actor, in pursuing the aims of his action, uses whatever means are available to him within the constraints of this objective position. Both the ends and means of action and the efficient relationship between them are, therefore, determined by the institutionalized class structure of the system itself. Action is, in consequence, primarily organized in terms of material interests. Moreover, class position is an objective source of power by virtue of the ownership or non-ownership of the forces of production that are vested within it.

The system, then, is characterized by a high degree of interdependence between the forces and relations of production in which the former determine the latter in so far as they later correspond to a definite stage in the development of the forces of production. Similarly, there is a high degree of interdependence between them (as the economic infrastructure) and the legal and political super-structure of the system which they determine by virtue of the extension of the ownership of the forces of production to the control of other spheres of social life. The system changes in so far as, within the course of the development of the economic infrastructure, the forces of production come into conflict with existing relationships of production. This in turn gives rise to class conflict by virtue of the way in which the new forces of production are accompanied by the emergence of a new class with a consciously vested interest in the overthrow of the old ruling class who attempt to maintain their position. The greater the degree of institutional incompatibility, the greater the degree of class awareness and class conflict to the point at which such incompatibilities can no longer be contained within the system and conflict, thereby, precipitates a social revolution in which the old ruling class is replaced by the new. Class conflict and revolution, then, are the product of objective conditions of the system which give rise to them. The basic institutional incompatibility within capitalism is taken to be that between socialized production and capitalist appropriation induced by the market economy. The market provides the objective conditions of exploitation and pauperization for the proletariat out of which arises their class consciousness and activity antagonistically directed towards the bourgeois who control the market. These conditions are further exacerbated by recurrent crises of over-production induced by market conditions of competition between the bourgeois as they attempt to maximize their profits through the sale of commodities.

What remains problematic with regard to this model is the manner in which the identified objective conditions of the social system are a managed accomplishment of the interpretive procedures of the Marxist observer on the basis of assumptions about the nature of the social world. Primarily, these are assumptions concerning the materialistic character of social action premised on philosophical arguments about man as "homo laborans" and commonsense observations of the importance men place on material desires. It is, then, another first-order construction of the social world, and not an "objective" account of real features of that world. Moreover, its application to the features of the social world manifests a considerable degree of ambiguity. Not only are terms such as the forces of production, the relations of production, infrastructure and super-structure used in an extremely abstract manner (that is, with only vague empirical reference to the actual activities of members) but they are frequently indistinct, if not interchangeable with one another. For example, the content of the economic infrastructure is frequently defined so as to include the ideational framework of technological arrangements in a manner which neatly preserves the materialist framework but arbitrarily side-steps arguments concerning the ideational determination of social action.[19] Or again, the Marxist concept of class is replete with ambiguity by virtue of its definition both variously and alternatively in terms of sources of revenue, position within the productive process, and organized consciousness. Moreover, it is never made exactly clear what is actually meant by the suggestion that property relations are not the relations of production but a normative expression of them.

This ambiguity is at its maximum in the discussion of the role of social consciousness as both determined and determining social action. It is never clear, for example, whether the proletarian revolution must inevitably come by virtue of its determination by institutional contradictions within capitalism or has to be brought about by organized consciousness or both. Now, if it has to be brought about by conscious activity, this assigns an autonomy to consciousness which is somewhat difficult to fit into the deterministic systemic framework. Moreover, Marx himself is aware of the problems associated with such a framework in explaining actual activity which deviates from his model, as his idea of false consciousness makes clear. The problem with such an idea resides in the assumption of the objective logic of institutional arrangements against which subjectively false characterizations of them, on the part of actors, can be contrasted as an explanation of their failure to obey this logic. But the apprehension of the objective logic of institutional arrangements is itself the product of the application of an interpretive criterion to them. As McHugh points out:

> To say "false consciousness" is to replace one criterion (common sense) with another (institutions according to sociology). All well and good, except that it is unreasonable to ascribe subjectivity to one and objectivity to another, since both are objective in their own terms—it is the relation between the two criteria which is distinctive. . . . This is not to say that the standards of the actors are always right. . . . It is only to say that the standards of the actor, his way of making definitions, are the bases of action, and that actions are the analytical bases of institutions (1968, pp. 10–11).

The point is that Marx never addresses the actual procedures by which the members of society recognize and describe the appearances of the social world and how ascribed meanings change over time with reference to such procedures. Rather, he presumes to settle these issues in terms of his own theoretical framework.

---

[19] Marxist and neo-Marxist literature is filled with attempts to fill the content of the economic infrastructure in a manner which subsumes criticisms of the materialist interpretation of social action.

This is not to suggest that the work of Marx and Marxist-oriented sociologists is without value but that such work might be read as some kind of second-order account of the interpretive procedures of the members of the particular social world self-recognized as capitalism. The work of Weber, too, could be read in a similar light. But not even the most nominalist-oriented interpretation of Marx could actually turn him into a phenomenologist, close as he comes to this position in his early writings. However, one critical direction in which the phenomenological paradigm might be developed to deal with the problem of the generation of particular commonsense worlds is in terms of a Marxist-tinged account of the dialectical relationship between praxis (self-conscious activity) and the historical circumstances of its emergence. Such an attempt has come to characterize the work of the Frankfurt school of sociologists of whom Habermas is probably the leading figure.[20]

We return then, to the reiterated requirement that sociology should treat the manner in which a preconstituted social world becomes available as the problematic focus of its concerns; a requirement that necessitates an analysis of the actual procedures by which the members of that world assemble it as a reality and which cannot be met by the reified abstractions of systems theory which settles, in theoretical terms, the character of that world.

SUGGESTIONS FOR FURTHER READING

BUCKLEY, W. (1967) *Sociology and Modern Systems Theory*, Prentice-Hall, Englewood Cliffs, New Jersey.

CICOUREL, A. (1964) *Method and Measurement in Sociology*, Free Press, New York.

GARFINKEL, H. (1967) *Studies in Ethnomethodology*, Prentice-Hall, Englewood Cliffs, New Jersey.

McHUGH, P. (1968) *Defining the Situation*, Bobbs-Merrill, Indianapolis.

MARX, K., ENGELS, F. *Basic Writings on Politics and Social Philosophy*, ed. L. Feuer, Anchor Doubleday, New York.

PARSONS, T. (1951) *The Social System*, Free Press, New York.

PARSONS, T., SHILS, E. (1951) *Towards a General Theory of Action*, Free Press, New York.

SCOTT, M. (1968) *The Racing Game*, Aldine, New York.

WINTER, G. (1966) *Elements for a Social Ethic*, Macmillan, New York.

---

[20] Readers are directed to an interesting presentation in these terms by Schroyer (1970) who attempts to account for the emergence and legitimation of technocratic consciousness in post-capitalist societies.

All perspectives in sociology, with the possible exception of symbolic interactionism, have taken their stereotype of natural scientific investigation as the model for empirical study of the social world. This has resulted in a reliance on a range of methodological techniques which are presumed to be neutral, mere techniques for disconfirming hypotheses about social life. A consequence of this view of methodology in sociology is the large gap between "theory" and "research"; the activities of theorizing and researching are taken to be independent sets of activities. Similarly the process of generating and operationalizing concepts, sociologists' means for making connections between the social world and their theories, remains unexamined and non-problematic. Phenomenological sociology gives primacy to the empirical character of sociology (to actual investigations of concrete situations and processes) and, in so doing, emphasizes the mutual dependence of theorizing, researching, and conceptualization. Language and meaning, which are taken-for-granted and used as unexplicated resources by other sociological perspectives, are treated as problematic and this constitutes an attempt to eliminate the gap between theory and research. This chapter discusses some problematic aspects of the relationship between theory and research in traditional empiricism and suggests the kinds of problems with which a phenomenologically oriented sociology must come to terms.

FIVE

Theory, Methodology and Conceptualization

MICHAEL PHILLIPSON

Sociology students frequently complain that they cannot relate the abstractions of sociological theory to their own experiences or to any social world with which they are acquainted; the interpretive leap from collected data (or armchair) to conceptualization, which sociologists somehow accomplish, remains unexplicated in their conceptualizations. During the period of undergraduate socialization into the thought-ways of sociology many students do come to take-for-granted a stock of common sociological concepts which are seen as portraying the social world "as it really is". Assimilation of sociological jargon and techniques of investigation is felt to provide access to the "actual underlying patterns" of social life, so that initial doubts about the relationship between sociological explanations and the worlds experienced by students and others are gradually dropped. By the time the final examinations are reached, most students, if not actually converted to the faith, have a sufficient working grasp of the common concepts to pass for members.

The phenomenological critique of conventional sociology lends support to students' initial fears and doubts by drawing attention to fundamental problems of analysis which are ignored in conventional sociology. In fact the critique suggests that, far from providing verbal constructions which reveal the world "as it really is", the linguistic architects of sociology have constructed vast edifices which bear unknown relationships to the social world which they purport to describe. Certainly these constructions provide shelter for verbose sociologists but, from the viewpoint of men engaged in practical activities in the world, they are more likely to appear as esoteric retreats whose doors are barred except to the converted. Phenomenological sociology points the way for a destruction of what Matza calls "the surrealist architecture of primitive sociology" (1969, p. 108) and for a reorientation of the discipline by grounding the sociological project firmly at the human level of meaning in the social world. In this chapter my main concern is with the means by which the surrealist verbal architecture is constructed, and I treat the interpretive leap from data to theory in conventional sociology as a central problem. Arguably the most important contribution of the phenomenological critique and the work which has stemmed from it is to have clarified the nature of the yawning chasm between theorizing and researching in sociology and to have provided ways for bridging it. The main theme of this chapter, therefore, is the problematic character of the gap between theory and methodology in conventional sociology; my aim is to draw attention to issues too frequently ignored which concern both the role of sociological theory and methodology and also the relationship between the sociological enterprise and the social realities which it purports to describe. In examining the character of the gap between theory and methodology, I focus on four problematic features of explanation and description in sociology. The problematic issues centre on: the confusion over the role of sociological theory, the character of the relationship between theory and methods of research, the nature of sociological concepts as links between theory and research, and the validity of sociological explanations.[1]

Although the concern of this chapter is a critical assessment of the relationship between theory and research in conventional sociology, it must be stated that the purpose of this assessment is to establish a base for the development of alternatives in subsequent chapters. The alternatives presented later take as their main analytical problems the clarification of the basic structures of social interaction and their content in manifest areas of social life, and how the sociologist can grasp these structures. Fundamental to the discussion in this and the remaining chapters is the assumption that sociology is an empirical discipline. By empirical, I mean two things. First, in terms of its subject matter sociology must concern itself with the ways in which everyday interaction is actually constructed by members of a society for members' consumption; the outgrowths or emergent properties of social interaction are normative preoccupations with normatively created acts (such as the public concern over "crime") and it is these outgrowths which have provided most of the subject matter for conventional sociology. Phenomenological sociology, by contrast, gives primacy of emphasis to *how* members accomplish social interaction; clearly this must not be confused with the conventional sociological preoccupation with *what* they have accomplished. In so far as the processes through which members accomplish social interaction are inadequately understood the concentration on what has been accomplished may be regarded as premature. The reason for this charge of prematurity should become clearer when I have examined how the conventional methods for investigating and describing social phenomena treat certain issues as nonproblematic; when the taken-for-granted assumptions of most conventional sociological investigation are treated as problematic, as in the phenomenological

---

[1] The problem of validity is considered more fully in Chapter 6.

critique, much of what passes for "adequate" evidence, data, and explanation in sociology must be called into question.

The second implication of the term empirical is that sociological understanding of how men construct their social worlds can only come through the study of actual social worlds; studies of the ways in which the everyday social world is actually accomplished by members is a prerequisite in the alternatives to conventional sociology. Sociologists' interpretations must be demonstrably derived from data gathered from the social world and not merely from their imaginations. Empiricism is only a means in sociology to the development of sociologically adequate and valid abstractions; but emphasizing the empirical character of the alternative approaches serves to draw attention to the tenuous or unknown links with social realities of much theoretical abstraction in conventional sociology. Unless we can establish the links between a particular sociological abstraction and the realities it purports to relate to, it should carry no special status for us, for it then remains merely another account of the social world or some part of it. Much of what counts as explanation or description in sociology fails to provide us with the means for establishing the nature of the links between it and the actual experiences of men in particular social contexts.

A basic premise of phenomenological sociology is that the inseparability of theory and research is ensured by treating methodology, not as the manipulation of a set of given research techniques, as is the case in conventional sociology, but as *the processes by which a sociologist generates an abstract view of a situation.* The processes of observation, selection, interpretation and abstraction constitute the sociologist's methods of constructing his "theory". In this sense, methodology comprises *how* the sociologist decides *what* social phenomena are relevant to his descriptive project at hand, and how he deals with these in developing his account or theory. Methodology, therefore, includes all the processes by which a theory is constructed. Unless we can reconstruct the processes through which the observer moves from his observations of the social world to his conceptual description of it we are in no position to evaluate this description; without this clarification our interpretation of his description has to rest on a series of taken-for-granted commonsense assumptions which allow us to implicitly assume that we "know what the observer means". Conventional sociology fails to treat these commonsense assumptions as problematic. At this stage I wish merely to point to the failure to treat this as a central problem in sociological explanation; its implications will be drawn out in this and subsequent chapters.

Defining methodology in this way makes a consideration of it essential in relation to any so-called theoretical statement by a sociologist, whether the statement claims to relate directly to a set of research observations or not. In fact, the less the statement relates explicitly to research observations the more crucial do the above methodological considerations become for our interpretation of the theoretical construction; if the theory does not relate to clearly defined sets of empirical observations and the theorizer does not describe his processes of theory generation, our interpretation of his theoretical abstraction becomes entirely problematic. In practice the problem is solved by our tacit reliance on commonsense knowledge. Thus the linking theme in the following discussion of the relationship between theory and research in sociology is the centrality of the problem of methodology.

Two fundamental and related problems which underlie the issues discussed subsequently are, first, the confusion and disagreement in sociology about the role and purpose of sociological theory, and second, the conventional practice among sociologists of regarding theoretical problems as quite separate from, and independent of, methodological problems. A result has been the gradual emergence and predominance of certain methods of theorizing and research which rest on taken-for-granted assumptions about the relationship between theory and research, about the kind of data which sociologists ought to collect, and about the kind of explanation they ought to offer. A reappraisal of these assumptions and an alternative way of looking at the relation between theory and methodology is required by the phenomenological critique.

CONTEMPORARY SOCIOLOGICAL THEORY

No agreement exists in sociology about either the definition of theory or its aims and purposes; disagreement on such basic issues clearly creates fundamental problems for research practice. There are no clearly articulated rules in sociology for either generating or recognizing sociological theory; given that sociologists both give centrality to theory in the discipline and also frequently distinguish between studies according to their theoretical or atheoretical character, it would seem reasonable to expect a set of rules which would tell us how to recognize and generate descriptions which would count as sociological theory. However, no such rules exist and the writers who view themselves as theorists— that is, those who explicitly claim to be writing theory or writing about it— typically make no attempt to explicate the rules or guides which they follow in theory construction; in the present context such rules would comprise their methodology. The nearest approach to the provision of such guides can be found in the various exhortations to sociologists to adopt stereotypical models of natural science hypothesis-testing procedures; this approach has been referred to by Glaser and Strauss (1968) as "the rhetoric of verification". But such guides are not concerned with processes of theory or concept construction, but rather with the empirical "illustration", "testing" or "verification" of concepts largely derived from writings of acceptable and accepted sociological theorists. Two related questions can thus be drawn from this confusion: first, what counts as "theory" in sociology? And second, what is it for? Some kinds of answers have to be given to these questions before we can develop criteria for deciding on the adequacy of any given theory. Unfortunately, when these questions are asked, large discrepancies are found between authors in the implicit and explicit answers they give to them.

The origin of some of the discrepancies lies in the fact that sociological explanations or theories are couched in natural language and not in a set of idealized symbols which are treated as objective and unequivocal for purposes of scientific explanation, as in the explanations of physics or chemistry. In natural language, not only is there clear variation in the meanings attached to different linguistic descriptions of the same phenomena, but there is also considerable variation in the meanings attached to the same words or phrases, both according to who interprets them and to the context in which they appear. The same words carry a variety of meanings and different words carry obviously greater variation. A slight variation between authors in the words used to define, say, the aims of sociological theorizing may carry radically different horizons of meaning and very different implications for the directions to be taken by theory and research. Thus, whether any given theorist intends his explanations or definitions to be synonymous with or to conflict with the writings of other sociologists, the variety of meanings inherent in the use of natural language provides a potential for confusion and differential interpretation.

The apparent inability of sociologists to come to terms with or address the problems which arise from couching their explanations in natural language seems to stem from the fact that, in conventional sociology, language is treated as a mere resource and not as a topic for investigation in its own right; it is the unquestioned medium through which "objective" sociological explanations can be presented. By contrast, the phenomenological critique treats language as a social phenomenon which is given primacy as a topic for sociological investigation. It is primarily through language that we constitute and communicate in social interaction the meanings which we attach to our experiences; thus, for phenomenological sociology, the constitution of socially meaningful realities, achieved largely through language, becomes a basic topic of investigation. By extension, as the observer can only study language through his own use of language, he must treat as analytically problematic not only the language use of societal members but also his own use of language as a participating member of a speech community. The importance of the sociological study of socially situated language use in relation to the problem of meaning is treated at length in later chapters. Given the openness of natural-language descriptions to an infinite variety of interpretations, this would seem to place rather sharp limits on the pretensions of some branches of sociology to develop laws or law-like statements about social phenomena. The way phenomenological sociology helps to clarify the limits of sociological theorizing is discussed in the next chapter.

Two recent conventional approaches to theory

The confusions and differing conceptions about what theory is are detailed in Walsh's discussions (Chapters 2, 3 and 4) of some of the dominant competing perspectives in sociology. Although the confusions are recognized within conventional sociology, they are resolved by sociologists' individual identification with one perspective rather than another, made on the basis of their intuitive reasoning about which is the "correct" perspective on the social world. An illustration of this confusion over the aims and role of sociological theory is provided by contrasting the ideas of two authors who have provided introductions to sociological theory.

I want to parallel the reasoning of J. Rex (1961) and P. Cohen (1968) in their sophisticated discussions of sociological theory with commonsense practical reasoning. Their sociology is "commonsense" in two ways: first, it shares with the "man in the street" a non-problematic definition of social reality and rests upon unquestioned assumptions about social life which are taken for granted by members of society in their everyday practical activities; in other words, it does not treat "commonsense", "what everyone knows", as problematic. Second, by treating theory in isolation and ignoring both methodology and the processes of theory construction, the authors reinforce the commonsense assumption within sociology itself that theory is something quite separable from research. Questioning these assumptions is central to the present critique.

However, before examining the implications of these assumptions in more detail it is important to note the kind of confusions which emerge from disagreements about the role of theory; sometimes these differences are manifest in only slightly different uses of language.

Rex argues that the sociologist has two main tasks:

> On the one hand there is the need to establish a valid model for the analysis of a particular social system which he is studying. And on the other hand, once such a model is established he may be faced with explaining some partial and particularistic form of behaviour in terms of the part it plays in the total system (1961, p. 185).

These two tasks subsume also that of verifying propositions about social interaction (ibid., p. 58). The tasks are to be achieved by the application of "scientific discipline" to a "very special set of determinants of human behaviour" (ibid., p. 19). His discussion of scientific discipline is limited to a brief consideration of three general scientific approaches: classification, the search for laws and the search for causes. The task of constructing a model of a social system and its defining interaction patterns is given a definite direction by Rex, for he argues that the starting point for the development of a model must always be the ends to which the system as a whole is directed. Because in industrial societies there is conflict over such ends, Rex advocates the adoption of a class-conflict model as the basic system model for contemporary sociology (ibid., p. 187).

It seems that theory is defined by Rex as the construction of a model of a social system (large or small) which shows the conflicts over ends; the aim of his model building is to reveal some of the determinants of human behaviour. Rex's presentation suffers from shortcomings which are especially relevant in the present context. He claims, through his adoption of an action frame of reference, to be a voluntarist in his approach to sociological explanation, but in spite of this claim much of his argument is couched in positivist terminology. Walsh discusses in Chapter 2 the problems faced by positivist explanation in sociology. Rex's concern with locating the social *determinants* of human behaviour through the application of scientific discipline is a denial of the voluntarism he claims to espouse. As this concern is expressed in the absence of any discussion about the relationship between theory and research processes, this suggests that Rex accepts that conventional methodology, which is itself founded solidly upon positivist assumptions about behaviour, will enable sociologists to locate the so-called determinants of behaviour. There is thus a contradiction between his claims to voluntarism and the language which he uses to support these claims.

Apart from the issue of positivism, Rex's presentation epitomizes the problem of talking about theory in sociology in isolation both from a discussion of actual situations and from the methodologies by which sociologists analyse such situations. It is another treatment of "theoretical" problems as separable from and independent of methodologies; there are few guides as to how the sociologists can build up the models Rex envisages, or as to how the assumed ends of the system can be located and analysed. Further, there is no attempt to explicate the relationship between the conceptual models and the particular research methodologies through which these can be empirically tested. Although verification is frequently cited as providing the criteria for accepting sociological explanations, Rex pays no attention to the empirical problems of verifying the kinds of explanations which he proposes. For Rex, the criterion of the validity of sociological explanations or descriptions is whether they have been subjected to the "test of disconfirmation" (ibid., p. 174), presumably through conventional methodological techniques; validity is established by the ability of a model to correctly predict empirical events (ibid., p. 174). Unfortunately no examples of the sociological prediction of empirical events are given. Although he mentions Weber's insistence on adequacy at the level of meaning, the methodological problems of how ultimate validity is established at the level of meaning are ignored.

Each of these omissions illustrates a general problem of sociology and one that seems peculiar to it among disciplines which make some claims to scientific status. This is the problem cited earlier of the accepted chasm between theoretical writing and research practice; perhaps sociology is the only discipline in which one can be either a "theorist" or a "researcher". If sociology is an empirical discipline much self-styled theoretical writing should be considered rather as essays in the philosophy of science, metaphysics or ideology. Similarly, if sociology is a "science", with claims to theoreticity, we must consider very carefully what kind of a science it can be; the problem of meaning requires a rejection of sociologists' attempts to develop a positivistic sociology. In the case of Rex's contribution, the irony is that his aim in his approach to theorizing is "to make empirical research both more exact and more free from concealed value judgments than much research which claims to stick to the empirical facts is at present" (ibid., p. 176). But in spite of his intention his discussion of theoretical issues remains abstract and almost entirely divorced from empirical research procedures, and there is no consideration of how the theoretical constructs he proposes can be meaningfully translated into research indicators. Methodology is not recognized as a problem for the "theorist".

Cohen's recent lucid analysis (1968) can be seen, in the context of my argument, as perpetuating the traditional gap between theory and research. His discussion of theory in isolation from any consideration of methodological problems and research processes reinforces the assumption found in the work of many who write about sociological theory that the two are separable and independent. The assumption seems to be that theorizing and researching are two independent sets of activities which carry their own quite separate problems. As with Rex, this is ironic, for Cohen concludes his book by drawing attention to the very problems he has failed to deal with; thus he says:

> There is a depressing tendency for social theorists to discuss the nature of social theory and not the nature of social reality (ibid., p. 242).

He then goes on to say that,

> The relationship between theory and research in sociology is far from satisfactory (ibid., p. 242).

His complaint is that,

> not enough empirical enquiry is used to decide between the rival claims of different theories, at least to establish whether these claims are or are not incompatible with one another (ibid., p. 242).

Unlike Rex, Cohen sees order and not conflict as the central problem for sociology, so that a basic aim of sociological theory is to suggest ways of explaining social order (ibid., p. 16). Although Cohen identifies "holism" and "atomism" as the two main approaches to the study of social phenomena (ibid., p. 13), the term "approach" does not coincide with the present use of the term "methodology"; the approaches outlined by Cohen are identified both by the assumptions they make about social phenomena and by those things they treat as problems, rather than by the processes through which they construct their explanations or models. The lack of concern with methodological issues comes through clearly in the three criteria according to which, Cohen proposes, theory should be assessed. These are:

> First, it should be able to explain, or suggest ways of explaining, why social phenomena have the characteristics which they do have; second, it should provide ideas for the analysis of complex social processes and events; third, it should aid in the construction of models of how social structures and systems operate (ibid., p. 236).

The most significant problem which these criteria fail to deal with is *how* sociologists can recognize and identify the characteristics that social phenomena have; this is a necessary prerequisite for any explanation but Cohen does not treat this as a problem. He assumes that we know unequivocally what social phenomena are; it is precisely here that the injunction of phenomenology to "get back to the things themselves" becomes of crucial importance by drawing attention to the problematic features of that which conventional sociology takes for granted.

A further problem of the criteria is that, quite apart from the fact that it is not at all clear in what ways they are independent of each other, they do not in themselves contain any suggestions as to how one can choose between different theories about the same social phenomena; in Chapter 1 of his book, Cohen, like Rex, accepts Popper's criterion of disconfirmation or empirical testability as the means for choosing between competing theories. In practice, sociologists typically judge between theories according to first, their internal logic and consistency; second, their external consistency with other theories; and third, the kinds of data used to support them. The last demands a consideration of methodology and it is this which Cohen ignores. Indeed the key theoretical and methodological problem of the validity of sociological explanations is reduced to the narrow terms of testability through conventional research procedures, thus ignoring the problem of validity at the level of meaning. Validity in this sense remains an issue internal to sociology; the meaning of the explanation in the social world is not seen as a problem. Cohen argues that the dispute concerning the validity of differing explanations in terms of social structure "is resolved by recognizing that sociological analysis necessarily makes use of models which isolate certain aspects of reality and interrelate them" (ibid., p. 238). He remarks that this can be done without "hopelessly distorting or idealizing the chaotic reality of social events" (ibid, p. 238). The processes of isolation and interrelation to which he refers involve selection by the sociologists, which in turn demands a methodology. To dismiss the problem of validity by pointing out that the sociologist in constructing his models has to select from "chaotic reality" does not help us to understand how the theories and their related methodologies relate to this "chaotic reality". The key problem of this approach to validity is that it treats as non-problematic the empirical research procedures and the empirical knowledge which they provide; that which "empirically disconfirms" and that which "empirically corroborates" are taken-for-granted.

Thus, like Rex, Cohen gives few guides to the methodological processes by which the sociologist's models are to be constructed, let alone validated, at the level of meaning. The question of validity is treated as a matter of the internal logic of the models and their susceptibility to disconfirmation by unquestioned research techniques; the research procedures themselves by which the data for constructing and/or testing models are collected are entirely ignored.

From these two examples, differences and agreements emerge which illustrate the confusion over the role of theory. Both writers refer to the sociologist's development of models, but Rex starts with conflict and Cohen with order. Neither of them provides grounds for enabling us to distinguish between the validity of their respective starting points. Although both use the term "model" it is clear that they attach somewhat different meanings to it and would focus on different phenomena in constructing their models; there is nothing wrong with this in itself, for not all models have to be the same, but, because the methodologies through which the models are constructed are ignored, we have no way of reconstructing their relationships to particular social realities or of judging their relative worth. Both discuss theory as if it was something quite independent of research; both ignore the methodological problems implicit in the processes of theorizing and conceptualizing, such as the problems of defining social reality and the nature of the relationship between concepts and the "chaotic reality" acknowledged by Cohen.

The separation of theory from research

Whilst these two texts on sociological theory are illustrative of the conventional way in which theory and methodology are treated separately, the separation takes several forms in sociological writing. At one extreme are those approaches to theory construction in which methodology, research processes and empirical studies are ignored completely because the author's main interests seem to be the construction of enclosed and internally consistent theoretical abstractions.[2] At the other extreme are the conventional research methods textbooks which, while urging the student to utilize theory in his research activities, devote their space to discussions of the accepted canons and mechanics of research practice and ignore the complexities of the ties between theorizing, research and social realities.[3]

Between these two extremes lies a range of approaches. Merton (1957), for example, in his presentation of a structural functional paradigm for sociological analysis urges sociologists to relate theory to research and vice versa; but his exhortations are couched in the limiting terms of the "rhetoric of verification", in which research simply becomes the testing and modification of hypotheses derived from an existing body of theory or from the researcher's new theory. This stereotypical view of research, as merely the testing of existing theory, is reinforced by the approaches of the cited research methods textbooks. There are, of course, several studies, such as Durkheim's *Suicide* (1952), in which the theoretical and methodological problems are recognized as inseparable, and these studies form the shaky empirical foundations of contemporary sociology. Unfortunately many of these studies combine theory and methodology in a way which, from the perspective of phenomenological sociology, rides roughshod over the very social reality they are trying to comprehend. The adoption of positivist methods of research, whatever the theoretical framework within which a sociologist works, affects what he selects for study, the ways these phenomena are studied, and the kinds of explanations he offers for them. *Suicide*, as Douglas has shown,[4] is a very good example of the way the methodology adopted failed to come to terms with the explanatory problems set by the theory. The result is not simply an isolation and abstraction of parts of reality but a remedy of that reality. Sometimes it is largely the theory, sometimes the methods, and sometimes it is the two in combination which unnecessarily remedy the social phenomena under investigation.

The problem is, then, to find a descriptive or analytical approach which

---

[2] See, for example, Parsons (1951); Berger and Luckmann (1966).

[3] For example, Goode and Hatt (1952); Galtung (1967); H. and B. Blalock (1968); Selltiz et al (1965).

[4] J. Douglas (1967); see also Walsh's discussion in Chapter 3 for further comments on Douglas's critique of *Suicide*.

incorporates a methodology that minimizes the remedy of social realities, that offers the possibility of validating explanations in terms other than merely their internal consistency, and that is firmly based in an adequate philosophy of investigation. While one can agree with Cohen that all sociological theory is involved in selecting from social reality, the problem is to develop a sociology which treats this reality as a phenomenon worthy of investigation in itself and which copes with it with the least remedy.[5] The enterprise of phenomenological sociology is directed towards exactly these issues and takes them as its central problems.

Sociological theory and social reality

Phenomenological sociology, because it takes meaning and hence the nature of social reality as its central problem, provides us with a criterion or baseline against which to set off other sociological perspectives. If one adopts the position that the peculiar character of the social world, that which differentiates it from the object- or natural-world, is its inherent meaningfulness, then this not only directs attention to the central subject matter and problems for sociology but at the same time provides a criterion for judging the range of competing sociological perspectives. The ontological presuppositions of phenomenological sociology, derived from the descriptions of phenomenological philosophy, posit a social world constituted and sustained through meaning, so that the prime characteristic of its model of man is man's meaning-giving ability; as Merleau-Ponty puts it, "we are condemned to meaning" (1962, p. xix). Other sociological perspectives can thus be assessed according to the way they deal conceptually and methodologically with the problem of meaning. If men act on the basis of the meanings they give to their world and the project of sociology is to understand men's actions, then the most adequate sociological interpretations will be those that minimize the remedy of those actions by ensuring continuity between their descriptions and the meaningful actions to which they relate.

By contrast, those perspectives that ignore meaning or ride roughshod over the issues it raises will unnecessarily remedy the realities to which they purport to relate; if their interpretations remedy social reality this raises the question of the nature of their validity. If it is very difficult to establish congruence between sociological descriptions and the realities societal members experience, their validity must immediately be called into question. If congruence cannot be established, the relationship that a description bears to any experienced reality remains entirely problematic. The problem of validity will be examined in more detail in Chapter 6, and it is sufficient in this context to note that within phenomenological sociology the level of human or experienced meaning provides the criterion for assessing alternative perspectives. One approach to understanding the nature of the remedies which arise from the selection and abstraction procedures of conventional sociological perspectives is suggested by Gibson Winter (1966).

---

[5] See Silverman's discussion of reflexivity in Chapters 1 and 7.

D

Grounding his discussion in phenomenological descriptions of conscious-ness, Winter contrasts the dominant social-scientific perspectives on the social world and seeks to clarify their relationship to the "lived world". By using phenomenological descriptions of man as his baseline or criterion of adequacy he is able to contrast the ontology of phenomenology (man as a meaning-giving being) with the various ontologies presupposed in other social scientific per-spectives. Winter is able to show that the model of man underlying most socio-logical theorizing and investigation is not congruent with phenomenological clarifications of consciousness. According to the terms of phenomenology most sociological description remedies the forms of man's being-in-the-world.

Winter starts from a recognition that the "world of the intentional self is not fully accessible to the other in even the most intimate relationship" (ibid., p. 119). We can never "inwardly experience in our consciousness the richness and particularly of the other's consciousness" (loc. cit.). The other has a unique perspective on the world which is always beyond our grasp. The recognition of man's intentionality not only places limits on a science of the social world but also raises again the question first raised by Weber (1949) and subsequently by Schutz (1967a) of how best to come to terms with intentionality while re-maining scientific. The typical sociological solutions to this problem, which remedy man's intentionality in varying degrees, are found in Figure 1 which

FIGURE 1 : SCIENTIFIC PERSPECTIVES ON THE SOCIAL WORLD[1]

STYLES	ACTOR	ORDER OF OBJECTS (UNIFICATION)	ACTION (FORM)
Behaviourist	Impulses	Balance of forces	Laws
Functionalist	Needs	Maintenance of system	Pattern variables
Voluntarist	Interests	Domination/ compromise	Ideal constructs
Intentionalist	Attention	Order of meaning	Projects
Implicit Level	Spontaneity	Intentionality (Embodied)	Schema (body-subject)

[1] From Winter (1966, p. 114). "The arrow running from bottom left to upper right indicates the increasing degrees of abstraction in these major styles of social science and the focus of the particular abstraction on one or another element of the basic structure of social reality" (ibid., p. 113).

contrasts four dominant social-scientific perspectives. Winter argues that here are several typical levels of abstraction which characterize the different styles of sociological theory. A level of abstraction is defined in terms of its model of man, the nature of the order of social objects which it presupposes, and the way in which it views social action; each level differs in terms of these and thus differs in what it takes as its explanatory problems and in the kinds of explanations which it offers. These levels of abstraction can be viewed as forming a hierarchy which depicts their relative distance from social reality, from the human projects they are trying to comprehend, from man's intentionality in the world.[6] While each level inevitably involves some kind of selection from that reality which it is trying to understand, a central point of Winter's argument is that the closer to that reality the selection process is the less the remedy will be and vice versa. Some of the defining features of each level's theoretical style are given in Figure 1, and the shortcomings of some of them have already been discussed by Walsh. The four dominant levels of abstraction found in social science deal with intentionality in very different ways. The behaviourist perspective, for example, operates at a level of abstraction at furthest remove from intentionality, and the actions of individual actors are viewed as mechanical responses to internal and external determining conditions; the order of objects under study is seen as a balance of forces, and action is to be understood in terms of "scientific" laws. The problem of intentionality, of social meaning, is completely ignored at this level, for behaviourists reduce mind to mere sensations. At the other end of the hierarchy the intentionalist style, that recommended by phenomenological sociology, gives primacy to the modes of attention the actor gives to his world, takes the problem of meaning as its starting point, and understands action in terms of men's meaningful projects.

The problem of a social science is to come to terms not merely with those social phenomena which are amenable to relatively precise formulation but, more importantly, with those which are not. Social meanings are just such phenomena. As Winter says, "the scientist can presuppose the meaning or inquire into it; he cannot escape it" (1966, p. 124). The behaviourist and functionalist levels of abstraction have presupposed meaning, treating it as a mere epiphenomenon of social forces or system needs; a consequence of their aims, assumptions and methods is that their explanations of social phenomena typically reduce or remedy social reality by trying to make it fit their scientific ideal. Moreover, because it is never made clear whose reality is being explained, the connections between the explanations and actual experiences of men are impossible to establish; there are no rules to show how the leap was made from observations to the particular level of conceptual abstraction chosen.

The alternative offered by phenomenological sociology is to take the intentional self as the starting point for sociological analysis and to take the human level of abstraction, the level of social meaning, as being the fundamental level for systematic sociological reflection and abstraction. This requires the development of new methodologies for getting close to and examining the everyday world. It is at this point that Winter stops short, for, while he spells out the character of phenomenological sociology's subject matter, he fails to clarify *how* this is to be done; the methodological problems and substantive investigations are left to others.

As a given perspective's level of abstraction defines the kind of theoretical problems that it faces, it follows that it also defines the kind of data to be collected, and hence has direct implications for the methodological style to be adopted.

---

[6] For a similar classification done for rather different purposes, see Wagner (1964).

Thus, for example, in order to make empirical generalizations at the level of the social system or whole society, the sociologist requires data which relate to the whole society. Apart from the fact that very few, if any, sociologists have the resources to generate such data themselves, data relating to some unit called "the society" are likely to be expressed in highly abstract and condensed forms, whether numerical (such as demographic rates) or linguistic (such as the formal statutes of the criminal law). If he wants to make statements about the society based on data rather than imagination, the sociologist is left with various kinds of condensed data which have been produced for practical and not sociological purposes. Such data are products of commonsense practical reasoning; the practical projects in the world through which and for which they are produced determine the form and shape which they take. Any coincidence between their actual form and shape and those required by sociology for the solution of its problems is entirely fortuitous. The typical solution of sociologists to the problem of using non-sociological data for sociological purposes is to treat them as approximations of the "actual underlying patterns"; numerical indices, for example, are treated as more or less accurate summary indices of events that "actually happened". This solution requires a taken-for-granted acceptance of the categories in which the data are fixed; the measurement categories of the data are assumed to bear a known and unequivocal relationship to the events to which they refer. Accepting the data in this way forces a coincidence between socio-logical interests and the practical interests which produced the data in the first place. Implicitly, the sociologist who accepts and works within the categories of the practically produced data is forced to share the commonsense definition of the situation; the definition of the sociological problem coincides with the definition of the social problem because of its reliance on data which reflect practical and unquestioned decision-making.

By contrast, phenomenological sociology treats as problematic the very things taken for granted within conventional sociology; the production of statistics for practical problem-solving purposes is viewed as a phenomenon requiring investigation in its own right. The categories used in practical collation of official data are viewed as practical social constructions which bear an un-explicated relationship to the events to which they refer.[7] An order is imposed on events by the categories chosen so that the order (expressed for example in official rates) can only be understood through an investigation of the categories used. This would suggest that the reliance of "macro-sociologists" or "system theorists" on data gathered for practical purposes and relating to the whole society requires them to take for granted the meaning of the data. Presupposing the meaning leads to an implicit coincidence of sociological and practical defini-tions of the situation. Reliance on practically produced data thus raises in an acute way the issues of what interpretive understanding means in sociology and how such understanding requires a suspension of commonsense values and

---

[7] For discussions of the problematic character of official data which illustrate these points see Cicourel (1968); Cicourel and Kitsuse (1963b); J. Douglas (1967); Sudnow (1968b).

beliefs. Questioning the meaning of the data on which sociological generalizations about "the society" or "the system" are based calls into question the meaning of the generalizations themselves.

Thus the level of abstraction with its particular analytical problems directs the sociologist to focus on some kinds of data rather than others and in so doing influences the methodological style. As one moves up through the hierarchy of theoretical levels, from intentionalist to behaviourist, the focus on consciousness and the problem of social meaning increasingly gives way to a focus on the "objective" and external features of action so that the summary indices of official data are viewed as an adequate resource for generalizations about "the society". The problems faced in coming to terms with intentionality are by-passed in favour of concentrating on those phenomena which are held to be amenable to the application of social scientists' stereotype of "the scientific method". A major consequence of the sociologist's perspective and methodology is a focus on very limited features of action. This is epitomized in the conventional field survey which follows the canons of "good survey research practice", where the logic of the method imposes an order on events and severely limits the features of action which are studied. The classification of sociological perspectives according to their distance from the level of human meaning serves to point up the remedial character of most sociology; those perspectives which treat men, for analytical purposes, as analogous to objects or organisms of the natural world, or simple carriers of attributes, remedy the forms of man's being-in-the-world and therefore of social realities too.

Two related problems are raised by those sociological perspectives which presuppose meaning and intentionality. A first problem concerns the relationship between the sociological venture and the encompassing society within which it takes place; those sociological perspectives which presuppose meaning, rather than treating it as problematic, provide explanations which are largely unrelated to the intentionalities of the societal members who accomplished the very events to be explained. By offering explanations of action which either deny or severely remedy intentionality, the meaning and therefore the relevance of such explanations becomes highly dubious for the members of the society. The philosophical issue of "freedom" versus "determinism" also expresses the dilemma concerning the nature of sociological explanation. If sociological explanation is couched in forms which describe members' actions as determined by structures, forces of production, or external social pressures of some kind there is clearly little members can do about it. Positivist explanations and methodologies view men in precisely these terms. But whether the members whose actions are explained in such deterministic terms can make sense of or accept such explanations is problematic; commonsense acceptance of the principle of choice, epitomized, for example, in the general notion of responsibility before the law, requires rejection of explanations which deny choice and draw attention away from its sources in intentionality. By contrast, perspectives and methodologies which explicitly recognize freedom and choice, as in phenomenological sociology, tell societal members that they can change situations if they so choose; sociological information and description here become possible sources for clarifying the bases of choice and bringing them more fully into self-consciousness.

In fact much sociological explanation, because it does not relate to the intentions and meanings through which social events are accomplished, appears to be very hard to translate into terms which have meaning for the members of society; where this occurs sociology becomes an esoteric game played by an alienated minority at the intellectual margins of society. To what end are the theoretical abstractions of sociology directed if they are not congruent with men's experiences? Can they be made meaningful to members if they are framed in terms which deny meaningful choices?

The second and related problem, that of validity, is dealt with more fully in the next chapter, but also draws attention to the external meaning of sociological description—that is, its meaning to non-sociologists; in the case of validity the relevant non-sociologists are those whose actions the sociologist is trying to understand. Within the phenomenological perspective it is not sufficient to have criteria of validity which are internal to the sociological enterprise, for validity is understood in much wider terms. To establish the external validity of an explanation requires the sociologist to develop methodologies which take sociological explanations back into the social world from which they were derived and which demonstrate that they do not unnecessarily remedy the members' realities to which they relate. Validity is established through demonstrating that sociological explanation is congruent with the meanings through which members construct their realities and accomplish their everyday practical activities.[8]

The interrelated issues of validity and the social meaning of sociological explanations require that sociology ground itself at the level of intentionality and inquire into and build on the social meanings out of which men construct their actions. By recognizing and trying to come to terms with the character of man's being-in-the-world, his intentionality, sociology offers the possibility of providing interpretations of human action which have wider validity than that recognized by the limiting canons of a stereotypical scientific method, and which, by their congruence with social meanings, not only remain meaningful to the members of the society but also bring such meanings more fully into consciousness.

The project of phenomenological sociology thus concerns itself with the development of methodologies and modes of description which dispense with the distinction between man as subject and man as object; if it is to be true to the phenomenological injunction to "get back to" and "be true to the things themselves", and if "the things themselves" are men's meaningful experiences of themselves and their social world, then its task is to reveal and describe "the things themselves". But the very nature of men's phenomenal experiences places limits on the kinds of methodologies and associated descriptions which can adequately reveal rather than remedy the phenomenal social world. A recognition

---

[8] See Silverman's discussion of validation in Chapter 7 and my elaboration of this point in Chapter 6.

of the problem of meaning as the central problem for sociology requires a concomitant rejection of the claim by observer/researchers that their descriptions are "objective" accounts of the social world. The observer, like everyone else, has to rely on his commonsense reasoning and his descriptions are products of his commonsense reasoning; he is already a member of the social world and cannot remove himself from it to become some kind of "objective" observer. He too is constrained by the implicit rules governing practical reasoning and conversation, and if he lays claim to some superior or detached "objectivity" in so doing he becomes a fake observer; by taking up the stance of the fake observer he obliterates the very things that must be investigated if sociology is to be true to its subject matter.

Everyday reasoning thus becomes the core interest of sociology. How people routinely acquire a sense of, produce and sustain those phenomena which sociologists call "social structures" are the central concern of the phenomenological perspective and a definition of this as the subject area for sociological investigation demands a recognition that sociologists themselves have access to these phenomena only through their practical reasoning. The implications of such a recognition for evaluating traditional research methods in sociology and the data they produce are far-reaching. Clearly, alternative modes of investigation are required to those dehumanizing techniques which treat man as object while relying on commonsense reasoning as an unexplicated resource.

From a phenomenological perspective, therefore, the main problems of sociological theory reside in, first, the lack of clearly defined aims of theorizing; second, the lack of clearly defined rules for generating theory; third, the ambiguity over what counts as theory; fourth, the assumption of the dual autonomies of theory and methodology which has led to the practical separation of the two activities; fifth, the unexplicated relationship between sociological theories and the social meanings from which human projects emerge; and sixth, the unrecognized implications of members' and sociologists' reliance on practical reasoning for making sense of the social world. All these problems point to the necessity of developing methodologies which come to terms with the problem of meaning and which enable sociologists to establish and demonstrate the validity of their explanations at the level of human meaning.

CONTEMPORARY METHODOLOGY

In discussing sociological theory I have argued that it is largely divorced from consideration of the methodological problems of doing research and investigating the empirical social world. A conscious and central aim of phenomenological sociology is to transcend the conventional dichotomy between theory and methodology. To complement the above discussion of problems of theory some of the main characteristics of conventional methodology which support this dichotomy are now examined; a clarification of these methodological problems should point to the necessary requirements of any alternative which might be developed.

The clearest illustration of the gap between theory and research processes is found in the limitation of contemporary methodology to the study of research techniques and the practical problems of survey research; thus the "methodologist" in contemporary sociology is someone who specialized in the design, management, and analysts of social surveys. Restriction to the mechanics of research organization omits that which ought to be regarded as the central issue of methodology. I have argued earlier for a redefinition of methodology to include all the processes by which the sociologist comes to construct an abstract view of a situation (his theory). The processes of observation, selection and transformation of aspects of social reality define the nature of the links between a resulting sociological interpretation and the realities under investigation. These processes, which comprise far more than what is conventionally regarded as "research methods", are literally the sociologist's "method" of arriving at an interpretation. Unless we can reconstruct these processes more or less adequately on the basis of information made explicit by the sociologist in his interpretation we are in a very weak position to assess its worth. From the phenomenological perspective, the methodological problem is to show how the sociologists' interpretations are constructed and how they relate to the meaningful actions they are trying to comprehend. Conventional esapproach to theory and methods ignore these issues.

The problem requires analysis and presentation of the form and content of sociologists' rules and decisions; we must know *how* any sociologist in constructing an explanation decides *what* is relevant to observe, select and transform. This refers not only to his activities in a fieldwork situation, but equally importantly to what he does before and after any fieldwork; the "before" and "after" are conventionally referred to as design and analysis. It is important to note that the processes which comprise this redefined methodology are common to all sociological perspectives and to all sociological attempts to provide explanations, irrespective of whether an explanation refers directly to a substantive empirical investigation or not. A brief look at some of the features of research methods in contemporary sociology may clarify the relevance of the phenomenological critique for an understanding of the unexplicated relationship between theory and research methods.

Views of the scientific method

The sociological assumption of the essential similarity of the natural and social worlds, discussed earlier by Walsh, led to the attempt by sociologists to develop research procedures which were analogous to those of the natural sciences. Even when there was a recognition of the peculiar character of social phenomena, attempts were made to approximate "the" scientific method by emphasizing quantification and precision in measurement; the natural-scientific paradigm was still viewed as the ideal for sociological investigation and was taken as the model for empirical research. Adoption of this paradigm as the ideal can be seen as one of the most important sources of the split between theory and research in sociology. This can be illustrated by following Rudner's (1966) distinction between "the context of discovery" and "the context of validation" in the research process. The "context of discovery" refers among other things to the context and processes through which the scientist comes to develop ways of seeing the natural phenomena under investigation; it alludes to the innovation of ideas within a scientific discipline and the means by which a scientist comes to construct an abstract view of a phenomenon (his hypothesis or theory). By contrast, the "context of validation" refers to the processes by which the scientist attempts to validate his ideas; in laboratory sciences the typical mode of validation is the laboratory experiment designed to disconfirm the hypothesis. Validation thus refers to research practices; these research practices are for the most part regarded as neutral techniques, that is they don't change or influence the phenomena studied except in ways controlled by the scientist. As natural phenomena are inherently meaningless, the claim to neutrality can be justified with few apparent exceptions.

Conventional sociology works largely in terms of this distinction between the two contexts; the processes by which the sociologist initially constructs an abstract view of social phenomena are viewed as independent of the means he subsequently adopts for testing his ideas. The means, conventional research procedures, are viewed as neutral ways of disconfirming or supporting his ideas. As I have suggested earlier the adoption of this stance serves to reinforce a situation in which some people are regarded primarily as "theorists", presumably the "real" innovators, while others are first and foremost "methodologists", or sociological equivalents of laboratory technicians. However, if, as it is a main purpose of this book to argue, the social world is pre-eminently a meaningful world, the relevance of the natural-scientific model of investigation (and especially the idea of neutral techniques of investigation) to the problems of sociology must be subjected to radical doubt. The context of validation, as exemplified in the recommended procedures of conventional social research, should be suspended and replaced by a revitalized and reformulated context of discovery; an alternative rhetoric to the "rhetoric of verification" is required.

In the discussion of Winter's classification of the levels of theoretical abstraction it was suggested that each level, because of its particular definition of what constitutes a sociological problem, would focus on particular kinds of data and would develop methodologies appropriate to its particular problems and data. One might resonably expect radical differences between theoretical levels in their data and methods because of the very different problems with which they attempt to grapple. However, if the actual research practices of contemporary sociology are examined, this expectation is unsupported, for it appears that, far from there being an appropriate methodology developed for each theoretical level, a research style or orientation has emerged which is used in common by sociologists writing at all levels of theoretical abstraction. There is an "ideal" set of research procedures which is recommended irrespective of the theoretical problem being investigated. The prescriptions of these research procedures appear to centre on sociologists' desire to achieve certain kinds of "objectivity", the particular conceptions of which stem from the attempt to apply a stereotype of "the scientific method" to social phenomena. Not surprisingly, the attempt to be "objective" has resulted in the development of an orientation to research, complementary to the range of theoretical perspectives, which reduces men metaphorically to objects. Research techniques, and the way in which their results are interpreted, reinforce the theoretical denial of man's intentionality and ignore the question of meaning. What the researcher who follows the conventional code of "good research practice" does is to take for granted the problem of meaning and ignore the fundamental issues it raises about what he is actually doing. In spite of the differences in theoretical problems between levels of abstraction, an approach to research has emerged which uncomfortably straddles the different perspectives and which is recommended irrespective of the analytical problems. Although they pay lip-service to the need for a theoretical approach, conventional research textbooks[9] pay no attention to the substantive analytical problems of sociology, for their aim is to describe a set of procedures which are viewed as independent of these problems and which in themselves are claimed to be neutral.

The phenomenological critique argues first, that these procedures, by treating the social world as an object-world and pretending that the problem of meaning does not exist, unnecessarily remedy the phenomenal social world, and second, that the very methods themselves contain implicit theories and assumptions about the phenomena being studied which should be problematic for the observer and not taken-for-granted by him. It is not merely theoretical perspectives, such as functionalism or behaviourism, that rest on assumptions about man and the social world but also, and equally important, research methods and procedures; embedded in the recommended canons of "good" research practice are unexplicated notions of man, social order and rationality. Thus even the "abstracted empiricists"[10] who reject the necessity of a theoretical, orientation to research, in fact operate with implicit and unexplicated theory because of their adherence to research procedures which provide ordering principles for investigating the social world. Some of these ordering principles are suggested in Figure 2 on page 103.

The attempt to emulate the natural-scientific ideal means that conventional research methods have the ultimate aim of generating laws or causal explanations; these are to be achieved through the careful testing of hypotheses which have been derived from stocks of conceptual knowledge. The concepts of a hypothesis are operationalized and conventional research procedures are followed, ostensibly in attempts to disconfirm the hypothesis. Thus Merton (1957), in recommending the close collaboration of "theorists" and "researchers", exhorts sociologists to develop and verify theories of "the middle range" as a necessary prerequisite to the higher-level derivation of theoretical constructs. This emphasis on theory verification as the central problem for sociology carries with it an

---

[9] See, for example, the texts cited in footnote 3, p. 86.
[10] This term is taken from C. Wright Mills, 1959, p. 50.

acceptance of existing methodological procedures which views them as non-problematic. The typical way of viewing the relationship between theory and methods among those who implicitly or explicitly subscribe to the natural-science ideal is to regard the basic methodological problems of sociology as solved; from this perspective, the most important developments and modifications will stem from a concern with theorizing in and for itself, so that all that is required from methodology is the steady development of increasingly mathematically sophisticated techniques for the more precise testing of hypotheses. The phenomenological perspective, by rejecting the relevance of the natural-scientific ideal for the analysis of the social world, attempts to transcend the dichotomy between theory and method and offers alternatives to the conventional sequence of hypothesis-derivation and verification.

Quantification and measurement

The unwillingness to question the basic assumptions on which existing research methods rest and to examine critically research procedures has meant that problems of quantification and the development of measurement techniques have become the central concerns of "methodologists".[11]

There are two related problems here. First, the major decisions in the design and analysis of most field research are dictated by the logic of the statistical method, especially in the related processes of sampling and significance testing. Statistical theory provides the criteria for deciding whether research is basically sound; if the procedures followed in any particular research project more or less satisfy the basic requirements of statistical theory, the data produced are then judged according to sociological criteria of relevance. This two-stage process applies both to the design and evaluation of research. Prime consideration is given to statistical prescriptions both when the investigation is designed and when it is evaluated; sociological considerations are treated as secondary in both stages. It is thus the logic of the statistical method which determines the form of an investigation and which provides the initial criteria for deciding whether it is even worth evaluating in sociological terms. The statistical method is regarded as a set of value-neutral procedures which sociology can use as a tool. Two problems stem from this. First, the assumption about the neutrality of statistics is faulty, for like any other body of theory it contains implicit ordering principles which impute values to the phenomena being studied; for example, in relation to social action, statistical theory imputes certain kinds of rationality to men which rest on notions of probability. Like any other perspective in sociology its ordering principles contain implicit models of man and of action; sociologists should thus consider whether the values attributed to the social process in statistical theory are congruent with the ordering principles of

---

[11] For example, compare the mathematical content of Goode and Hatt's textbook, published in 1952, with that of H. M. and B. Blalock, published in 1968.

their chosen sociological perspective let alone with members' "rationalities". The second problem of viewing statistics as a value-neutral tool of sociology is that, in practice, far from being a mere tool of sociologists it has swelled to such proportions that it now rules its master; the important decisions about research design and evaluation are made from a statistical and not a sociological frame of reference.

The irony is that many things that are statistically very significant are sociologically completely insignificant. The statistical results of an investigation do not speak for themselves; theoretical judgments and interpretations are required for making sense of the data and for deciding on their relative importance. These interpretations are carried out only marginally on the basis of explicit theory and they rest mainly on implicit values and a reliance on commonsense or "what everyone knows". An examination of the values implicit in the statistical method and a recognition that interpretation of its results rests on commonsense assumptions calls into question the relevance of the statistical method to the analytical problems of sociology. Blumer, writing from within the conventional symbolic interactionist perspective, has convincingly argued that there are many research situations in which this logic obscures the issues of sociological concern.[12]

The second major and related problem of the emphasis on numerical measurement is the sociological "sickness" given the apt name of "quanto-phrenia" by Sorokin (1956, ch. 7); there are several relevant aspects of this obsession with number and measurement in sociology and the most important centre on those things that are obscured or passed over as a result of the obsession. Not only does the increased mathematical content in research reports cast a veneer of scientific respectability and apparent precision over sociological projects, it also serves to increase the distance between the sociologist and his actual and potential audiences. The more that attention is drawn to and placed on the internal characteristics of a piece of research, for example in relation to the elaborate character of its research techniques, the less likely is attention to be given to the external meaning and validity of the completed project in either a sociological context or as knowledge in the wider society. Quantification is therefore politically convenient for the sociologist because it obscures the meaning of his project. The increasing concern to quantify meanings and values is in itself a further step in the dehumanizing process of contemporary sociology, for the more men's intentionalities are reduced to numbers and are severely distorted in the process, the more difficult it becomes to recognize their intrinsic qualities. The suffocating grip of quantification in sociology strangles emergent meanings at birth; as soon as meanings appear in the world the aim of the quantophrenic sociologist is to slap numbers on them.

Cicourel's critique of sociological methods of investigation is most relevant here. A general problem raised by Cicourel is the relevance of measurement

---

[12] Blumber (1969). See especially Chapter 1 and his discussion of "exploration" and "inspection", pp. 40–7.

techniques in sociology to the phenomena being studied. His central thesis is that:

> Present measurement devices are not valid because they represent the imposition of numerical procedures that are external both to the external social world empirically described by sociologists and to the *conceptualizations* based upon these descriptions (1964, p. 2).

Neither the commonsense meanings of everyday life nor the concepts based upon them by sociologists have inherent numerical properties. Thus what we now have in sociology, Cicourel argues, is measurement by fiat; the measurement systems and their categories which sociologists use have a forced and arbitrary correspondence to the social phenomena they are trying to grasp. As the prime characteristic of the social world is its meaningfulness, and as shift and ambiguity are prime qualities of meaning, so must the sociologist develop methodologies for comprehending the social construction of meaning; the static and logically consistent properties of mathematical languages seem remarkably inappropriate for this task. To obtain any data at all the sociologist must form minimally meaningful relationships with other men; the data obtained from such relationships thus emerge from a process of mutal interpretation in which meaning must always be regarded as problematic. As this mutual interpretation is accomplished through the typifications of natural language, which only rarely uses numbers for expressing meaning, the sociologist must somehow demonstrate the congruence of his constructs with members' constructed meanings. Such congruence is impossible to establish if the sociologist turns meanings into numbers because the links between the sociological number categories and the meanings of the social world are achieved by fiat. The sociologist makes an unexplicated leap from the commonsense categories of practical reasoning to the number categories of mathematics. Thus the problem faced in the process of conceptualization is the nature of the equivalence between the observer's concepts and the social phenomena he selects for study and which are subsumed under the concept.

In fact Cicourel prefers to leave the problem of measurement an open question and starts off from the assumption that,

> it is possible to establish equivalence classes at the conceptual level which correspond to correlatives of an observed environment (ibid., p. 4).

This follows the example of Schutz who argues that the second-order constructs of the sociologist should relate directly to the first-order constructs of the lived world—the linguistic typifications of commonsense practical reasoning.[13] The problem of measurement recedes and the more general issues of the character of the relationship between sociologists' concepts and what they observe come to the fore. For Cicourel,

> . . . arguments about whether sociology is a "science" or its theories and findings amenable to quantification are premature if we cannot agree on what is theory and

---

[13] Schutz (1962, pp. 62ff). See the following chapter for an expansion of this point.

whether our theories can be stated so that they generate numeric properties that will have correlatives in an observable world (ibid., p. 5).

An essential aspect of Cicourel's critique is to draw out the methodological implications of studying commonsense practical reasoning, the taken-for-granted social world, which have previously been unrecognized by sociologists. A recognition of the ways in which practical reasoning implicitly structures all research practice requires a reappraisal of existing research practices. One major prerequisite in any research project is for the observer/researcher to attempt to make explicit his own system of relevancies which provides the horizon of meaning for the decisions, choices and selections he makes. Unless the reader knows the nature of a researcher's resources he has to rely on his own commonsense for filling in what "he knows the researcher means". By failing to make his relevance structures explicit, the researcher trades on what he assumes "everyman" to know unequivocally.

The unknown process whereby the meanings which are the empirical indicators of sociologists' concepts are transmogrified into numbers serves both to mystify the research process by giving it a spurious aura of "scientific" respectability and exactitude, and also to reinforce the gap between data collection and conceptualization.

The key question, therefore, becomes: What is measurement for in sociology? In spite of Weber's early location of meaning as the central problem for sociological analysis, sociologists have carefully side-stepped the problems involved in showing how quantification clarifies or diminishes the difficulties which arise in interpreting social meanings. If Cicourel's thesis of measurement by fiat is correct, then, while questions concerning the meaning and relevance of quantification are being debated, we might consider substituting a simple alternative; the recommendation of phenomenological sociology is that numerical measurement in sociology be limited to social phenomena that are inherently measurable, and that we try to deal more adequately on the conceptual level with non-numerical phenomena. It is all right to count the number of times people attend church, but it does not make any sense to impose seven-point scales or other numerical devices onto the meanings given to religious experience. Using observers' categories (for example, age, sex, class or occupation) to subdivide a studied group according to their differential responses to given observers' questions is not going to contribute to an understanding of members' and observers' meaning construction unless such observers' categories are used by members in their accomplishment of the social world.

The problem of meaning

How does conventional research methodology deal with the problem of meaning at the intentional level? In general research techniques treat meanings as mere epiphenomena of other "external" social factors; thus, for example, attitudes are explained in terms of group membership or gross factors such as "technology".[14] Survey research treats members' linguistic typifications, some of which are employed in their handling of questionnaire items, as if they are "obvious" and unequivocal responses to unambiguous stimuli. These methods completely miss the intersubjective processes of interpretation in which group members together create and share meanings, and make situations accountable in commonsense terms. A practical result of treating the attachment of meaning to an object as a given rather than as analytically problematic can be seen in the questionnaire/interview research method. Cicourel points out that the traditional empiricist has to assume, usually on the basis of very limited pilot interviews, that all the questionnaire respondents attach identical meanings to each of the questions and that these coincide with the observer's intentions in framing the questions. He argues that the lack of a developed social theory (that is, one that specifies how to translate concepts into empirical indicators) forces researchers to employ commonsense concepts that reflect knowledge which is assumed to be known to both sociologists and "average members of the community"; thus the "obvious" meanings of operationalized questionnaire items will incorporate properties that have only been vaguely defined, if at all, in social theory but which are nevertheless either taken-for-granted as relevant to the research or ignored altogether. In making sense of and interpreting his data the researcher relies on his commonsense knowledge of the respondents' commonsense, and the guides or rules he intuitively uses in coming to commonsense decisions are not a problematic issue for him. Yet it is precisely through these commonsense reasonings that the research and the mundane social world is accomplished.[15] Conventional methodological procedures contain no injunctions to the researcher to attempt to reveal his reliance on taken-for-granted meanings as unexplicated resources.

Perhaps the most problematic feature of the way conventional research procedures handle the problem of meaning stems from their origins in the "context of validation"; the very shape and form of the research techniques (questionnaire, self-completed schedule and so on) impose an order and pattern on the realities being investigated and in so doing *create* meanings. Far from simply laying bare what is "already there", the instruments of the observer create the very order they are supposedly designed to reveal. Any research instrument ready for use in a particular study reflects a compromise between the researcher's ideals, the design requirements of the statistical method, and the practical problems of doing research in a particular setting; the researcher is nevertheless seeking to locate the "real underlying patterns" or "order" referred to in his basic hypotheses and the instruments are designed to reveal such order. The conventional concepts of sociology presume an idealized regularity in the social world and research techniques are designed to "reveal" this regularity. As Cicourel puts it:

---

[14] See, for example, Turner and Lawrence (1965) and Silverman's critique of "technological determinism" (1970, Chapter 5). For a further discussion of conventional methodology, with illustrations from substantive studies, see Chapter 8.

[15] See Cicourel (1964, pp. 19–24).

When researchers seek the "underlying patterns" to manifest materials, they employ an implicit abstracting procedure for discovering a few ideals to explain large masses of unintelligible manifest data, rather than develop a theoretical apparatus that would explain and generate everyday behaviour. . . . The search for hypothetical "underlying patterns" precludes the discovery of socially meaningful action by invoking the researcher's ideals as an unobservable explanation (1968, pp. 332–3).

Thus, where meanings are studied directly, as in attitude research, they are viewed as "objective" products of underlying structural conditions and are used as data to illustrate or be fitted into the sociologist's existing stock of concepts; the very structure of the research instruments used imposes a form on the data and in so doing creates new data which are taken to be more or less adequate indicators of the assumed "underlying patterns". In the design and analysis of instruments and data the problem of the way the observers own taken-for-granted meanings and practical reasoning continually structure his perception and decisions is ignored; his analysis of the data rests on the assumption of the identical attribution of meaning to questions by himself and all respondents.

A further problem of conventional methodology is its lack of concern with social processes, with shift, change and the dynamic character of social life; the constantly shifting character of relationships and the continuous subtle changes in social meanings present challenges to sociological research which conventional methodology has largely ignored. Analysis of social processes is bypassed in favour of providing limited static descriptions of a population at one point in time. The nearest that conventional methodology comes to attempting to deal with process and change is in the panel study;[16] but even this provides only a series of descriptions of the "same" population at different points in time. When done carefully, as in Converse's panel study (1964), the results suggest that many typical sociological assumptions, concerning, for example, the stability of political opinion, may be totally misplaced. The one method which would seem to provide the greatest opportunity for studying the processual character of social life, participant observation, is the technique most frowned upon and regarded with suspicion in the canons of conventional methodology, because it fails to satisfy their limited criteria of objectivity. Unfortunately this has meant that participant observers have been put on the defensive; the result has been that most defenders have been put in the position of justifying the technique according to the terms of conventional methodology, rather than developing an independent case for it.[17] From the phenomenological perspective the problem of participant observation is whether the observer can reconstruct for the reader what he did and how he came to select some things out as important; he must be able to demonstrate how he accomplished a level of competent performance in participant situations and the resources he employed for the accomplishment.

---

[16] See, for example, J. W. B. Douglas (1969).

[17] See, for example, many of the essays in McCall and Simmons (1969); the exceptions are Blumer (1969) and Bruyn (1966) both of whom make out a positive case for participant observation from within the symbolic interactionist perspective.

FIGURE 2 : PERSPECTIVE UNDERLYING CONVENTIONAL METHODOLOGICAL STYLE FOR THE ANALYSIS OF THE SOCIAL WORLD

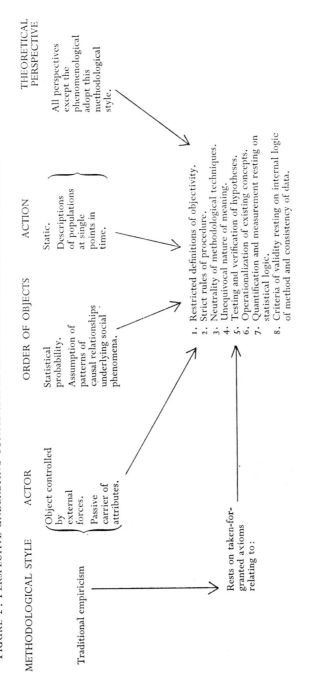

METHODOLOGICAL STYLE

ACTOR

ORDER OF OBJECTS

ACTION

THEORETICAL PERSPECTIVE

Traditional empiricism

Object controlled by external forces.

Passive carrier of attributes.

Statistical probability.

Assumption of patterns of causal relationships underlying social phenomena.

Static.

Descriptions of populations at single points in time.

All perspectives except the phenomenological adopt this methodological style.

Rests on taken-for-granted axioms relating to:

1. Restricted definitions of objectivity.
2. Strict rules of procedure.
3. Neutrality of methodological techniques.
4. Unequivocal nature of meaning.
5. Testing and verification of hypotheses.
6. Operationalization of existing concepts.
7. Quantification and measurement resting on statistical logic.
8. Criteria of validity resting on internal logic of method and consistency of data.

By treating meanings as if they were objects of the natural world to be tapped by his "precision" instruments, the sociologist who operates according to the canons of conventional research imposes a spurious order on the social world through his instruments, and neglects the study of social realities as inter-subjectively meaningful accomplishments; the crucial methodological weakness is the failure to recognize his own taken-for-granted reliance on meanings and practical reasoning as tacit resources. When meanings are taken-for-granted the social world is viewed as an unequivocal given, thereby passing over the fundamental problem of how members construct and accomplish meaningful social interaction.

SUMMARY

Some of the main characteristics of conventional methodology are brought together in Figure 2 to illustrate how its guiding principles and canons contain implicit theories of the social world, in the same way as the theoretical per-spectives classified in Figure 1. The taken-for-granted axioms underpinning this style are used for assessing the worth of practically all the research currently carried out in sociology; as long as sociologists continue to model their explana-tions and research on the ideals of natural-science investigation by following some approximation of the style summed up in Figure 2, the related problems of meaning and validity will be ignored. The import of the phenomenological critique is to suggest that bypassing the problem of meaning automatically renders problematic the social meaning of the sociological enterprise.

The inability of the conventional methodological style to come to terms with the problems of intentionality and meaning requires a new orientation for sociological analysis. The required alternative must both transcend the traditional dichotomy between theory and research in a coherent way and address the problems presented by meaning and intentionality in ways which remain true to the phenomena studied. Phenomenological sociology attempts to meet both these requirements, and recent work by the ethnomethodologists suggests some solutions. Some of the empirical work of the ethnomethodologists is discussed by Silverman (in Chapters 7 and 8) but it is worth noting here one of their basic orienting assumptions concerning the generation of sociological explanations: ethnomethodologists start from a recognition that anybody, whether in the natural attitude of everyday life or the scientific attitude, has access to the social world only through a reliance on commonsense practical reasoning; accounts, socio-logical or otherwise, of any aspect of the social world are a product of such reasoning and consist of linguistic typifications which are assumed to be clear and unequivocal. We all operate with the assumption that for all practical purposes others "know what we mean" in our accounts; it is this assumption along with others which allows social interaction to flow in a relatively unhindered way.[18] But our assumption that we know what the other means in his account relies

---

[18] See Schutz's discussion of the "reciprocity of perspectives" (1962, pp. 11ff.).

on our filling in or fleshing out his account with horizons of meaning in order to "make sense" of it. Accounts, descriptions, conversation, plain "talk", are effectively shorthand depictions because they all rely on the other being able to fill in material that enables him to make sense of them. This is referred to when ethnomethodologists talk about the inherent indexicality of accounts. Meaning is always more than is or can be stated.[19] The accounts of traditional sociological theory are no exception to this rule of social life, for they too require us to fill in the details for ourselves if we are to make any sense of them; the student familiar with sociological jargon claims to know what a particular theorist means because he can fill in the empty concepts used in explanation. However, because theorists and researchers in conventional explanation do not reveal their relevancies in using particular concepts, we have no way of establishing the congruence between our fill-ins of the text and those presupposed by the author; nor would I know whether your fill-in was congruent with mine.

While for practical reasons congruence is assumed, it should be regarded as problematic because of the very vague character of sociological concepts. Because there are no rules for generating or interpreting sociological concepts, assumptions about the congruency of interpretations are forced assumptions whose validity is untestable in the current state of sociological explanation. The only way we can approach congruency of meaning in sociological explanation is by making explicit the structures of relevance or background expectancies which provide the grounds for the emergence of the sociologist's selections, choices and transformations. Only in this way can the reader more or less establish that his fill-ins, how he makes sense of the description, are congruent with the researcher's horizons of meaning in generating the description. Even when this is done[20] the reader's fill-ins can only approximate the researcher's intentions because of their inherent indexicality. In this context, however, the most important feature of making relevancies explicit is its contribution to the transcendence of the theory/research dichotomy. The final short-hand account of a study, the "theory", is an attempt to sum up, in an apparently unambiguous way, all the complex processes out of which the study emerged; the theory is being produced throughout the project in a largely implicit way through interaction with the subjects of the study and others, through processes of reinterpretation, and through unanticipated organizational contingencies. Only if we can reconstitute, from the manifest data, the processes by which the observer jumps from his observations to his theoretical interpretation can we know for all practical purposes what his theory means. Thus by making explicit his relevancies at every stage of interpretation, by showing how his interpretation relates to the data, the sociologist demonstrates that theory is an emergent product and not something separate from the research process; it cannot stand by itself, it can only stand in relation to a body of data which are collected and made sense of in an ongoing process of interpretation and reinterpretation. The final theoretical

---

[19] See especially Chapters 7 and 9.
[20] See, for example, Cicourel (1967).

account must somehow document these ongoing interpretive processes so that the reader can see for all practical purposes "what happened". Unless the reader can reconstruct the ongoing interpretive process, the meaning of the theory remains problematic. Within this perspective, therefore, theory is not and cannot be divorced from the research and conceptualization processes to which it relates; the problem is to make manifest the ways in which any theoretical abstraction is an emergent accomplishment arising from the ways in which observers make sense of research contingencies. The observer must treat as problematic not only the everyday accomplishments of those he is observing but also his own accomplishments in doing research.

CONCEPTS IN SOCIOLOGY

Phenomenological sociology raises two initial and fundamental questions about concepts in sociology; it asks, first, what counts as a sociological concept? That is, what gives concepts their specifically *sociological* character and enables us to differentiate them from other kinds of concepts, such as those of commonsense? Second, and related to the first, it asks, what are the rules, if any, which socio-logists follow in generating and using their concepts? The sociological literature on theory construction and methodology gives very little help in answering these questions; the assumption seems to be that if one is doing sociology then one must be using sociological concepts. In the absence of such guides and rules, and for the present purpose of drawing attention to some problems of conceptualiza-tion in sociology, I adopt the pragmatic approach of defining concepts in terms of their actual usage by sociologists. I regard those words that sociologists use in framing what they regard as "theory" as sociological concepts. This immediately raises an interesting problem which arises from the natural-language character of sociological theory; the linguistic expression of sociological theory follows the ordinary rules of grammar and syntax so that those words which are speci-fically regarded as sociological concepts, such as "role", "status" or "norm", are always embedded in sentences composed of other words; it is only by stringing sociological concepts together with ordinary language according to the rules of conventional grammar that we can impute a meaning to the theory. If we can make sense of sociological concepts only when they are embedded in a context of meaning that relies on our commonsense understanding of grammar and ordinary language, it becomes clear that we cannot regard concepts as neutral expressions or different from, or separable from commonsense reasoning. We have meaningful access to them only when they are situated in contexts of meaning which provide us with the means for making sense of them (grammar and ordinary language). As concepts are always situated in this way it becomes very difficult to distinguish them from non-concepts or commonsense. The problem is that, of all the words which appear in sociological theory texts, only a small number are specifically regarded as sociological concepts, yet these are compre-hensible only because they are locked into contexts of commonsense meaning; how, therefore, can we distinguish sociological concepts from commonsense?

Concepts and commonsense

A recognition of this problem of conceptualization serves to call into question sociologists' claims to have revealed the "real, underlying patterns" of the social world; it would seem that the necessary reliance on practical commonsense reasoning for any understanding of sociological theory, and a realization that this reliance on commonsense leads to infinite interpretations of the theory, requires a rejection of the special status claims by sociologists to have provided an "objective" account of the social world. A sociological account thus becomes just another account of the social world, done from a very particular perspective and resting upon very special assumptions about that world. Cicourel states the ethnomethodological view of sociological accounts in the following way:

> In recognizing that we can generate only different glosses of our experiences, the ethnomethodologists try to underscore the pitfalls of viewing indexical expressions as if they could be repaired and thus transformed into context-free objective statements (forthcoming).

In other words to take members' accounts of their acts or social worlds and assume that they can be transformed by the sociologist into an "objective" statement of "what actually happened" or the "real underlying pattern of events" is to mistake the nature of the social world and members' accounts of it. Sociological theories are indexical accounts by sociologists of the social world and, like anybody else's accounts, they are glosses of the experiences which comprise that world. In this sense they carry no special privileged status as being more "objective" or nearer the "truth" than the accounts of anybody else.[21]

Fortunately for sociologists, some members of society, usually those with financial or political power, can see practical uses to which sociological accounts and accounting procedures can be put; by ensuring the continued financial support of sociology they allow sociologists to cling fast to their beliefs to have portrayed the world as "it really is", and they are also in a position to select out from sociological accounts those items they deem relevant to their practical interests without disturbing the comfortable beliefs of the sociologists. In a sense, sociologists' beliefs about the "objectivity" of their accounts are of no importance to anybody but other sociologists because practical men are not only highly selective in their use of sociological accounts, but are also concerned with action rather than achieving a specifically sociological understanding.[22]

These strictures about sociological conceptualization in general and about the problems of defining a sociological concept provide a setting against which to discuss some of the prime characteristics of the sociological use of concepts. In referring to concepts as "sociological" I am following the standard sociological

---

[21] A. Schutz's discussion of "multiple realities" is helpful for revealing the relativity of sociological accounts; the sociologist's account is simply an alternative reality accomplished from a very particular "here and now" (1967a, pp. 207ff.).

[22] For a discussion of these issues in relation to crime, see Phillipson (1971b, Chapter 6).

practice of differentiating out concepts from the contexts of meaning in which they occur while acknowledging that this differentiation is arbitrary.

The ambiguity of concepts

Perhaps the most notable characteristics of sociological concepts are their vagueness and ambiguity, and the ambiguity in this context does not result merely from the ambiguous character of social realities but also from sociologists' neglect of the process of concept formation. By vagueness, I am referring to the lack of explicit rules for deciding both the relevant contexts of use for concepts and also the content of the empirical indicators. In spite of their vagueness, sociologists take a nucleus of concepts for granted; they assume in practice that other sociologists both know what they mean by a given concept and attach identical meanings. For practical purposes there is assumed identity of understanding in the use of such concepts as "society", "system", "structure", "class", "status", "role" and others. It need hardly be added that it is this assumption of common meaning which allows discourse and communication within the discipline to proceed relatively freely. Yet when examined critically this assumption seems somewhat ill-founded; several features of the use of concepts in sociology suggest that the discipline has yet to come to terms satisfactorily with the conceptualization process.

Concepts are used by all theoretical styles or levels for they are the indispensable tools of theorizing. But it is clear that the range of use of even the same concepts in sociology is enormous; not only are the same concepts given different meanings in different theoretical perspectives (for example, "role" as used by symbolic interactionists and structural-functionalists), but they also select out different empirical indicators and therefore have different methodological implications. The confusion within sociology about the use of even the common concepts is enormous.

Concepts and social reality

Apart from these internal confusions and disagreements about the meanings and uses of particular concepts, a more significant problem from the phenomenological perspective is their relationship to the social realities they are trying to capture. If one asks the question: To whose realities and in what ways does a given concept refer? it is frequently very difficult to provide a satisfactory answer. The "underlying patterns" or "regularities" ostensibly subsumed under particular concepts are often not experienced by members in ways described by sociologists, although sociologists typically argue that these patterns determine members' experiences. In fact the "patterns" may have no meaning whatever for members in the form in which the sociologist describes them. The sense in which such "patterns" can be seen as determining experiences thus becomes problematic. An illustration is provided by the concept "social class"; the so-called "objective" indices of class, such as occupation, income or terminal age of education, often clash with individuals' conceptions of their class position. Sociologists typically give greatest emphasis in their analysis to the "objective" variables (for example, the arbitrary Census occupational groups or the Registrar-General's social class groupings) and play down the use of social meanings in the definition of class and class position. The social meanings of social class are ignored in favour of those unambiguous categories which are thought by sociologists to be indicators of the "real, under-lying patterns" or "causes of action"; the nature of the relationship between these gross commonsense categories used in analysis and the meanings, if any, which people give to these categories, is rarely viewed as a problem. In this particular example, practical convenience seems to be the most important criterion, for the typical "objective" indicators of social class present fewer measurement problems than the elusive, subtle and shifting meanings attached to class. Indeed it may be that for some members the concept of "class" has no meaning at all, in which case its empirical relevance to their construction of reality is non-existent. Thus in developing practically convenient indicators and categories for the analysis of social class, the problem of the meaning of the sociologist's explanation, which utilizes the concept of "social class" in conjunction with other concepts, to the members of the society is immediately raised.

A fundamental premise of phenomenological sociology, based on Schutz's discussion (1967, pp. 34ff.) of concept and theory formation, is that there should be direct and demonstrable continuity between sociological concepts and the linguistic typifications men use to index their social experiences. This would ground any sociological description at the level of meaning and would ensure that such descriptions were always translatable back into the terms meaningful for the very subjects whose experiences were being described. To the extent that this continuity between commonsense meanings and knowledge of everyday life and sociological concepts is not maintained, the relationship between explanation and experience will remain problematic. Most concepts in sociology do not appear to meet this requirement of continuity, for they are typically extreme short-hand terms for subsuming large masses of disparate phenomena. Although some of the terms may be used fairly frequently by members in their everyday talk (for example, status, value, role) sociologists typically make no attempt to show the relationship between their various uses of such terms and the multiplicity of meanings attached to these terms by members. Their relationship to the lived-world thus remains unexplicated. Cicourel's excellent outline of the ethnomethological paradigm (1970a) contains a valuable critique of two common concepts in sociology, status and role, which illustrates the problems emerging from their conventional usage.

Operationalization

A related aspect of the use of concepts has already been cited as a general problem from the conventional perspectives on both theory and method; this is generally known as "operationalization", or the procedures by which a concept is trans-lated into a research tool, such as a question or a scaling device. Operationalization is a problem in conventional sociology because of the natural-science ideal of hypothesis verification. In the natural sciences operationalization is not too difficult because of the inherently meaningless and manipulable character of the data; agreement on the meaning of concepts is easier to reach in these conditions. But in sociology, where the very data themselves consist of other meanings, none of which can be assumed to be constant or unequivocal, the problems of operationalization are acute.

The purpose of a research tool is to illustrate or define the concept empirically. As operationalization is the means by which a concept is actually linked to phenomena in the social world, the process would seem to be highly relevant to the theoretical perspective adopted and the kinds of concepts used. A description of operationalization would show how the theory or hypothesis was to relate to the empirical social world. But this process, whatever the theoretical level adopted, has been almost entirely ignored by those who call themselves theorists.[23] The problem is that the procedures used and decisions taken in operationalizing concepts and obtaining indicators of them have been regarded as commonsense; sociologists have not thought it necessary to reveal their horizons of meaning, what they were taking-for-granted, in operationalizing any given concept. The assumption seems to have been made that the operationalization process, because it was commonsense, could be regarded as in some way independent of the particular observer involved and therefore neutral.

In this way operationalization is regarded as a mechanical means for making abstract concepts refer to phenomena in the social world. But the fact that the process rests on the observer's unrevealed commonsense reasoning and relies on any reader's commonsense reasoning for making some sort of sense of it means that we cannot regard the process as neutral or mechanical. Operationalization is literally the meaning of the empirical concept because it involves the observer's reasoning as an unexplicated resource at every stage. The indicators and empirical referents of a concept, which are then used in the research process of hypothesis verification, are the products of the observer's commonsense reasoning, so that the manifest "public" hypothesis he claims to be empirically investigating cannot be seen as independent of the "private" practical theories he has used in operationalizing his concepts. A methodological prerequisite of phenomenological sociology, therefore, is that the researcher develop ways of making his practical reasoning accountable and observable to the reader of his research reports; only in this way can the researcher show the links between his concepts and the social phenomena he claims to be investigating. Operationalization thus cannot be viewed as something independent of "theorizing" or "conceptualizing"; it is itself a conventionally unrecognized part of the conceptualization process.

Specifying concepts' meanings

Even when judged according to the conventional scientific criteria of conceptual

---

[23] See, for example, Rex (1961) and P. Cohen (1968).

adequacy, sociology falls short, as a discussion by Kaplan (1946) illustrates.[24] Kaplan notes that there are two aspects to the specification of meaning of concepts in science. First, there is the problem of definition; the definition of a concept is typically an abstract statement concerning the logical equivalence between the concept and an expression whose meaning has already been specified. However, a definition is inadequate by itself for it presents a static account of a concept and does not meet the challenge of the process of inquiry in which concepts undergo modification as inquiry proceeds; similarly any given concept has various meanings in different contexts so that it is inappropriate to talk about "the" meaning as is done in a definition. Thus definitions remain abstract and general and do not help to specify the empirical referents which represent the concept in particular inquiries. Second, there is the specification of meaning of a concept through indicators and it is here that Kaplan's argument is relevant to my previous discussion of operationalization. The range and clarity of indicators of the concepts within any discipline suggests that concepts are going to form a continuum of vagueness.

As an example Kaplan takes the concept "species" from biology and shows that although there is no agreement among biologists as to the definition of the concept this does not prevent its use in inquiry, and in different contexts of inquiry a wide variety of indicators for the term are specified. The key criterion for the presence of a concept like "species" in a discipline is its indispensability. In Kaplan's terms a concept's introduction into a discipline is valid "if it does not constitute merely a convenient short-hand for commonsense locutions" (1946, p. 284). It must mark an advance in the discipline's theory in the sense that "the various characteristics serving as indicators and references of the concept have an empirically significant relatedness" (loc. cit.). In biology, the concept "species" meets this criterion in that its indicators have such an empirically significant relatedness. If a concept does not subsume empirically related indicators then the question of its eliminability must be raised for it is simply a convenient short-hand term to replace "cumbersome locutions". For Kaplan, then, a concept may well be vague but its meaning can be found in the empirical overlap of its set of indicators, each of which may relate to a slightly different empirical "region". In this sense every term in a discipline designates a "family of meanings" representing a pattern of empirically overlapping references. Although Kaplan does not specify this, the empirical overlap would presumably be established statistically in the natural sciences; I have already suggested that empirical overlap in sociology, as measured by statistical correlations, remains entirely problematic because of the interpretation to be attached to the correlation.

However, if Kaplan's question concerning the eliminability of concepts is applied to the concepts of sociology, it may prove to have answers which, even according to the conventional criteria of conceptual adequacy, have awkward implications for much conceptualizing in sociology. Although sociological concepts share the characteristic of vagueness with some concepts in other dis-

---

[24] See also Kaplan (1964).

ciplines, the specification of their meaning through a pattern of empirically related indicators seems much harder to establish. Even for many of the discipline's most fundamental concepts, not only is there little agreement over the kinds of indicators to be taken, but the indicators of a concept used by sociologists in different theoretical perspectives may logically conflict with each other. This suggests that their empirical relatedness, measured presumably by statistical correlation coefficients, may be fairly low. The indicators of such concepts as "class", "status", "role" or "structure" do not simply differ in their emphasis within the different theoretical styles, they also clash with and contradict each other. The range of theoretical perspectives within sociology means that the same concepts are given different and often conflicting meanings and indicators between perspectives. Because of the clash in the specification of meaning of basic concepts, it would seem difficult to satisfy Kaplan's criterion of eliminability. It would seem doubtful whether sociologists from different perspectives could agree, in terms of definition and specification of indicators, on the indispensability of more than a handful of concepts, especially as there is no agreement, as we have seen, over the purposes of theory in the first place. In this sense, Kaplan's argument is akin to Cicourel's remarks concerning the shorthand character of sociological description as a means of subsuming vast masses of unintelligible manifest data.[25]

While Kaplan's discussion is useful in providing a conventional critique of problems of conceptualization in sociology, it should be emphasized that he does not show what the realities of doing research are and he offers no practical prescriptions for coming to terms with the issues he raises. Moreover his concern with the problem of meaning is different to that of the phenomenological sociologists, for he is not concerned with the role of commonsense reasoning in generating and applying concepts. Following natural scientific ideals, his interest is in the relation between the concept as a given and the range of empirical indicators to which it refers. The phenomenological sociologist is interested not simply in this equation but more importantly in the commonsense reasoning processes through which the sociologist accomplishes a "fit" between a concept and selected social phenomena. Because it is through this process that concepts acquire their meanings for the researcher, the process itself must be treated as problematic.

An interesting distinction made by Kaplan is relevant for our understanding of the research and conceptualization processes although he himself did not develop the implications in this direction.[26] Cicourel draws attention to this distinction in his ethnomethodological analysis of the sociological usage of the terms "status" and "role" (1970a, p. 22). Kaplan distinguishes between "logic-in-use" (a member's practical reasoning while participating in some form of social interaction or action) and "reconstructed logic" (a member's reconstruction of the same events after he leaves the scene). The observer/researcher

---

[25] Cicourel (1968, p. 332).
[26] Kaplan (1964, p. 8).

too must employ both these forms of reasoning in providing an account of events in the social world. While carrying out the research (for example, interviewing, observing) he employs a "logic-in-use" which is subject to a wide variety of situational contingencies; subsequently in analysing his data and constructing an explanation he employs a 'reconstructed logic' for making sense of the events in which he was involved. Conventional sociological accounts do not tell us "how the social analyst as observer and/or participant translates the "logic-in-use" of his fieldwork into the 'reconstructed logic' of his theorizing" (Cicourel, 1970a, p. 22). In deciding what is relevant for his theory, the sociologist draws upon both his "logic-in-use" and his "reconstructed logic", both of which in turn reflect his past experiences as a commonsense member and as a scientific observer (ibid., p. 36). The problem for the reader is how to separate the "commonsense component" from the scientific component when both forms of logic rest typically on unexplicated horizons of commonsense meaning. No observer can avoid this problem because he can only communicate his findings to others through the medium of language which provides for an open horizon of interpretation; the observer has to rely on the basic rules of linguistic communication in his culture and this reliance requires the assumption that others "know what he means". He can however support his assumption by making his resources explicit rather than taking-them-for-granted:

> The observer cannot avoid the use of basic or interpretive rules in research for he relies upon his member-acquired use of normal forms to recognize the relevance of behavioral displays for his theory. He can only objectify his observations by making explicit the properties of basic rules and his reliance on them for carrying out his research activities (ibid., p. 36).

Concepts and sociological rhetoric

Some rather different characteristics of conceptualization in sociology are discussed by Bruyn in his essay on participant observation (1966). By focusing on the rhetorical devices of sociology he helps to clarify the limiting features of many sociological concepts and provides a framework for their analysis. Sociological language relies to a considerable extent on a variety of rhetorical devices, such as metaphor, simile, paradox or irony. Each of these, and others, enables the sociologist to draw attention to and emphasize certain aspects of social phenomena; but Bruyn argues that the very character of these literary techniques places rather narrow limits on their use. Some of these techniques can be illustrated by looking at the sources of many sociological concepts. Sociologists have frequently stolen their concepts from other disciplines; the result is that the concepts bring with them not only the particular meanings which led to their selection by sociologists, but also certain references, implications and horizons of meaning which derive from their original use and which are impossible or very difficult to eliminate. These references are intrinsic to a concept and are part of its meaning. The sociologist in transferring these concepts from other disciplines makes use of some of the devices listed by Bruyn, such as the metaphor or simile. Concepts like "structure", "system", "pressure", "forces", "mass" or "role" (each invariably prefixed with the word "social") are used metaphorically in sociology; the references of such concepts, intended by sociologists to carry highly particular meanings in given contexts, also carry generalized meanings which have implications for the way social relationships as a whole are viewed. Thus concepts drawn from biology carry concomitant horizons of meaning which liken society to a biological organism; an interesting example here would be the term "social pathology" which was used for many years as a basic orienting concept in the area of social problems; its horizons of meaning, drawn from its origins in medicine, have very particular implications for the kinds of action programmes to be developed in relation to social problems.[27]

Other main orienting concepts in sociology which rely on organic, mechanical or dramatic analogies (for example, function, forces and role, respectively) carry with them horizons of meaning likening society to an organism, a machine or a play. Metaphors and analogies, if carefully chosen, do have a limited value in drawing attention to highly selected aspects of the social phenomena under investigation, but to use them as total explanatory devices or as the basis for overall perspectives on the phenomena is to remedy rather than to clarify the nature of the social world. Thus the rhetorical use of concepts derived from other disciplines in sociological explanation requires a concomitant awareness of both their partial and selective character and their generalized symbolic implications.[28]

A rather different conceptual limitation of sociology is also discussed by Bruyn; it is quite clear that sociological concepts have failed completely to come to terms with the variety of man's experience of being-in-the-world. Not only are the concepts partial and selective, they also deal typically with those features of social life which seem to approximate "scientific" definitions of rationality and logic.[29] The "emotional" experiences of men and the passions of love, hate, fear, and commitment, from which significant social events may arise, are largely untouched by sociologists' barren conceptualizations; the typical methodological device is to reduce the richness of social life to a series of five-point scales. As Bruyn points out, the sociological vocabulary is built largely on sense and logic and we now need to think about the theoretical and methodological problems of dealing with the basic forms in culture which are lacking apparently in what sociologists conceive as sense and logic.[30] Bruyn recommends a concentration on "concrete" concepts in sociology which maximize "the expressive meaning of particular sentiments through the explication of procedures for knowing them intuitively" (1966, p. 40). Such concrete concepts are outside the vocabulary of traditional social science but are essential for accurate knowledge of man in

---

[27] See Mills (1943, p. 165).

[28] An extended discussion of the problem of themes and horizon in relation to meaning can be found in Schutz (1970).

[29] The relationship between sociological theory and the rationalities of everyday life is discussed in Schutz (1964, pp. 64ff.) and in Garfinkel (1967, Chapter 8).

[30] See Schutz and Garfinkel, ibid.

society; their absence from sociology may help to explain why some novels sometimes seem much better able to provide a more vivid understanding of some situations than sociological analysis. One possible area where this occurs is that of race relations where white sociologists may find it understandably difficult to take the role of the black man. The novels and essays by men such as Richard Wright, Ralph Ellison, James Baldwin, Eldridge Cleaver, Stokely Carmichael, or George Jackson project the meaning of being black in American society with incomparably greater immediacy and starkness than the scores of field studies undertaken by white researchers.

The methodological device recommended by Bruyn for providing sociological description which comes to terms more adequately with the richness of the social world is participant observation. However, Bruyn couches his discussion of methodological procedures (1966, ch. 7) in the language of the "rhetoric of verification" and ends up viewing participant observation as the "subjective" complement of the so-called "objective" traditional empirical procedures; Bruyn's discussion thus serves ultimately to reinforce the dichotomy between "subjectivism" and "objectivism" in sociology while failing to raise the issue of the reliance of the participant observer and his subjects of study on a tacit commonsense reasoning. Bruyn's statement contains little to help the participant observer who wishes to make his background expectancies explicit.[31]

CONCLUDING REMARKS

My concern in this chapter has been to examine the dichotomy between theory and research in conventional sociology and to suggest that the reorientation to sociological analysis found in phenomenological sociology transcends this dichotomy. I have argued that the split has its origins in and is reinforced by misguided attempts to apply natural-scientific modes of investigation to the social world, the result of which has been the failure of sociology to come to terms with the problem of meaning. The neglect of the analytical issues arising from the problem of meaning has produced a tradition of sociological investigation which, from the phenomenological perspective, uses inappropriate methods for addressing the wrong problems. By treating meaning and social reality as problematic, phenomenological sociology offers new directions for sociological analysis; the promise of this reorientation is that it will help to clarify those issues which have been characterized by confusion and disagreement in conventional sociology.

In taking the commonsense world of everyday life as its subject matter, phenomenological sociology attempts to clarify the phenomenal social world as an ongoing meaningful accomplishment of members. In so doing, the perspective also contributes to our understanding of the limits of sociological explanation, the nature of theory generation and its relationship to methods of investigation,

---

[31] See A. V. Cicourel (1964, Chapter 2) for further critical comments on conventional approaches to participant observation.

and the validity of sociological explanation in terms of its relationship to the social world it attempts to comprehend. By emphasizing the empirical character of sociology, phenomenological sociology rests on the fundamental assumption that qualitative changes in our comprehension of the social world can come only through empirical investigation of that world. All theory emerges from a methodology, a way of generating the theory, but the distinction between valid sociological theory and speculative meta-theory is that, in the former case the links between the theory and particular experienced social realities have been established and are demonstrable, while in the latter case they have not.

SUGGESTIONS FOR FURTHER READING

Cicourel's (1964) book on methodology is the most valuable phenomenological critique of the relation between theory and methodology. Douglas's (1967) study of suicide and Cicourel's (1968) work on juvenile justice provide two examples of this general critique and both show the problematic character of the sociological use of official and research statistics. Winter's (1968) book, while presuming some knowledge of phenomenology, is one of the few attempts to make explicit the links between phenomenological philosophy and sociological theory; it is available in paperback. Bruyn (1966) makes a strong and very readable case for the development of participant-observation in sociology. The papers on "rationality" by Schutz (1964, pp. 64ff.) and Garfinkel (1967, Chapter 8) reveal the intractable problems faced by observers of the social world who analyse social action according to their own ideals of "rationality".

The criticisms levelled in the previous chapters at the range of sociological perspectives and their adopted research methods have their origins in phenomenological philosophy. As this philosophy differs radically from the philosophies which are conventionally used to justify social scientific activity, such as logical empiricism or Popperianism, an outline of some of its main themes and their implications for sociological analysis is called for. Both the substantive problems and questions of sociology and the means through which these are investigated are redefined if the injunctions of the phenomenological critique are followed. The aim of the redefinition is to generate a sociology which is truly reflexive in its stance towards both itself and the social world. This chapter suggests some of the ways in which such a reflexive sociology can develop by following the methodological imperatives of phenomenology.

Part 2 Phenomenological Alternatives

SIX

Phenomenological Philosophy and Sociology

MICHAEL PHILLIPSON

The thesis of this book is that phenomenological philosophy provides the grounds and the impetus for a reorientation of sociological analysis. To support this thesis some account of this philosophy and the possible ways in which it impinges on the sociological enterprise is in order. This chapter outlines briefly some of the main themes of phenomenological philosophy and suggests ways in which its investigations provide a system of relevances which redirects sociological analysis.

Some qualifications and clarifications of the aims and limitations of this chapter are necessary prolegomena to the subsequent discussion. First, any attempt to summarize the ideas of any philosophical movement would remain an inadequate gloss of its achievements and failings. In the present case only a rough outline of some of the main themes of phenomenology can be sketched and these inevitably fail to do any kind of justice to the complexities and diversities of the phenomenological movement.[1] There is no "one" phenomenology just as there is no "one" sociology; the movement comprises several strands which all complement each other and also disagree over certain issues.[2] In order to suggest the diversity of the movement I have attempted to draw the recurring themes and concerns of phenomenology mainly from two writers who represent contrasting wings of the movement, Husserl, the founder of modern phenomenology, and Merleau-Ponty, the more recent existential phenomenologist. Extensive quotations from these two authors are included both to provide a grounding in the terminology of phenomenology (for many of their concepts are relevant to

---

[1] H. Spiegelberg (1969) gives a comprehensive account of the phenomenological movement and Farber (1943) gives an outline of Husserl's philosophy.

[2] For an expansion of this point, see Phillipson and Roche (1971).

the development of a phenomenological sociology) and to minimize distortion of their ideas.

A second point is worth raising at this stage. It must be emphasized that sociology is *not* phenomenology. From the standpoint of contemporary sociology, phenomenological philosophy is to be viewed as a clarifier of the sociological task and a resource of ideas for sociological analysis. As I shall suggest, the tasks of the two disciplines, although in some senses mutually dependent, are quite distinct. If sociological problems are the prime interest, the over-involvement in phenomenological philosophy should be avoided; it is very easy to be side-tracked by the voluminous literature of phenomenology with very little extra pay-off for the sociological project-at-hand.

Third, the development of a phenomenologically based sociology is in its earliest stages; the methodologies and concerns of those sociologists already following phenomenological injunctions must be regarded as the first attempts to develop a radically new sociology which suspends its belief in and withdraws its grant of legitimacy to existing problems and methods. In this sense acceptance of the phenomenological critique of conventional sociology opens up an enormous field for sociological development and inquiry, for all conventional problems and methods require reformulation. Thus the work of sociologists like Garfinkel and Cicourel are not to be viewed as boundary markers for phenomenological sociology; nor do they offer prescriptions for the content and methods of study. They are the first attempts to deal empirically with the problems set by the phenomenological critique and as such they provide guides for ways into phenomena previously unexplored by sociologists. In developing new methods of investigation and in rephrasing sociological questions Wright Mills's exhortation to sociologists again becomes relevant; in recommending avoidance of the "fetishism of method and technique" he suggests the following precept:

> Let every man be his own methodologist, let every man be his own theorist; let theory and method again become part of the practice of a craft (1959, p. 224).

Abandoning the dogma of conventional theory and method in favour of the open horizons of phenomenological sociology facilitates the implementation of Wright Mills's exhortation.

THE ORIGIN AND AIMS OF PHENOMENOLOGY

The foundations of modern phenomenology were laid by Edmund Husserl during the first thirty years of this century; his extensive writings present the main concerns and problems of phenomenology and provide a background against which to set off the writings of other contributors to the movement.[3] The main contrast of ideas within the movement can perhaps be drawn between Husserl's attempt to develop a "transcendental phenomenology" and the work of the

---

[3] Husserl's own ideas changed considerably during the course of his investigations; see Farber (1943) and Pivcevic (1970).

existential phenomenologists, such as Sartre and Merleau-Ponty.[4] Husserl's transcendental phenomenology may be regarded as a form of "idealism" while the ideas of the existential phenomenologists may be regarded as "realist". Although they differ in their understandings of what it is that experiences, what is experienced, and whether experiencing activity can be analysed in isolation from the world of experienced and existent objects, they do start from and share a common interest in the problem of consciousness. Einstein's paradox that the least comprehensible thing in the world is that the world is comprehensible[5] points to a central concern of all strands of phenomenology, namely that of the nature of our consciousness of ourselves and the world. In Merleau-Ponty's elegant terms, "as a disclosure of the world . . . phenomenology's task was to reveal the mystery of the world and of reason" (1962, pp. xx-xxi).

The term "phenomenon" refers to that which is given or indubitable in the perception or consciousness of the conscious individual; phenomenology thus comprises the attempts to describe the phenomena of consciousness and to show how they are constituted, although the descriptions and constitutive analyses of the various strands of the movement differ in the way they regard consciousness.

The earlier writings of Husserl were very much a reaction to psychologism and can be seen in part as attempts to provide a sound philosophical base for psychology, the sciences of man, and the natural sciences. Those sciences of man, whether "psychologism", "sociologism" or "historicism", which explain men's experiences as *determined* by external or internal causes, fail, as a consequence, to deal with the following problem as Merleau-Ponty points out:

> If, indeed, the guiding thoughts and principles of the mind at each moment are only the result of external causes which act upon it, then the reasons for my affirmation are not the true reasons for this affirmation. They are not so much reasons as causes working from the outside. Hence the postulates of the psychologist, the sociologist, and the historian are stricken with doubt by the results of their own researches (1964, p. 44).

For Husserl, naturalistic psychology, which models itself on the natural sciences, as does sociology, fails to recognize its own limitations because it misses the very "sense" of the phenomena it investigates:

> . . . it is a victim of a presumably facile confusion between pure and empirical consciousness. To put the same in another way: it "naturalizes" pure consciousness (1965, p. 92).

Husserl argues that the unclarified and confused concepts and methods of psychology, because they exclude the phenomenal "givens" of experience, impose a content and a form on experience; psychology,

> . . . has not considered what lies in the "sense" of psychological experience and what "demands" being (in the sense of the psychical) of itself make on method (ibid., p. 102).

The true method for Husserl, "follows the nature of the things to be investigated

---

[4] See, for example, Sartre (1969) and Merleau-Ponty (1962).
[5] See Merleau-Ponty (1964a, p. 193).

and not our prejudices and preconceptions" (loc. cit.). In relation to human consciousness the point is that those things we call "psychical phenomena" are "precisely phenomena and not nature" (ibid., p. 106). Attempts to model psychology on natural science lead to the absurdity of the reification of consciousness, and the need is for alternative methods which come to terms with the phenomena of consciousness themselves:

> It goes without saying that research will be meaningful here precisely when it directs itself purely to the sense of the experiences of the "psychical", and when thereby it accepts and tries to determine the "psychical" exactly as it demands, as it were, to be accepted and determined, when it is seen—above all where one admits no absurd naturalizings (ibid., p. 108).

Naturalizing consciousness misses the very sense of the phenomenal things of consciousness themselves; the concepts, theories, and methods of psychology impose forms on the "phenomenal givens" whilst failing to demonstrate the relevance of their own processes of imposition to the things themselves, the self-evident data of consciousness:

> Self-evident data are patient, they let theories chatter about them, but remain what they are. It is the business of theories to conform to data, and the business of theories of knowledge to discriminate the fundamental types, and to describe them in accordance with their distinctive nature (Husserl, 1967, p. 89).

Husserl's critique of psychology applies with equal force to those sociological approaches, whether "meta-theoretical" perspectives or plain "methods", which take the natural sciences as their model; they too have missed the "sense" of the phenomena of consciousness and utilize methods inappropriate to those phenomena. The Husserlian critique of the human sciences thus requires a radical redefinition of sociological problems, methods and explanation; the main orienting dictum of such a redefinition would be the methodological imperative of phenomenology to "get back to the things of consciousness themselves".

In Husserl's later work the focus widened in an attempt to develop phenomenology as the "first philosophy" which would delineate the domain of "pure experience" in which all other sciences were ultimately rooted.[6] Phenomenology would be "first" because it was to inquire into those forms of conscious experience which other philosophies and sciences took-for-granted and on which they built. It attempts to reach and describe the ultimate grounds of experience through its use of a particular method—the phenomenological reduction. The aim of this method is to describe pure experience; emphasizing the descriptive method of phenomenology helps to distinguish its project from the analytic methods and forms of explanation which characterize other philosophies and sciences. Phenomenology, then, as an attempted presuppositionless (and therefore "first") philosophy, would describe the objects, the phenomenal givens, of

---

[6] See Farber (1966, p. 13).

consciousness.[7] Merleau-Ponty outlines the project of phenomenology in the following way:

> It is a matter of describing, not of explaining or analysing. Husserl's first directive to phenomenology, in its early stages, to be a "descriptive psychology", is from the start a rejection of science. I am not the outcome or the meeting point of numerous causal agencies which determine my bodily or psychological make-up. I cannot conceive myself as nothing but a bit of the world, a mere object of biological, psychological, or sociological investigation. I cannot shut myself up in the realm of science. All my knowledge of the world, even my scientific knowledge, is gained from my own particular point of view, or from some experience of the world without which the symbols of science would be meaningless. The whole universe of science is built upon the world as directly experienced and if we want to subject science itself to rigorous scrutiny and arrive at a precise assessment of its meaning and scope, we must begin by re-awakening the basic experience of the world of which science is the second-order expression (1967, p. 356).

The project of phenomenology, therefore, is the description of the phenomenal precisely as it appears to us in our consciousness:

> It is a question of finding a method which will enable us to think at the same time of the externality which is the principle of the sciences of man and of the internality which is the condition of philosophy, of the contingencies without which there is no situation as well as of the rational certainty without which there is no knowledge (1964b, pp. 51–2).

If consciousness is both the means to and the object of phenomenological investigation, how is it viewed in phenomenology?

Consciousness

Husserl followed Descartes by taking as his starting point the stream of experience of the thinking ego. For Husserl, consciousness is always consciousness of *something*; there are thus two complementary aspects to consciousness: first, the process of being conscious (the *cogito*) which may take different forms (remembering, perceiving, evaluating) and second, that which is the object of consciousness (*the cogitatum*). However, the phenomenologist's investigation of consciousness is done by means of a special method, the phenomenological reduction, which attempts to lay bare a realm of being ("pure" consciousness) that remains untouched by the reflections we carry out in our natural attitudes.[8] A principle insight of phenomenology is thus to view consciousness as a region of being "which is in principle unique" (Husserl, 1967, p. 113). Husserl argued that this region could be revealed by the phenomenological method and at the same time that it would not be distorted or changed by the method:

---

[7] Whether Husserl achieved his presuppositionless philosophy is called into question by Farber (1943, p. 521).

[8] The natural attitude is discussed shortly. A major problem of Husserl's work centres on his attempt to develop a "transcendental phenomenology" in which the focus is on a "pure ego" (nonexistentially situated); this is a major point of differentiation between Husserl and the existential phenomenologists.

Consciousness in itself has a being of its own which in its absolute uniqueness of nature remains unaffected by the phenomenological disconnection (loc. cit.).

Unaffected by the method of phenomenology which makes it available for study, consciousness thus comprises the region of study for phenomenology; Husserl outlines the subject matter of the discipline in the following terms:

> We shall consider conscious experiences *in the concrete fullness and entirety* with which they figure in their concrete context—the *stream of experience*—and to which they are attached through their own proper essences.
>
> It then becomes evident that every experience in the stream which our reflection can lay hold on has *its own essence open to intuition*, a "content" which can be considered in its singularity in and for itself (1967, p. 116).

Consciousness is seen as both the source and the correlate of all being and its essential features can never be grasped by the factual or naturalistic analyses of psychology or sociology which reify it. The original grounds of being, "pure" consciousness, are open only to the intentional and intuitive description of the phenomenological method.

Intentionality

The notion of "intentionality" is also central to phenomenology. Intentionality is extended in phenomenology to refer not only to action (that is, that men *act* in terms of the goals, projects, motives and so on, that they entertain) but also that *consciousness* is intentional; mind or consciousness is viewed as some kind of relationship between a subject and object and the notion of intentionality is an attempt to describe this relation. This view of mind as intentional, which views the realm of consciousness as "perfect freedom",[9] is diametrically opposed to the determinism of the naturalizing human sciences which would reduce mind to a determinate object.[10] Intentionality thus describes an essential feature of the consciousness that is to be investigated, namely that consciousness is always consciousness of *something*; the objects of consciousness are always "meant" objects. Intentionality describes the meaning-giving feature of consciousness:

> ... *every* intentional experience—and this is indeed the fundamental mark of all intentionality—has its "intentional object", i.e.: its objective meaning. Or to repeat the same in other words: to have a meaning, or to have something "in mind", is the cardinal feature of all consciousness (Husserl, 1967, pp. 261–2).

The terms, "noesis" and "noema", are used by Husserl to refer to the complementary aspects of intentionality; a particular mode of intentional consciousness ("I think", "I perceive") is the "noesis", while the objective correlate, "that which I think or perceive", is the "noema". The objects of consciousness, its content,

---

[9] Husserl (1967, p. 107).

[10] A sociology which recognized mind as "perfect freedom" might as well take as its motto George Gurwitsch's definition of sociology: "Sociology is the science of human freedom and of all the obstacles which this freedom encounters and overcomes in part." Quoted by Strasser (1967, p. 528).

thus have great importance for phenomenology, for the modes of thinking, perceiving, remembering and so on, can be described only by investigating that which is experienced in any given mode. Intentionality thus constitutes consciousness, investing its content with meaning; the ego is oriented to the world through the intentionality of consciousness. Merleau-Ponty describes how the world is an intentional object of consciousness:

> If we actually reflect on our situation, we will find that the subject, thus situated in the world and submitting to its influences, is at the same time he who thinks the world. No world whatsoever is conceivable that is not thought by someone. Hence while it is true that the empirical subject is a part of the world, it is also true that the world is no more than an intentional object for the transcendental subject (1964b, p. 57).

The two complementary aspects of intentionality, the noesis and the noema, can also be related to the methodological tasks of phenomenology, describing the objects of consciousness (the noema), and showing how they are built up or constituted (the noesis).

The life-world and intersubjectivity

The world towards which the intentional consciousness is directed is what Husserl calls the "life-world"; this life-world is that to which we all belong in the pre-scientific natural attitude and is the basis of all meaning for all the sciences and for phenomenology. Thus the life-world is our "intuitive environment" in which, in Schutz's terms,

> . . . we, as human beings among fellow-beings, experience culture and society, take a stand with regard to their objects, are influenced by them and act upon them (1966, p. 116).

Moreover this life-world is seen by Husserl as an "intersubjective" world and it is the notion of intersubjectivity which crystallizes the relevance of phenomenology for sociology.[11] Although Husserl himself was somewhat ambiguous about the status of the notions of the life-world and intersubjectivity in his own thought and only granted them central importance in his later writings[12], their centrality to the work of Alfred Schutz is unequivocal. And it is Schutz who has drawn out the relevance of phenomenology for sociology. The notion of intersubjectivity broadens the base of the phenomenological critique and provides the grounds for its application to all human sciences.

The term intersubjective is used to describe some aspects of our mutual interrelatedness as beings in the life-world; intersubjectivity points to the inherent sociality of consciousness and to the experience of the world by self and others as a world in common. Schutz's discussion of intersubjectivity clarifies its relevance for sociology; in analysing its dimensions he points to some funda-

---

[11] Husserl's most detailed discussion of intersubjectivity is in his Cartesian Meditations (1970, pp. 89–150).

[12] See for example, Husserl (1965, pp. 149–92).

mental features of sociality. The thesis of the "reciprocity of perspectives" describes the basic form of intersubjectivity, and involves two idealizations.[13]
These idealizations are taken-for-granted "rules" of social life. First, there is the
"interchangeability of standpoints" through which each of us takes-for-granted
that: "I and my fellow-man would have typically the same experiences of the
common world if we changed places, thus transforming my Here into his, and his
—now to me a There—into mine" (Schutz, 1962, p. 316). We assume our ways
of experiencing the world would be identical in such a transposition of places.
The second idealization is that of "the congruency of the system of relevances";
through this I and my fellow-man assume that, in spite of our unique biographical situations, the differences in our systems of relevances "can be dis-
regarded for the purpose at hand" and that: "I and he, that 'we', interpret the
actually or potentially common objects, facts, and events in an 'empirically
identical' manner, i.e. sufficient for all practical purposes" (loc. cit.). The
"general thesis of the alter ego" is a further dimension of intersubjectivity described by Schutz and he suggests that, in itself, it is a "sufficient frame of
reference for the foundation of the . . . social sciences"; the thesis describes
some aspects of the ways in which we experience the "other" in the "vivid
present". The simultaneity of our experience of each other in the vivid present
means that in certain ways I know more of the other than he knows of himself
in that present:

> In so far as each of us can experience the other's thoughts and acts in the vivid present
> whereas either can grasp his own only as a past by way of reflection, I know more of the
> other and he knows more of me than either of us knows of his own stream of con-
> sciousness (ibid., pp. 174-5).

The emphasis here on the temporal mode of our experiencing illustrates an
important concern of phenomenology with time and its relationship to consciousness.[14] Other aspects of the intersubjective character of commonsense
knowledge discussed by Schutz are its social origins and distribution and its
location in the typical constructs of language; the concern with language has
been followed up by the ethnomethodologists.

In further comments on Husserl's writings Schutz makes the following
points concerning the inherent sociality of consciousness:

> We could not be persons for others, not even for ourselves, if we could not find with
> others a common environment as the counterpart of the intentional interconnectedness
> of our conscious lives. This common environment is established by comprehension,
> which in turn is founded upon the fact that the subjects reciprocally motivate one
> another in their spiritual activities. . . . Sociality is constituted by communicative acts
> in which the I turns to the Others, apprehending them as persons who turn to him, and
> both know this fact (1966, pp. 28-9).

It is worth noting that the analysis of intersubjectivity by phenomenologists

---

[13] Schutz (1962, pp. 315-16).
[14] See, for example, Husserl (1966).

confirms, extends, and sophisticates Mead's thesis (1934, 1959, 1964) concerning the social nature of the self. The coincidence of symbolic interactionism and phenomenology on this point suggests a basis for a synthesis between the two traditions; in view of their similar interests in the problem of meaning and the incomparably greater sophistication of phenomenology it seems likely that symbolic interactionism will increasingly be subsumed under phenomenological sociology.

The natural attitude

Reference has already been made at several points to the "natural attitude"; as with the thesis of intersubjectivity, the natural attitude provides the common ground or is at the intersection of phenomenological philosophy and sociology. For Husserl the "general thesis of the natural standpoint" referred to the ". . . *entire natural world therefore* which is continually 'there for us', 'present to our hand', and will ever remain there, is a 'fact-world' of which we continue to be conscious" (1967, p. 110). The natural attitude is the "naïve" attitude of the situated ego and is characterized by the mundane practical reasoning of everyday life in which his worlds, social and natural, are indubitable, simply "there", and taken-for-granted. Whilst Husserl's descriptions and clarifications of the "natural standpoint" were necessary preliminary exercises for his investigations of the transcendental realm of "pure" consciousness, in so doing he paved the way for the meeting of phenomenology and the human sciences. Phenomenological philosophy's project involved a suspension of belief in, or "bracketing" of, this natural standpoint; its concerns were with a non-situated "pure" ego. The method for attempting to reveal this realm of "pure" being is discussed shortly.

However, the existential realists, such as Sartre and Merleau-Ponty, returned in their work to the investigation of the naïvely situated mundane ego; similarly Schutz, in drawing out the threads of the relationship between sociology and phenomenology, showed how a focus on the natural attitude pointed directly to the concerns of sociology. Sociology was concerned not with the transcendental realm but with the mundane level—the intersubjective world of everyday life. While phenomenology for its own purposes bracketed the "general thesis of the natural standpoint", the task of sociology was to describe and show how this mundane social world was constituted.

The phenomenological reduction

The method through which phenomenology investigates conscious experiences is one of its key defining features and an understanding of this method facilitates the clarification of the relationship between the social sciences and phenomenology. A variety of terms have been used to describe this method, including: the reduction, the épand, putting the world out of play, suspension of belief in the world, and bracketing the world; the present discussion uses the term reduction.

The method is based on Husserl's distinction between the natural attitude, which characterizes both the commonsense attitude of everyday life and the attitude of the naïve natural and cultural sciences (for all of which the worlds they investigate are "there" indubitably), and the attitude of "radical doubt" leading to a suspension of belief in the world achieved through the phenomenological reduction.[15] By eliminating my taken-for-granted natural-attitude beliefs about what I assume, for my practical purposes, to be the characteristics of other subjects and objects in the world, I am left with the intentional objects of my own pure consciousness. Everything that I find there is thus "true" or "objective" by definition for it is indubitable for me as an object of my consciousness. The residuum of the reduction, that which is left to me after I have performed it, comprises the datum of my intuitive experience and it is this which phenomenology attempts to describe. Now it may appear that undertaking the reduction in relation to any particular object of consciousness must necessarily distort the object, but the intention of Husserl was that the method would preserve the essential characteristics of the object. As Farber puts it:

> The abandonment of the natural attitude does not result in the surrender of any meanings. They are transformed through being reduced and constituted. The first step is to transform all experiences into reduced experiences (1943, p. 564).

The aim of this transformation, achieved by the reduction, is the abandonment of all prejudgments so that nothing may be taken as pregiven. Thus transformation occurs because I have suspended all the judgments about the object which I made within the natural attitude; such a suspension leaves me with the thing itself as absolutely given to my consciousness. It can be seen that the phenomenological method is clearly intuitive, for in carrying through a reduction the phenomenologist is laying bare not the experience of others but the grounds of his own pure experience:

> This reduction is the decision not to suppress but to place in suspense, or out of action, all the spontaneous affirmations in which I live, not to deny them but rather to understand them and make them explicit. . . . When I carry out the phenomenological reduction I do not bring back information concerning an external world to a self that is regarded as a part of being, nor do I substitute an internal for an external perception. I attempt rather to reveal and make explicit in me that pure source of all the meanings which constitute the world around me and my empirical self (Merleau-Ponty, 1964b, p. 56).

The import of Merleau-Ponty's remarks here is to indicate that making the intuitively experienced meanings explicit should preserve and not distort their character. It should be noted that the problematic character of the reduction has been commented on by several authors[16] and Merleau-Ponty himself has

---

[15] What the limits of the attempt to bracket the world are remains problematic for pure phenomenology; the structure of language which provides the means by which the intentional objects of consciousness are to be described cannot be "thought away", but it can be inquired into. See the later discussions of the ethnomethodological concern with language in Chapters 7, 8 and 9.

[16] See Farber (1966).

suggested that the absolute reduction must remain an ideal rather than an actual possibility:

> The most important lesson the reduction teaches us is the impossibility of a complete reduction. This is why Husserl is constantly re-examining the possibility of the reduction. If we were absolute mind, the reduction would present no problem. But since, on the contrary, we are in the world, since indeed our reflections are carried out in the temporal flux on which we are trying to seize . . . there is no thought which embraces all thought (1967, p. 365).

Essences

The reduction, then, is the means of describing the noeses and the noemata of consciousness, but the intuitive method is concerned not merely with the data which are immediately given to consciousness but with their *essences;* to describe the essence of any noema or noesis stands as the central aim of the reduction. For this reason the reduction is often referred to as "eidetic" reduction, using the Greek word for essence or nucleus—eidos. The concrete phenomena of pure consciousness are thus examined to identify their essential characteristics; the question is asked of any given object of consciousness: What could be omitted from our description of the object so that what remained was still identifiable as the same object? The essential characteristics of a phenomenon are the least number which enable it to keep its identity as a given object. To establish the essence of a phenomenological object of consciousness the method of "free variation" is used; the object is imaginatively "rotated" or varied intuitively until the essential conditions, the necessary core, are established. In his comparison of Husserl and Merleau-Ponty, Kwant (1967, p. 390) shows how Husserl's thesis of intersubjective truth rests on the idea that the essential core of an object is the same for all men. The aim of the eidetic reduction as propounded by Husserl is thus to reveal the ultimate or absolute grounds of being. In this sense the search for the absolute in Husserl's phenomenology can be seen as an attempt to refute relativism. Merleau-Ponty, by contrast, appears to have adopted a secular version of Tillich's contention that "the only absolute is that there are no human absolutes"; this presents us with the paradox that the only absolute is absolute relativity.[17]

It is worth noting that Merleau-Ponty does not accept Husserl's distinction between pure essences, established through free variation, and facts. For Merleau-Ponty the primary realm of our being in the world is a unity of facts and essences, and while we may make valuable distinctions (such as between fact and essence) they only occur within a fundamental unity of being. In analysing the development of Husserl's phenomenology, Merleau-Ponty notes the transition from his distinction between fact and essence to his recognition of their inseparability; an attempt to describe an essence both arises from a factual experience and is in

---

[17] For an excellent discussion of Merleau-Ponty's view of history as contingency, placed in the context of the rest of his ideas and intellectual development, see Rabil (1967) especially Chapter 10.

itself an experience in the world. A recognition of the historicity of the pheno-menological search for essences suggests that there are no literal absolute essences beyond the facts of experience. The description of an essence is always temporally grounded, and the radical reflection attempted by Husserl, "finally discovered, behind itself, the unreflected as the condition of its possibilities, without which it would have no sense" (Merleau-Ponty, 1964b, p. 92).

There would, therefore, seem to be no ultimate incompatibility between the study of facts by the social sciences and the study of essences by pheno-menology; the two are not merely complementary but inseparable. Indeed the validation of a phenomenological description of an essence would seem to be establishable only by moving back from the attitude of radical reflection to actual experience:

> . . . though a knowledge of facts is never sufficient for grasping an essence and though the construction of "idealizing fictions" is always necessary, I can never be sure that my vision of an essence is anything more than a prejudice rooted in language—if it does not enable me to hold together all the facts which are known and which may be brought into relation with it (Merleau-Ponty, 1964b, p. 75).

Referring the essence back to our experience in the life-world both confirms the historicity of the phenomenological description and attempts to minimize the prejudices which enter into it. The search for essences is limited by the grounded experiences which it is trying to describe and which can never be fully grasped in reflection:

> It belongs to the nature of my reflection to gain possession of myself and in consequence to free myself from determination by external conditions. But in reflecting in this way, and just because I am doing it with the purpose of escaping external temporality, I at once discover a temporality and a historicity that I am. My reflection is taken over from preceding reflections and from a movement of existence which offers itself to me. But, Husserl said, it always involves a certain degree of naïveté. It never lifts itself out of time (ibid., p. 93).

Phenomenology thus has implications for and refers to the study of the factual and experiential realm while the social sciences contain within themselves some insight into essences. The direction of Merleau-Ponty's critique helps to suggest also why most of Husserl's own phenomenological investigations dealt with very particular kinds of phenomena; in his description of essences, the bulk of Husserl's own work was concerned with the essence of "ideal" phenomena and "ideal [intentional] objects" such as constitute mathematics and logic. That which is "ideal" refers to that which is "meant as the same in repeated experiences"[18] and can be objective without being "real", "existential" or "factual"; thus the ideal forms of mathematics and logic are objective in the sense that they mean the same in repeated experiences, without being real in the same sense as natural objects. A good example of an "ideal object" would be that of a melody which is the same although played in different keys, on different instruments, or by

---

[18] Farber (1966, p. 50).

different players.[19] It will be clear that phenomena such as geometry and logic lend themselves more to essential description than, say, social processes.

The distinction in phenomenology between "real" and "ideal" objects of consciousness is central to a consideration of the relationship between phenomenology and sociology. In the natural attitude we come to terms with the natural and social world through first-order typifications and idealizations; however, while most of the phenomena of the natural world are sensorily locatable or take some kind of sensory form, the phenomena of the social world exist only in and through their meanings. In this sense they are ideal objects like the objects of mathematics and logic; if social meanings, social processes, and cultural items are ideal, in that they are "meant as the same in repeated experiences" and thus are objective, are they amenable to the phenomenological reduction and essential description? What is the relationship between phenomenological and sociological investigations?

PHENOMENOLOGY AND SOCIOLOGY: ESSENTIALISM VERSUS EMPIRICISM

On the basis of the preceding brief outline of the interests of phenomenological philosophy, some distinctions can be drawn between it and sociology. In the previous chapter the starting point for examining the relationship between theory and methodology was the assumption that sociology is an empirical discipline. By contrast, phenomenology, in spite of Merleau-Ponty's demonstration that facts and essences refer to the same source, is not empirical; the descriptions of phenomenology, undertaken through the reduction, are not concerned with real objects of existence but essences. In order to find the essential features of an object of my own consciousness I imaginatively play around with it and vary it in order to find what is essential and what is superfluous. Essential descriptions deal not with real but with possibly imaginable things. As Schutz says, the reduction is a methodological device for the very specific task of describing essences:

> The phenomenologist . . . does not have to do with the objects themselves; he is interested in their meaning, as it is constituted by the activities of our mind (1962, p. 115).

Thus evidence, for the phenomenologist, unlike the sociologist, is the self-givenness of an object in the experience of the phenomenologist.[20] For the sociologist, evidence is gathered from sources other than simply his own intuitive experience.

Apart from major differences in what counts as evidence in the two dis-

---

[19] I am grateful to Maurice Roche for this illustration.

[20] See Farber. Of course the phenomenologist does not merely, or only, describe his *own* consciousness, he also describes the life-world; see, for example, Merleau-Ponty's extensive writing on art and politics. For an interesting comparison of Merleau-Ponty's and Sartre's writings on art, see Kaelin (1962).

ciplines, there is another difference in their criteria of objectivity. The concern with essences in phenomenology and the non-empirical character of its method does not mean that its descriptions are not objective. As I have pointed out, it deals with the intentional objects of consciousness, whether real or ideal, and in so far as any object is meant as the same in repeated experiences it is something objective without necessarily being real or "out there"; such is the case with mathematical propositions. In fact the criteria of objectivity of mathematical propositions are agreed within and presuppose the natural attitude. Mathematicians and natural scientists who use mathematical languages work within the natural attitude in their mundane scientific activity. "Objectivity" in phenomenology therefore has very different meanings to its use in sociology; the descriptions of the essential features of the intentional objects of consciousness which are indubitable for the experiencing ego are by that very fact "objective". In sociology, the limited criteria of objectivity rest in the sociologist's ability to demonstrate that his interpretation is consistent with men's experiences; "adequacy" in explanation is achieved, following Schutz, by showing that the sociological model is consistent with the way actors think. Sociological evidence and interpretation must be taken back into the life-world for confirmation. This point is expanded in the subsequent discussion of validity.

If phenomenology is non-empirical in its concern with essences and if it therefore has methods which are peculiar to it as a philosophy, its relationship to and relevance for sociology must be considered carefully. I propose to draw out some of its implications by following selected features of Schutz's programme for social-scientific investigation; my intention is to suggest how empirical sociology differs from phenomenological philosophy whilst treating it as a valuable resource.

The primary goal of the social sciences, according to Schutz (1962, p. 53), is "to obtain organized knowledge of social reality" where social reality is defined as

> the sum total of objects and occurrences within the social cultural world as experienced by the commonsense thinking of men living their daily lives among their fellow-men, connected with them in manifold relations of interaction.

The first methodological task of sociology, therefore, is *to explore the general principles according to which daily life is organized.* After discussing various features of the commonsense world of everyday life, focusing particularly on the dimensions of the natural attitude, Schutz provides us with a more refined and explicit statement of the task of what he calls "general sociology", which is,

> to reactivate the process (of consciousness) which has built up the sediments of meaning . . . [and to] explain the intentionalities of the perspectives of relevance and the horizons of interest. . . . To accomplish this on the level of mundane intersubjectivity is the task of the mundane cultural sciences, and to clarify their specific methods is precisely a part of that constitutive phenomenology of the natural attitude (1962, pp. 136–7).

This presents the kernel of the sociological task and at the same time suggests the forms of its relationship to phenomenological philosophy.

Whether one regards Schutz as primarily a phenomenological philosopher or primarily a sociologist it is clear that his own investigations of the natural attitude have opened up new avenues of investigation for empirical sociology. He himself takes a somewhat ambivalent stance towards Husserl's transcendental philosophy; whilst continually acknowledging his debt to Husserl he quite clearly addresses almost all his own efforts towards the investigation of the natural attitude, the very phenomenon bracketed by Husserl in his transcendental reduction. Moreover he quite explicitly rejects transcendental phenomenology as a foundation for the mundane cultural sciences; in pointing to Husserl's notion of the "life-world" as directing the way for the social sciences he says:

> We may say that the empirical social sciences will find their true foundation not in transcendental phenomenology, but in the constitutive phenomenology of the natural attitude. Husserl's signal contribution to the social sciences consists neither in his unsuccessful attempt to solve the problem of the constitution of the transcendental intersubjectivity within the reduced egological sphere, nor in his unclarified notion of empathy as the foundation of understanding, nor finally, in his interpretation of communities and societies as subjectivities of a higher order the nature of which can be described eidetically; but rather in the wealth of his analyses pertinent to problems of the *Lebenswelt* and designed to be developed into a philosophical anthropology (ibid., p. 149).

The central point to be taken from Schutz's proposals about the task of "general sociology" and his comments on transcendental phenomenology is his distinction between the "mundane cultural sciences" (sociology, anthropology, economics, psychology), the constitutive phenomenology of the natural attitude, and transcendental phenomenology. It is clear that he sees these as three distinct but complementary areas of investigation. However, whilst he pays lip-service to the primacy of Husserl's transcendental phenomenology, his own investigations are clear attempts to reorient phenomenology to an investigation of the life-world and the natural attitude; he sees his constitutive phenomenology of the natural attitude as providing a clarified philosophical grounding for the mundane cultural sciences. In this sense he is calling into question the direct relevance of much of Husserl's writing for the cultural sciences.

The constitutive phenomenology of the natural attitude, which is to be a methodological aid to the cultural sciences by clarifying their methods, concepts, and assumptions, is not to be confused with pure phenomenology because, while sharing some of its aims and techniques, its focus is not on pure consciousness or transcendental subjectivity but on how the natural attitude is constituted and the implications of this for social scientific investigation. Finally there are the mundane cultural sciences whose concern is the clarification of mundane intersubjectivity—the life-world; this most nearly approximates the level of sociological investigation as it is conventionally understood. However, it is clear from the programme for sociological analysis developed by Schutz that he intended the clarification provided by the constitutive phenomenology of the natural attitude to lead to a substantive and methodological reorientation of mundane sociological investigation. The questions and methodologies of mundane sociology would be radically altered by the phenomenological critique. It would seem that for Schutz, pure phenomenology can still undertake primary investigations relevant for philosophy in general and therefore for all the sciences, while the link between it and the mundane cultural sciences is provided by a constitutive phenomenology of the natural attitude.

The constitutive phenomenology of the natural attitude which is to be used to clarify the sociological task is quite distinct from the phenomenology developed by Husserl and later phenomenologists such as Merleau-Ponty. It is thus quite wrong to assume that sociology could or should take over the methods, terminology, and problems of pure phenomenology; philosophy self-consciously addresses philosophical problems using distinctive methods and terminology, while sociology addresses sociological problems and develops appropriate methods and concepts. Schutz is quite explicit about this and rejects a sociological takeover of phenomenology in the following terms:

> It must be clearly stated that the relation of phenomenology to the social sciences cannot be demonstrated by analysing concrete problems of sociology or economics, such as social adjustment or theory of international trade, with phenomenological methods. It is my conviction, however, that future studies of the methods of the social sciences and their fundamental notions will of necessity lead to issues belonging to the domain of phenomenological research (ibid., p. 116).

The problem is, then, to clarify how the constitutive phenomenology of the natural attitude impinges on and helps to reorient sociological analysis.

An initial distinction can be drawn between the contribution of natural-attitude phenomenology to first, the study of *methodological procedures* in sociology; and second, the sociological study of *particular substantive areas* such as race relations or deviance. Phenomenology has different relevancies for these two complementary concerns of sociology. This does not mean that the two are separated in practice; the observer concerned with a given substantive area should be so concerned with his methodology, his implicit and explicit rules of procedure followed in formulating an explanation, that the two should be inseparable and problematic in any given project.

Phenomenology and methodological procedures

As I have pointed out, Schutz gives primacy in his discussion of the constitutive phenomenology of the natural attitude to its relevance for the clarification of methodological procedures in sociology. Whilst it is clearly of fundamental importance for the substantive investigations of sociology, especially in its proposal for a sociology of the commonsense world of everyday life, the first task is to clarify the nature of sociological investigation itself; sociological methods, he argues, "can only become fully intelligible by means of the far-reaching investigations of a constitutive phenomenology of the natural attitude" (ibid., p. 138). Schutz is therefore posing questions about the very rationale of the discipline. What are sociological problems and how can we investigate them?

How can we form concepts for interpreting the social world, and what relationships should these concepts bear to the world? In regarding these as questions about methodology, I am following the approach (adopted in the previous chapter) of defining methodology in terms of the processes through which a sociologist generates an interpretation of the social world or some aspect of it. To illustrate the import of the phenomenological critique for methodology three problematic areas are suggested: clarification of concepts, the process of concept generation, and methods for investigating language and meaning.

CONCEPT CLARIFICATION

The first methodological imperative of phenomenology is to describe the phenomenal objects of consciousness; this imperative might usefully be applied to the clarification of concepts in sociology. My suggestion is that a partial "reduction" with its concomitant task of description can be applied fruitfully to the common concepts of sociology. Schutz himself has pointed to the possibilities of clarifying concepts through the phenomenological method[21] and, in his investigation of the natural attitude, has begun the work of clarification of concepts which have great relevance for the development of mundane sociology.[22] Similarly, Merleau-Ponty, in his discussion of the relationship between phenomenology and psychology suggests a comparable line of approach:

> We may take certain concepts, like image and perception, from common usage and then apply them without careful attention in interpreting psychological facts. But in so far as we have not given a coherent and adequate sense to these notions by reflecting on our experiences and perceptions, we will not know what they mean and what the facts concerning image and perception really show (1964b, pp. 58–9).

and again:

> It is a question, rather, of replacing habitual concepts, to which we pay no careful attention, by concepts which are consciously clarified and are therefore less likely to remove us from experience as it is lived (ibid., p. 61).

Many sociological concepts are "habitual concepts" which are used typically in loose and ambiguous ways; a particular problem of the use of these "habitual concepts" in sociology is that they bear unknown and/or variable relationships to the social phenomena to which they refer. Sociologists rarely articulate or make explicit the rules or procedures they follow in either generating or applying concepts. The relationship between the life-world and sociological concepts takes on a problematic status. Where the phenomenological approach to concept clarification differs from that common to other philosophical clarifications of scientific concepts is in its insistence on attempting to establish the connection between a concept and the life-world. Concept clarification can all too easily take one away from the life-world, while phenomenology's aim is to establish the empirical grounds of concepts in the life-world.

---

[21] See Schutz (1966, pp. 48–51).

[22] See, for example, his discussions of "multiple realities" (1962), "intersubjectivity" (1966) and "systems of relevance" (1970).

This phenomenological clarification of the concepts of sociology is clearly an infinite task, for new concepts are constantly being introduced (as, for example, those derived from phenomenology itself) and existing concepts undergo constant and subtle changes of meaning. The concern would not merely be with the problems of explication or definition discussed in the previous chapter but more especially to describe a given concept's career of meaning; transferring Schutz's terminology for analysing projects of action to the clarification of concepts, the current "biographically determined situation" of a concept can be understood only through an examination of the sedimentation of all its previous meanings and its origins in pre-scientific thinking. Current concepts are always abbreviated in their references, they are given specific meanings according to the relevancies of the sociological project at hand; yet every concept carries with it an horizon of meaning which remains implicit in its current usage and, unless this horizon is clarified through a process which examines the sedimentation of its meaning, sociological usage of the concept will remain vague. The horizon of meaning will be relatively open rather than relatively closed. The point is clearly made by Schutz in his discussion of the need for clarification of geometrical axioms and propositions and can be transferred directly to sociological concepts:

> The meaning-producing activity which has led to their sedimentation can be re-executed. But reactivation in this sense is also explication of the meaning which lies implicated in the abbreviations of this sedimentation, by referring it back to the primal evidence. The possibility always remains open for examining the primal evidence of a tradition, for example, of geometrical or of any other deductive science, which works on through the centuries. If this does not occur then the original activities which are found within the fundamental concepts of this deductive science and their foundation in pre-scientific materials remain undisclosed. The tradition in which these sciences are handed down to us is then emptied of meaning, and the basis of meaning to which these sciences refer, namely, the life-world, is forgotten (1962, pp. 128–9).

The members of any scientific community or discipline develop "second-order" constructs to understand the first-order phenomena, natural or social, which comprise the subject matter of their discipline. These constructs are generated within the scientific attitude of reflection on the world; this attitude can be regarded as a move towards the phenomenological reduction, for it is a partial move out of the practical commonsense attitude of everyday life. In talking of this move in sociology, Berger (1966, pp. 170–1) calls it "ecstasy", or the attempt to step outside the taken-for-granted routines. Nevertheless these partial "reductions" are still performed, as Husserl has pointed out, within the "natural standpoint"; all sciences are naïve in this sense for they take the world, their subject matter, as indubitable. Whilst they may adopt an attitude of radical reflection they do not adopt the phenomenological attitude of radical doubt. Now, because they remain within the natural attitude, their reliance on the commonsense reasoning which characterizes the attitude and through which their concepts are generated still requires investigation if the relationship of their concepts to the world is to be clarified adequately. This clarification can be provided by a constitutive phenomenology of the natural attitude; the need for clarification is particularly important in sociology where the subject matter, social meaning, is an emergent, negotiated, ambiguous, and ever-changing phenomenon. In this sense the constitutive phenomenology of the natural attitude becomes a sociology of sociology when it subjects the latter's methods and concepts to a partial reduction; the radical (or not so radical, according to the perspective espoused) reflection. of sociology is subjected to the partial reduction to clarify its relevance to the life-world.

Unless we can establish how concepts had their foundations in, emerged from, and relate to the pre-scientific life-world, their meanings will remain ambiguous both for observers and for those who read observers' interpretations. However, apart from Schutz's own work, there have been very few attempts to either clarify the existing stock of sociological concepts or to generate new ones through the constitutive phenomenology of the natural attitude.[23] One concept central to sociological explanation, which has received considerable attention from Schutz and other ethnomethologists, is that of "rationality".

By rendering meaning problematic for sociology, phenomenology also calls into question sociological use of the notion of "rationality". Phenomenology, by regarding all consciousness as intentional or meaningful for the actor, adopts a highly descriptive use of the term rationality, regarding this meaning-giving activity as rational for the actor. This contrasts strongly with the highly normative use of the term in conventional sociology which passes judgment on action as either rational, irrational, or non-rational according to some ideal means-ends schema. Sociology imposes definitions of rationality on actors[24] while pheno- menology exhorts sociologists to *inquire into* the various forms of rationality followed by actors.[25] As much sociological model or ideal-type construction rests on the presumption of rationality, the phenomenological critique poses serious questions about the relationship of these models to the lived-world.[26] Moreover, it is not only actors' rationalities that are to be inquired into, but also those of sociologists in their activities as observer-researchers; the presumption that the processes of sociological investigation somehow conform to "scientific rationality" is called into question when the processes are actually subjected to pheno- menological clarification.

The infinitely remote aim, therefore, of this first methodological task of the constitutive phenomenology of the natural attitude is to grasp "in perfect clarity . . . all possible conceptual essences" (Schutz, 1962, p. 50). By following the first phenomenological imperative of description, the task of concept clarification is to describe the range of empirical meanings of concepts and their relationship to men's experiences in the life-world.

---

[23] A valuable exception is Cicourel's (1970a) critique of the concepts "role" and "status".

[24] See, for example, Parsons (1937).

[25] See Schutz (1964, pp. 64–90), Garfinkel (1957, Chapter 8) and Scott (1968, app.).

[26] For a further discussion of these issues, see Phillipson and Roche (1971).

THE PROCESS OF CONCEPT GENERATION

The second methodological imperative of phenomenology is that of showing how the phenomenal "givens" are built up; this is the task of "constitution" or "reconstruction" and it refers to the meaning-giving processes of consciousness. In relation to the generation of sociological concepts, a concern with the process of constitution would direct attention to the everyday activities of sociologists qua sociologists; in any kind of mundane sociological activity the sociologist is involved in abstracting from his own and others' experiences and producing second-order interpretations consisting in part of what he and other sociologists take to be sociological concepts. Most often these will be existing concepts with careers and horizons of meaning, but occasionally new concepts are introduced to deal with emergent analytical problems. It is these processes of concept selection, application, operationalization and use in sociological projects that are treated as problematic in the phenomenological study of concept generation; the problem is to reconstruct or reconstitute the human activities and meanings out of which the concept and its applications emerged. Only by revealing the human meanings from which the concept emerged can its relevance to the life-world be clarified. If we are to understand the methodologies of sociology and be in a position to evaluate their products (theories and data), a clarification is required of concept constitution.

How do sociologists move from the first-order constructs of commonsense interpretation to the second-order constructs of sociological interpretation? This process will vary according to the research style and the nature of that aspect of the social world which the observer focuses on and from which he selects. To give an elementary example, the sociologist in constant face-to-face interaction with the subjects of his investigation will generate concepts in a different way and of a different kind to the sociologist undertaking analysis of documentary evidence such as official statistics. Thus clarification of the processes of concept generation in different research styles would seem to be an essential complement to the clarification of specific concepts; the problem again would be to show how the processes through which concepts are constituted and built up relate to the human activities and meanings in the life-world to which they refer. The concern of the project of concept constitution is to show the connection between actions in the world and concepts where they exist and to demonstrate their absence where none can be established.

The phenomenological clarification of concept generation leads to the study of methodology in general, and here the work of Cicourel has clarified many of the assumptions with which sociologists using a range of research techniques operate. His penetrating analysis of the use of measurement in sociology (1964) and his critique of sociological assumptions of equivalence between the logical/ideal categories of mathematics and the social categories of everyday language strike at the heart of conventional methodology and require a re-orientation towards it. The basic problems that meaning and language set for the observer-researcher require him to treat as problematic not only data acquired from the subjects of his study but equally his own unexplicated reliance on commonsense for producing and making sense of the data.

Cicourel's work could be followed up in relation to methodology by subjecting sociologists' taken-for-granted rules of procedure to a form of phenomenological reduction. Current research methods textbooks lay down a set of "ideal" prescriptions for doing "good" research; these typically divide the research process into a number of formal stages (hypothesis generation, pre-pilot, pilot, the survey itself, analysis, report) within each of which certain rules ought to be followed. As these rules result in research instruments, such as questionnaires, which both create and impose an order on the data which the sociologist collects, it would seem essential to clarify the taken-for-granted commonsense assumptions on which they rest. It is interesting that almost the only technique in which the oberver feels that it is necessary to give some kind of explanation of his assumptions occurs in participant observation.[27] This necessity to justify his decisions and data selections, which the participant observer alone seems to accept, would appear to stem, to a great extent, from the suspicion with which this technique is regarded by the proponents of conventional research techniques; it is the technique which appears to be the least amenable to the ostensibly "precise" rule-governed procedures of conventional survey methods, and as a result its users see themselves as having to undertake special pleading by trying to make explicit some of their assumptions. Even when this is done, as Cicourel (1964) shows, their revelations fall short of that which would be required in a phenomenological investigation because their systems of relevancies are not those of a constitutive phenomenology of the natural attitude. The methodological problems and questions opened up and clarified by the adoption of a phenomenological standpoint are outlined by Schutz in the following terms:

> How can I, in my attitude as a man among other men or as a social scientist, find an approach to all this if not by recourse to a stock of pre-interpreted experiences built up by sedimentation within my own conscious life? And how can methods for interpreting the social interrelationship be warranted if they are not based upon a careful description of the underlying assumptions and their implications? (1962, p. 117).

The answer to Schutz's questions about methodology is to be found in the application of the constitutive phenomenology of the natural attitude to the processes of concept generation and methodology; this is a further meeting ground of sociology and phenomenology. The everyday activities which comprise the role of the sociological observer-researcher can only be understood by bracketing belief in them and subjecting them to the same kind of phenomenological investigation as the data produced through these activities. By following the second methodological imperative, that of constitution, the phenomenologically orientated sociologist can show how concepts are built up in the activities of actual research practice and thus the forms of their links with the life-worlds of the subjects of sociological investigation.

---

[27] See, for example, the appendix to Whyte's *Street Corner Society* (1966).

NEW DIRECTIONS FOR METHODOLOGY

The constitutive natural-attitude phenomenology clearly does provide a substantive focus for sociology even though Schutz gave primacy to its relevance for methodology. That focus is on the natural attitude of everyday life within which the social cultural world is "experienced by the commonsense thinking of men living their daily lives among their fellow-men" (Schutz, 1962, p. 53). As I have noted, the "exploration of the general principles according to which man in daily life organizes his experiences" (ibid., p. 59) is, for Schutz, the first task of the methodology of the social sciences. Schutz's request is, in effect, for a substantive sociology of everyday life, a subject strangely ignored by conventional sociology; ethnomethodology is the attempt to build up a sociology of everyday life and is discussed in more detail in the subsequent chapters by Silverman and Filmer. However, a sociology of everyday life requires a reorientation to methodology and calls for new approaches to sociological investigation. How can sociologists explore "the general principles" of the commonsense world of everyday life? What difficulties and limitations are created for them by the fact that they too operate within the natural attitude even in their sociological activities? How does their own reliance on commonsense impinge on their inquiries into members' reliance on commonsense? How far can sociologists achieve the "ecstasy" or radical reflection apparently required in the suspension of commonsense beliefs about the social world?

These are practical questions relating to how the phenomenological sociologist can accomplish sociological investigation. Schutz, in recommending a clarification of methods, only pointed the way; his outline for a general sociology of everyday life is programmatic but empirically empty. He did not work out the actual methodological problems involved in the empirical sociological investigation of the constitution of the natural attitude. Nor did he provide any detailed recommendations about how the substantive issues of mundane sociology could be investigated in a phenomenologically reorientated sociology. Unfortunately he did not offer a critique of conventional methods in sociology or their reliance on the logic of the statistical method. As a result the ethnomethodological approach to the analytical problems posed by Schutz is currently involved in developing its own methodologies.

A prime interest of ethnomethodology in exploring the commonsense world is in natural language. Language is the most sophisticated means through which social realities and meanings are intersubjectively constituted and communicated.[28] If language is basic to the social processes of meaning-constitution then new ways of exploring the acquisition of language, and through it a sense of social structure,[29] and situated language use must be developed. Unlike the linguist, the sociologist does not posit some kind of "ideal speaker-hearer" whose

---

[28] This is not to say that the body and its gestures are not recognized as fundamentally important in meaning-giving processes (for example, when we say "his look spoke worlds"); phenomenology has been particularly concerned with the body and the problem of meaning. See Merleau-Ponty (1962).

[29] See, for example, Cicourel (1970b).

language use is context-free, but rather focuses on the context-bound contingencies of actual language use. His interest is in how members and sociologists together make sense of and accomplish the social world through various kinds of languages (oral and embodied) in situated interactions. Methodologically the problem is to reveal these mutual processes of reality negotiation, construction and maintenance. This requires the capture of natural language use in its natural settings. The recording of language interactions together with detailed ethnographic description of the settings, the participating members and the sociologists' own background relevancies and stocks of taken-for-granted knowledge, offers one kind of approach which some ethnomethodologists have adopted.[30] These and other approaches to the development of a sociology of everyday life are discussed in more detail by Silverman in Chapters 7 and 8.

The constant emphasis on the necessity for the observer to reveal *his* reliance on commonsense understandings in making sense of his observations and data reveals how sociological interpretations are built up through the contingencies of research practice. This ongoing explication of sociological activities is a kind of sociology of sociology but not of the conventional kind; the emphasis in ethnomethodology is on what sociologists *actually do* and on how they account the world. Ethnomethodology, through its concern with language, also draws attention to the limitations that the problematic character of language itself imposes on the kinds of interpretations or accounts sociology can offer of the social world. The "objectivity" of sociological accounts becomes problematic when the implications of couching theory in language are examined. A theory or interpretation based upon empirical investigation is always a negotiated theory, for it emerges from the observer's negotiated interactions not only with the subjects of his study, but also with many others such as those who provide access to data, ancillary research assistants, and other sociologists. Whatever the techniques used by the sociologist for revealing the processes of members' construction, accomplishment and maintenance of their realities, the methodological problem is to make the processes of negotiation explicit enough to allow for their adequate reconstruction by a reader. Only through this revelation can we know how the research, and hence the theory, was accomplished through the negotiation of contingent events.

Phenomenology and the sociological study of substantive issues

The question of the nature of the relationship between the essentialism of phenomenology and the empiricism of sociology has already been raised and requires particular clarification when phenomenology's relevance for the sociological analysis of substantive aspects of the social world is considered. Schutz argues that sociologists, like all other naïve scientists, remain partially within the natural attitude in their investigations because those aspects of the social world which encircle the phenomena they investigate are indubitable for

---

[30] For example, Scott (1968) and Cicourel (1968).

them; this simply reaffirms the Husserlian distinction between the naïve sciences and the attitude of radical doubt adopted in transcendental phenomenology.[31] Sociology is therefore naïve in that it is forced to take certain things for granted about the life-world. But a distinction can be drawn between the natural attitude characterizing sociological investigation and the commonsense attitude of practical reasoning which characterizes our stance towards the everyday world; although both are within the natural attitude, the two styles or stances are quite different. The distinction can be illustrated in terms of the differences between the two attitudes in two of their constituent features—their systems of relevancies and their stocks of taken-for-granted knowledge; these partly describe the nature of a member's stance towards his social world. First, the relevance system of sociology and any mundane science is quite different from that of the commonsense attitude; the orientating questions and problems of the sociologist, that which is relevant for him qua sociologist,[32] are quite different from those of men in their everyday practical activities, for they derive from the analytical interests of sociology; they are derived from the feature of the relevance system which prescribes the sociological aim of certain kinds of *understanding* of the social world, and not from involvement in the practical activities of daily life. Second, the stocks of taken-for-granted assumptions and knowledge of the sociologist is different from that of men in their practical activities. The phenomena taken-for-granted by the sociologist consist both of that which counts as "adequate", "established", "acceptable" knowledge in the discipline, and also those things which are irrelevant to his sociological project at hand. It is the biographically determined situation of sociology which determines what the stock of taken-for-granted knowledge is for the sociologist, whereas the stock of knowledge of the man in his commonsense attitude is determined by his personal biographically determined situation.

In this sense, the sociologist, in studying a given sociological problem, is still partially within the natural attitude, for he has suspended his belief in only certain aspects of the everyday world. Those phenomena which he is inquiring into and wishes to understand are the very things about which he suspends his belief. The sociologist thus observes a situation, metaphorically speaking, wearing blinkers which exclude some things from his sociological vision. These excluded phenomena are necessarily taken-for-granted by him. However that which is left within his vision is subjected to a suspension of belief which renders it available for investigation. In this reduced vision his aim is not the derivation of essences (nor is it the solving of "social problems") but the generation of typifications which are always derived and, through this derivation, removed from the life-world. These typifications are Schutz's second-order constructs. The typifications generated by sociologists in the partially reduced natural attitude differ from the essences sought in the phenomenological reduction although, as Merleau-Ponty has pointed out, they both refer to each other.

---

[31] See Pollner's (1970) account of the "folk" nature of all sociology, discussed in Chapter 1.
[32] See Schutz (1962, p. 63).

Sociological typifications are not generated through intuitive free variation, but through certain kinds of empirical investigation into aspects of the life-world of other selves. Both disciplines may be objective in terms of criteria peculiar to each, but sociology is empirical in a way which differs from phenomenology; that which counts as evidence, the uses to which it is put, and the criteria for evaluating it differ in the two disciplines. If one were to attempt an essential intuitive description of social phenomena perhaps the first finding would be that their very lack of clarity, their vagueness, and the disparity in the meanings attributed to them, would seem to preclude the derivation of their essences; certainly the ordinary language through which social meanings are communicated differs radically from the formal languages, such as mathematics, which formed a large proportion of Husserl's investigations. Understanding of social phenomena can be reached only through an empirical analysis of the socially distributed meanings through which these phenomena are created, negotiated and sustained. Schutz's programme for achieving sociological understanding through certain kinds of concept and theory formation is designed to provide the basis for just such an empirical sociology.

Substantively the problem is one of developing ideal-typical constructs of social meanings which provide a second-order description of the realities of given areas of social life. The objectivity and validity of these descriptions should be ascertainable according to criteria to be discussed shortly. Given the general aim of phenomenological sociologists to generate certain kinds of second-order interpretations of social phenomena in the form of typifications grounded at the level of members' meanings, what directions could such investigations take? As Schutz's writings contain many pointers for sociological investigation it is worth drawing out some further aspects of his description of the natural attitude before suggesting how the phenomenological imperatives impinge on substantive sociological studies.

In describing the natural attitude Schutz notes some of the key characteristics of the everyday world of practical activities. At the level of social reality in the living stream of a member's intentionalities, the world is experienced by him in terms of typicalities; the linguistic constructs by which we categorize and communicate our experiences are "first-order" constructs which define the particular objects of our perception in terms of their typical features, the features they share with other objects of the same category. The everyday world, he notes, is necessarily an intersubjective world and this makes meaningful communication possible. Moreover, knowledge is socialized in various ways; we enter a world in which there is a stock of taken-for-granted socially shared knowledge, and through the sedimented meanings which comprise this stock we can take part in the social world. Social action flows from and is sustained through meaning— that is, from the first-order constructs through which the actor makes sense of his world. As the life-world comprises such meanings, sociology, if it is to provide organized knowledge of social reality, must come to terms with the meanings from which social action emerges. The problem is that sociology, in laying claims to a "scientific" status, must aim at some kind of objectivity which would require procedures of verification, testability, and validation. Thus Schutz argues (1962, p. 62) that the most serious question facing the social scientist is how to form objective concepts and objectively verifiable theories of meaning structures.

In answering this question he recommends that the sociologist should start from the level of meaning; the concepts and constructs of the sociologist then become "second-order" constructs, for they are constructs of the actual common-sense first-order constructs of actors in their daily life. They are objective (subject to verification) ideal-typical constructs based on the first-level common-sense constructs and as such are of a different order from the constructs used in commonsense thinking; the procedural rules for forming and deriving these constructs will be looked at further in the subsequent discussion of validity. In inquiring into the character of the social meanings which men give to their practical activities in the world, the sociologist is removing himself from the continuous flow of practical activities and is undertaking very particular kinds of reflection on this flow.

From this perspective the focus and the starting point for any sociological inquiry is the level of meaning of men (including the sociologist himself) in their commonsense mundane activities. Concrete experiences are the starting points for the peculiar reflection of the sociologist. As Strasser says in a discussion of the relationship between phenomenology and the social sciences, "The starting point . . . has to be a real experience concerning man and things human" (1967, p. 528). The investigation has to arise out of direct experience. The corollary of this is that to start from abstract hypotheses, theories or models is quite inappropriate; Husserl calls these "opinions unrelated to the matter"[33] and such "opinions" are not proper reference points for the pursuit of a human science. By making explicit through description the character of the direct experience which is the reference point of an inquiry, the social scientist prepares the way for the further development of his inquiry. Development subsequent to the experienced reference point may proceed through interpretations, hypotheses, models or theories, but the phenomenologist will evaluate the development by asking: "What really has been experienced in the course of an empirical inquiry and what has been introduced merely as an hypothetical concept" (Strasser, 1957, p. 527). Strasser's point provides further support, from a phenomenological standpoint, for a social science which derives its concepts and interpretations from direct experience, thereby contributing to the elimination of the gap between theory and research.

The processes in which the concrete experiences and meanings are transformed into the second-order constructs of the social sciences are called "idealization" and "formalization"; much formalization in sociology has involved the transformation of social phenomena into mathematical objects—numbers—and phenomenology calls into question the relevance of this process of transformation for sociological interpretation. Clearly a forced transformation can always be

---

[33] Quoted in Strasser (1967).

effected but the key question is what the transformation does to the phenomena being investigated. Phenomenology requires a suspension of belief in mathematization of social phenomena in sociology because mathematical objects and languages do not correspond to the social processes of meaning construction. Mathematization may appear elegant but it obscures the problems of meaning and language and thus mystifies the events the sociologist is trying to understand. The formal elegance of mathematics is a stark contrast to the social realities of the lived-world.

The sociological processes of selection, idealization and formalization, arise from the scientific problem at hand of the disinterested observer; for these purposes the observer must metaphorically depart a certain distance from the living stream of intentionalities. This self-removal from the situation is more than the mere thought process of reflection which we all perform frequently during our practical activity in the commonsense attitude, for the sociologist suspends his practical interest in the situation and substitutes a scientific interest. Referring to this suspension by the sociologist Schutz says,

> to make up his mind to observe scientifically this life-world means to determine no longer to place himself and his own condition of interest as the centre of this world, but to substitute another null point for the orientation of the phenomena of the life-world (1962, p. 137).

The lived intentionalities and meanings of men in their commonsense attitudes thus become the raw data for the sociologist; the very things that are regarded as "obvious" and are taken-for-granted in the commonsense attitude become problematic for the sociologist. It is these which he is trying to reveal.

Schutz's clarification of the dimensions of the natural attitude, and especially his distinction between the scientific and the commonsense stance towards the world, not only provides a methodological critique and basis for sociology but also offers a frame of reference for the substantive analysis of meaning-structures. Many of the concepts developed by Schutz and others for describing the natural attitude orient sociology to putatively universal features of social consciousness and social processes. Like Mead's earlier analysis of the "reflective self", which pointed to the inherent sociality of consciousness, the more sophisticated and differently oriented phenomenological descriptions point to invariant features of direct relevance to sociology.[34]

Starting from Husserl's description of intersubjectivity Schutz has drawn out a variety of concepts which should facilitate analysis of meaning-structures. The dynamics and content of the natural-attitude stance of members in their everyday activities can be described through the following concepts, the life-world, the reciprocity of perspectives, multiple realities, finite provinces of meaning, background relevance systems, taken-for-granted assumptions, stock of knowledge at hand, the sedimentation of meaning, "in order to" and "because of" motives, the strata of anonymity, and many others.[35] Each of these directs the

---

[34] For an excellent phenomenological critique of Mead's analysis of the self, see Winter (1966).
[35] See the various cited works of Schutz for discussions of these concepts.

observer's attention to features of meaning in concrete situations and they provide sociology with a series of concepts which are grounded at the level of meaning and have been partially clarified in phenomenological investigations. As yet, few studies in sociology have used Schutz's concepts in an integrated way.[36]

The fundamental import of the preceding discussion of the relationship between phenomenology and sociology is that it is necessary to demonstrate the connections between sociological accounts and the lived world. The argument of this book is that traditional empiricism fails to come to terms with the problems of empirically grounding concepts in the life-world. Concepts are irrelevant unless they are grounded in concrete experiences and unless they refer to the realities of men in their life-worlds; concepts which merely refer to the realities or imaginations of sociologists, as in the case of abstract system builders, are not grounded at any level of meaning other than that of the professional sociologist. It thus becomes impossible to trace any connections between such abstractions and the multiple realities of men in their everyday practical activities. The phenomenological imperatives of description and constitution point to ways in which phenomenology is relevant to substantive sociological investigation and ensure the grounding of interpretation at the level of meaning. An outline of their relevance is given here while Chapters 7 and 8 discuss selected aspects in greater detail.

THE DESCRIPTION OF SOCIAL PHENOMENA

As phenomenological sociology starts off from the assumption that social phenomena are negotiated and sustained through the intersubjective process of meaning construction, members' realities are the contingent outcomes of these processes. A prerequisite therefore is to define what counts as a social phenomenon for members and sociologists; the problem is to decide the nature of social phenomena in themselves and to describe them as they are experienced by men in their everyday activities. Sociology's substantive focus on shared, typical and recurring phenomena is radically reformulated in phenomenological sociology. While the subjects of interest and relevance to phenomenological sociology do not appear to be very different from those of traditional sociology but the *ways they are to be addressed* are radically different, for the problem is to offer second-order accounts which reveal the context-bounded character of both the accomplishment of social phenomena and the accounting activity itself. This is to be done by examining how situated members construct their realities, how they account them, and what they account.

As language is the main vehicle for the communication of meaning, a central concern would be to investigate the way situations are negotiated and hence

---

[36] Exceptions would be Cicourel (1968) and McHugh (1968). However, the intending user of this perspective should perhaps bear one caveat in mind before embarking on social-phenomenological investigation. It would seem that any publications which may emerge would be likely to run the risk of an ideologically based professional ostracism; Cicourel's book on juvenile justice has yet to be reviewed in an American sociology journal.

mutually constructed through situated language use. The "phenomenal givens" to be described in this kind of project would be those phenomena which are taken-for-granted in any interaction situation; those things relating to the social world, self, and others, which are accepted as given or unequivocal for all practical purposes, allow interaction to proceed. That which is taken-for-granted thus becomes fundamentally problematic for phenomenological sociology, for it is an inherent feature of members' reality-constituting activity. Ethnomethodologists have already begun the investigation of the "given" nature of the social world for its members and this provides one way in to revealing the principles according to which we organize our daily life.

The descriptive imperative thus directs sociologists' attention to the nature of social phenomena in themselves and requires sociologists to attempt descriptions of these intersubjective phenomena which are indubitable and given for members. This requires a reformulation of the ways sociologists approach their accounting and conceptualization. Rather than starting with a vague definition of a concept such as class, status, role, or whatever and a series of disparate phenomena which are taken as "objective" indicators of the concept, the problem is that of establishing whether the concept has any meaning for members themselves. Do they use it, and if so in what situations, to refer to what sorts of phenomena, and with what horizons of meaning? If the concept is not a members' term then the sociologist is going to face the greatest difficulty in showing its connections with concrete lived experiences. Only by investigating the way members themselves constitute those things which sociologists lump together under their concepts can the content of the lived world be adequately revealed. The substantive study of "deviance" provides clear examples of the sorts of investigation required.

Recent emphasis on "social control" processes or "societal reaction" by sociologists of deviance[37] has given importance to the "labelling process" and public rituals of "stigmatization". But the authors' use of each of these and other concepts in this area rests on their assumption that we know unequivocally to which processes they are referring; none of them, however, provides us with directives or rules for applying these concepts to particular social phenomena or for showing how they were derived. Their use rests on the taken-for-granted assumption that the reader "knows what the author means" when he uses a particular concept. What is required, therefore, is careful detailed description of what moral "labels" mean to those labelled, to the labellers, to the social audience and to sociologists. Only by this kind of investigation can the relationship between such concepts and the life-world be established. The field of social deviance, with its strong symbolic-interactionist emphasis and its consequent interest in the problem of meaning, would seem to be ripe for conversion to the phenomenological perspective in sociology.[38]

---

[37] See, for example, Becker (1963), Lemert (1967), A. Cohen (1966), Erikson (1966) and Matza (1969).

[38] See Phillipson and Roche (1971) for a more detailed discussion of these points.

THE CONSTITUTION OF SOCIAL PHENOMENA

The constitutive imperative of phenomenology asks: How are the pheno-menological "givens" built up or constituted? The emphasis is placed on the *processes* of consciousness. From the sociological position the interest lies in the ways in which social phenomena are constructed by members so that the socio-logical task, its interpretive aim, is that of the second-order *reconstruction* of these processes. In terms of substantive study, the imperative requires the sociologist to treat Goodenough's definition of "culture"[39] as the criterion for judging the adequacy of the interpretation. Interest thus centres on members' "cookbook knowledge" (their "recipes" for action) and the typical ways this is invoked in the situated interaction of everyday life. The object of reconstructing the conscious processes of members' constituting practices is to reveal how everyday behaviour is generated and sustained; in this sense the object is general (the study of action in general) and does not primarily relate to particular "institutional" spheres such as "the family" or "work organizations". However, if the sociologist has a substantive interest in such an area, the project of reconstruction can clearly be geared to clarifying both the foundations of everyday life in general and also members' reciprocal and ongoing negotiation of reality in particular institutional contexts. The distinction between everyday life in general and the substantive study of particular "issues" has led to the ethnomethodologists' distinction between "basic" and "surface" rules.

"BASIC" AND "SURFACE" RULES

The distinction, referred to in the previous chapter, between basic and surface rules helps to crystallize the foci of phenomenological sociology and to draw out its contrast with conventional sociology.[40] Basic rules are the main interest of a sociology of everyday life; they refer to the implicit resources we employ in our mutual construction and negotiation of our everyday practical activities. I have already mentioned Schutz's delineation of the "reciprocity of perspectives" as one example of such a basic rule. They comprise the rationalities of common-sense and are our means for making sense of and for sustaining our belief in the world.

Conventional sociology has ignored the analytical problems posed by commonsense reasoning and in its empirical investigations has restricted itself to rather inadequate documentation of aspects of *the content of surface rules*. Surface rules would include, among other things, the kinds of phenomena typically subsumed by sociologists under such terms as "values" and "norms". In spite of its concern with "values" and "norms", conventional sociology has been remarkably unproductive in providing good descriptions of particular surface norms and showing the conditions in which they do and do not apply. Reliance on methodological techniques which hardly scratch the surface rules

---

[39] See p. 11 for the full quotation from Goodenough.
[40] See Cicourel (1970a).

of social life would seem to be the major reason why sociology has so little to show at the surface level.

The distinction between basic and surface rules is analogous to that between *form* and *content*. In so far as sociologists maintain an interest in content—that is, in substantive issues or surface rules (such as comparative life-styles, the content of socialization, moral or political beliefs and ideologies)—the phenomenological injunction is to develop methodologies which reveal the actual meanings used by members and to show how they are constructed. It demands a focus on members' situated uses of the norm's contents themselves. Such methodologies would require the observer himself to make explicit his own reliance on certain meanings and commonsense reasonings in his attempts to lay bare the substantive meanings of everyday life.

Form and content thus become complementary and ultimately inseparable spheres of interest of phenomenological sociology. While form may in some senses be seen as a primary concern (it is the basic rules that allow meaningful action to proceed) they are meaningless unless placed within the particular contingencies of the contexts of their everyday use. Content is always important and relevant for members and should thus be the same for sociologists in their investigations.

The ways in which the phenomenological imperatives impinge on both the methodological and substantive interests of sociology require a new approach to the problem of validity, and, again, the sources of such an approach are to be found in the writings of Schutz.

THE PROBLEM OF VALIDITY

In Chapter 5 the point was made that the validity of most sociological explanations is assessed in terms of: first, the internal logic of the explanation and method; and second, the availability of sociological data from the same or other studies which confirms or supports the explanation. The problem with limiting the criteria of validity to issues internal to sociological activity is that this takes no account of the relationship between the activity and the social realities which it is trying to comprehend; it becomes very difficult, if not impossible, to show the relationship and connections between the reconstructed logic of the explanation and the logic-in-use of the members who created the realities. Phenomenological sociology specifically concerns itself with these connections and offers a new criterion of validity; from this perspective the ultimate validity of a sociological interpretation rests on how far the sociologist's idealized and formalized second-order constructs truthfully reconstruct the essential processes of meaning-construction from which the project to be understood actually emerged. In other words, to establish validity the following question must somehow be answered: What is the relationship between the retrospective reflections of the sociologist and the past realities he is trying to understand?

The abstract beginnings of an approach to validation which add a new dimension to the internal criteria of conventional sociological explanation are presented by Schutz in the form of three criteria for both constructing and evaluating social-scientific model constructs of the social world. In trying to develop "objective" explanations of meaning-structures Schutz argues that the thought-objects of the social sciences, their second-order constructs, have to remain consistent with the first-order constructs of commonsense which men form in creating and sustaining social realities. In order to do this, the typical constructs of social science must satisfy the following postulates:[41]

axioms

1. *The postulate of logical consistency:* this includes the clarity and distinctness of the constructs and their compatibility with the principles of formal logic.

2. *The postulate of subjective interpretation:* this includes the construction of a model of the individual mind and its contents which can explain the data the sociologist has gathered; this builds in the possibility of referring all kinds of human action or their result to the action's subjective meaning for the actor.

3. *The postulate of adequacy:* each term or concept in the model of action must be constructed so that an act actually performed in the world in the way indicated by the construct would be understandable *for the actor himself* and for his fellow men in terms of commonsense schemes of interpretation. This ensures consistency of social scientific constructs with those of everyday commonsense experience.

Of the three postulates the first two are unremarkable and it is the third which is crucial for the establishment of validity; it is this postulate which requires a reorientation of what sociologists mean by validity and in so doing poses new methodological problems. However, it must be said that there is a certain tension between the first and the third postulates as Schutz expresses them.

As existential psychiatrists, cognitive dissonance theorists, linguistic philosophers and ethnomethodologists have all demonstrated that common-sense practical reasoning does not conform to the rules of formal logic, Schutz's postulate of adequacy points to some of the limitations of social-scientific theorizing and interpretation. By adopting the first postulate, the sociologist is recognizing his inability to capture the "vivid presents" of the subjects whom he studies with his second-order constructs. This inability places his reflective retrospective interpretations outside of the living stream of intentionalities; the "objectivity" of sociological interpretations which is achieved partly through their conformity to formal logic suggests their distance from the social realities to which they refer. Actual methodological practices would seem to require a slight modification of this first postulate to that of achieving logical consistency *for all practical purposes.* As an observer, I adopt the "scientific attitude" for my sociological project at hand and in doing this I try to rule out inconsistencies and ambiguities in my interpretation; however, I must recognize that my own

---

[41] Adapted from Schutz (1962, pp. 43–4).

theorizing is constrained by the practicalities of my setting and ultimately by my own reliance as a member on the commonsense reasoning common to all members. A sociological awareness of the "infinite regress" feature of all accounting (whether by sociologists or members) of the social world can lead to the use of this regress as a methodological resource in itself.[42] The postulate of logical consistency, therefore, may for all practical purposes be modified, for the requirements of a sociologist, to a requirement to be consistent in the way he recognizes and reports the occasional character of the way members deal with their world.

The basis for the new orientation to validity is found in the *postulate of adequacy* which directs attention to the meaning of sociological interpretations for those members whose actions the sociologist is retrospectively trying to understand. Not only must the sociologist refer back to the meanings of action (postulate 2), he must also create second-order constructs from these meanings that have continuity with members' commonsense experience; his interpretations must be translatable back into the terms which the members themselves used to give meanings to their actions. If interpretations fail to do this, they are invalid at the intentional level. According to the phenomenological definition of the term, validity is to be established by ensuring continuity and compatibility between the sociologist's interpretations and members' commonsense interpretations. The sociologist's models have to be faithful to the ways in which members themselves decide adequacy in everyday terms. In this way the consistency of the model with commonsense experience is ensured.

Validity is established by developing methods which show that, for all practical purposes, the sociologist's reconstructions are consistent with members' constructions.[43] Winter, in his phenomenological critique of sociological theory, follows up Schutz's postulate of adequacy and clarifies its meaning. In discussing the criteria for the validity or adequacy of interpretation, he starts from an analysis of the meaning of the project for the members who create it and outlines the relationship between this and the interpretive constructs of social science. Starting from the level of meaning, the level of the intentional self in his everyday activities, he argues that,

> The decisive criterion for the "meaning of action" is the project of the actor—the anticipated state of affairs in his own preremembrance or the retrospective recovery of that project as elapsed; that is, meaning is "what is meant" or "what was meant" (1966, p. 131).[44]

---

[42] For further discussion of the "infinite regress", see Cicourel (forthcoming) and Chapters 7 and 8.

[43] For some ways of tackling this problem see Sutter (1969).

[44] It is worth noting that Winter recognizes that the meanings of a project, members' intentions, are not always clear to members but this does not prevent the project being the criterion of meaning: "Even the subliminal processes which cannot be explicitly made conscious are not alien to consciousness but form the 'lived' expression of that consciousness in its attention to the world. The criterion of meaning is the synthesis of recognition of the intentional consciousness, even though any particular person may at one or another stage of his experience be very unclear on his intentions" (1966, p. 131).

F

At the most general level, the common culture itself is the criterion of adequacy of any social-scientific interpretation; Winter follows Garfinkel in his definition of the common culture as,

> the socially sanctioned grounds of inference and action that people use in their every-day affairs and which they assume that other members of the group use in the same way (ibid, p. 123).

It is these grounds of inference, the world taken-for-granted, which stand as the ultimate criteria of validity; it is essential to assert this for while most of the sociological vocabulary "externalizes" culture it must be remembered that social structure is "meant" and does not comprise some "objective" unity. As mentioned earlier, for certain scientific purposes and problems the social scientist can (and indeed must) presuppose and take-for-granted some aspects of this meaning, provided always that he recognizes that the social structure, or any other social phenomena conceptualized as an objective, external, independent variable, is a result of intentional social "work" by the members of the culture. Thus,

> the culture is the sedimented project of the society and is the decisive criterion for the adequacy of any interpretation of social processes (ibid, p. 138).

The abstract problem of validity, therefore, with which sociologists have to come to terms in particular empirical studies, is to ascertain the congruence of their interpretations with commonsense interpretations. Winter expresses this in the following terms:

> the criterion of adequacy for any scientific grasp of these typical patterns is the projected meaning of this world for the consciousness of that world (ibid, p. 137)

And again:

> A social pattern or symbol or institution can be viewed as a sedimentation of meaning through which consciousness is shaped and may thus form a theme for scientific schematization. The particular social science will then proceed to idealize elements of this pattern and the occasion of its occurrence according to its own interests. However, the understanding of the meaning of this regularity is *ultimately verifiable only by exploration of the intentionality in which it is constituted and actualized* (ibid., p. 140, my italics).

Stating the problem in these ideal and abstract terms however does not provide any guides to how such validity for all practical purposes can be achieved in everyday research practice. Neither Schutz nor Winter offer such practical advice. Language itself confounds the achievement of the abstract ideal of validity because of the infinite regress of accounts of the world so that some approximation, decided according to the practical contingencies of a given research project, has to suffice. The central aim in such a validation exercise is to satisfy for all practical purposes *members' conceptions of adequacy*, whilst recognizing that "talk" itself precludes satisfaction of the abstract ideal. Language is more than just oral language, for gestures and bodily movements are intentional, are saturated with meaning, and this raises problems for and sets limits on sociological description. The sociologist can never, therefore, "tell it like it was" for it is not the case that everything experiencable is expressible linguistically; in this sense even a partially validated description remains simply a gloss of commonsense experience.

CLARIFYING THE LIMITS AND THE RELEVANCE OF SOCIOLOGY

The phenomenological critique, apart from pointing to new directions for sociological analysis, helps to clarify both the limits of sociological interpretation, by inquiring into its aims and procedures, and also the relevance of sociology to the world of practical activity. In the following discussion, I draw heavily on Winter's discussion of the relationships between different styles of social-scientific theorizing and the world of everyday life.[45]

The problem is to understand the limits of what might be called sociology's "explanatory power". Coming to terms with the limitations of social science, clarifying what it can and cannot do, is especially important if we are to understand its relevance to the practical issues and problems of men in the world. Social scientists are being employed increasingly by governments, foundations and private enterprise to provide evidence on a wide range of practical problems; the sponsors of this kind of research now seem to take-for-granted the "scientific" nature of sociology, perhaps because of the veneer of respectability provided by the growing mathematical and statistical content of sociological research reports. This is reinforced by the willingness of sociologists to accept such commissions and by so doing to imply both a satisfaction with their own methods and a belief that the promise of sociology (and the demands of the sponsors) can be fulfilled through the existing methods. The phenomenological critique questions the relevance and the application of much current theorizing and research in sociology to the practical problems of men in the commonsense attitude of everyday life.

The conventional sociologies, which fail to recognize or to treat the problems inherent in intentionality, meaning and language, produce explanations of the social world which are largely irrelevant to the members of that world in their practical activities. This is ironic because, in spite of typically staying within the commonsense attitude themselves in terms of the problems they address (that is, by treating reality as a "given" and by *accepting* members' problems rather than *inquiring into them*), they then proceed to analyse these problems with inappropriate assumptions, concepts and methodologies. The relevance to members' commonsense understanding of their worlds of those sociological perspectives which explicitly or implicitly adopt a deterministic view of man must be questioned for two related reasons. First, because they rest on assumptions about the intended meanings of the common culture which are neither acknowledged nor verified, the grasp of human intentionality which their models evince is inadequate; this limits their significance and their relevance to members in their living stream of intentionalities. Winter acknowledges that it is invariably

---

[45] See Chapter 5 for an outline of Winter's classificatory scheme for social-scientific perspectives.

necessary, for scientific reasons, to take some typifications of the common culture for granted in pursuing scientific problems, but he points out that this gives "no warrant to deny the significance of what is taken-for-granted".[46] Second, not only do they rest on unquestioned assumptions about the common culture but they also fail to provide a methodology to deal with the central problem posed by phenomenological sociology of grasping meaning in a valid schema of interpretation; they are thus inadequately grounded at the level of meaning. This inadequate grounding rules out their validity at the intentional level and this in itself calls into question the relevance of their contributions to members' intentional activities.

Traditional empiricists would presumably claim that although their explanations were inadequately grounded at the level of meaning (and therefore phenomenologically invalid) they were adequately grounded scientistically in terms of their empirical corroboration by accepted and unquestioned research procedures. Even this latter claim to adequacy by traditional empiricists would be presumptuous given their signal failure to generate other than commonsense predictions about the social world.

By focusing on the distinctions between the scientific attitude and the natural attitude of everyday life, Winter is able to suggest both the main characteristics of the relationship between them and also the limits of a social science. He argues that science, "is a diagnostic attempt to account for the present in terms of the past—to relate the present order of a class of events to antecedent events of that class" (1966, p. 71); in this way, "social scientific formulation gives an account of processes and projects in the *present* on the basis of *antecedent* processes" (ibid., p. 72). Through his analysis of the different social scientific perspectives, Winter helps to clarify the possibilities and limitations of their accounts. The implication of his argument is that, rather than taking-for-granted the scientific status of sociological formulations and simply continuing to refine existing methodological tools, sociologists need to reassess their aims and strategies and the relationships of these to men's practical activities. The outlines of the limits of social-scientific explanation are sketched by Winter although he does not discuss the radical implications of these limits for methodology.

According to Winter the limits of social-scientific explanation are indicated principally by two phenomena. First, there is the character of the human project itself, the project of the intentional self in its practical activities; the human project is defined as the "intended meaning of action" and it is the intended meanings of any members' actions which set a limiting condition on the knowledge which the social sciences can achieve of these actions and hence on the kinds of valid interpretations they can offer (ibid., p. 156). In other words, the meanings given to human action by members are the ultimate data with which the social sciences must concern themselves. As they are the well-springs of action, social science cannot meaningfully go beyond them in its explanations. The assertion that members' meanings are the well-springs of action is the primary pheno-

---

[46] Winter (1966, p. 134, n. 20); see his Chapter 5 for an expanded discussion of these issues.

menological "a priori" or basic axiom. It is, however, no more axiomatic (and a lot more attractive) than the alternative positivistic procedural rule concerning the exclusion of mentalistic/intentional terms and concepts. The ideological content of social-scientific explanation can be measured by the extent that it goes beyond the meanings and intentions from which action emerged and incorporates phenomena and concepts which are dredged from the murky shallows of sociologists' imaginations.

The second major limitation on explanation is the temporal mode in which the human sciences work (ibid., p. 157); those cultural regularities which provide the basis for some kind of social science can be understood only through *retrospective* reflection:

> the human sciences find themselves engaged in retrospective reflection on a social reality which is prospective in its dynamic character (ibid., p. 140).

From their stance in the present they look back on completed projects, thus taking the projects for granted by viewing them as elapsed, and attempt to account for the constitution of human projects in terms of prior conditions and experiences; these prior conditions ought to be seen by all sociologists to be "the sedimented meanings and styles of the common culture" (ibid., p. 157). The temporal mode of the human sciences is to give an account of the conditions within which these meanings appeared. Thus, while practical action in the world is forward-looking or prospective in character, social science is a process of retrospective reflection and this limits social science to an interpretive role.[47] As Winter puts it:

> Even as the regularities and coherences of common culture make a human science possible, the dependence of these regularities on a consciousness which cannot be objectified as an immanent object of reflection for the observer limits human science to an interpretive role (ibid., p. 140).

The attempt at interpretation by the social scientist is not a causal task in the sense of locating antecedent forces and conditions that *determined* the project. However, much sociological explanation through its terminology does give this illusion of empirical social determinism;[48] the actions of men are described as *actually* determined by social conditions. The mistake is to assume that men are as sociologists have typically described them:

> When such reflective interpretations are confused with the prospective movement of the intentional self, a retrospective reflection creates an illusion of social determination (ibid., p. 163).

The problem is to show the relationships between the sociologists' models

---

[47] As a corollary one could argue that positivist sociology, incapable of interpretation, has to limit itself to a predictive role in which so far it has had little success.

[48] This "real" or empirical determinism, which seems to characterize much sociological explanation, differs from the logical empiricists' view of determinism; the latter apply the term "deterministic" to theories to refer to a theory's logical properties. See Rudner (1966, pp. 90–1).

of men (Schutz's homunculi) and their projects, and those intentional projects of men communicated through first-order typifications to which the models refer. These two features, the intentional meanings of the project and the temporal mode of scientific explanation, define the limits and the possibilities of social-scientific explanation.

This clarification of the possibilities of social science enables us to understand more easily its relevance to practical activities. At the most general level social science can be seen as,

> an interpretive attempt to bring the project and its conditions more fully into the scope of meaning for consciousness and the society (ibid., pp. 156–7).

In this sense sociology's contribution is to clarify for members their involvement in the social world. However, in viewing the main perspectives on the world[49] Winter's fundamental thesis is that the social sciences have increasingly lost touch "with the concrete processes of the society and man's history-making through their preoccupation with abstract models" (op. cit., p. 280). In Chapter 5 I noted that each of these perspectives rests on a basic ordering principle which emphasizes and selects out some aspects of social process to the exclusion of others. These ordering principles, or "comprehensive images", impute particular values to the total social enterprise; thus, for example, the functionalist perspective imputes the value of equilibrium resting on integration, while the voluntarist perspective imputes conflict arising from the ordering principle of dominance and compromise. A particular meaning or value is thus imputed to the social process itself through the basic ordering principle adopted by the social scientist in his interpretations of it. As noted earlier, the conventional sociological reliance on internal consistency and unquestioned methods and data for "verifying" or "validating" theory falls short of the phenomenological criteria of adequacy.

If the relevance of sociological explanation to members' realities is to be clarified, then other criteria are required by which to evaluate them. How, Winter asks (ibid., p. 211), is one to select among these evaluative perspectives, which often conflict in their interpretation of the social world, for an understanding of "what is the case"? Quite apart from the difficulties raised for such perspectives by the ethnomethodological argument, based on the infinite regress of accounts, that there is no "what is the case", the phenomenological answer is that an understanding of the relative significance of the alternative models "can be achieved by testing the grasp of human intentionality which the models evince" (ibid., p. 203). This provides a basic test for assessing the relevance of sociological perspectives to men's experience of their worlds.

The abstract schema of much conventional sociology emphasize, by their reduction of the intentional self into a passive carrier of attributes, their own detachment from the world and thus present intractable problems of translation into terms which are meaningful for members of society in their practical

---

[49] See Figure 1, page 88.

activities. Members in the commonsense attitude of everyday life judge social scientific explanations pragmatically in terms of their pay-off for practical problem-solving from particular value standpoints; the further away from intentionality the interpretations are the more irrelevant will they be judged to be. Various positivist competitors have been discussed by Walsh in Chapters 2, 3 and 4 and all of them, whether it is Lundberg's "social behaviourism", Popper's "unintended consequences" analysis, Marx's "false consciousness" analysis or Merton's "latent function" analysis, suffer when judged according to this criterion. Ultimately, as Winter points out, commonsense experience is the "criterion of adequacy for any social-scientific perspective" (ibid., p. 200). This leads him to suggest that an intentional style of analysis has two main purposes. First, the richness of the social world and its significant problems are available only within this method:

> Precision and quantification can be achieved in the social sciences only by screening out the richness of experience and the problems of significance to man; for certain purposes, this reduction of social phenomena may be useful, but what it gains in precision it will lose in adequacy (ibid, p. 200).

Second, this level of analysis enables us to set the other levels, each claiming to be *the* perspective, within a wider and more adequate frame of reference by testing their relevance within the everyday world. It allows us to see their limited and partial relevance by applying the test of adequacy at the level of commonsense experience. Intentionality is therefore the starting point and the finishing point for phenomenological sociological analysis in that it both prescribes the proper area of focus for sociological analysis and provides a criterion for the evaluation of sociological interpretations.

The necessity for a reconsideration of the relevance of sociology can be judged from the enormous amount of research undertaken by sociologists which is commissioned by non-sociologists for specific practical purposes; sociological data and explanations are used increasingly in practical decision-making in society.[50] If such data and interpretations are not grounded at the level of meaning (or do not make explicit their assumptions about the meanings on which their retrospective idealizations rest), if they are not therefore phenomenologically valid, then their relevance to practical decision-making must be regarded as dubitable and problematic.

Even if continuity between interpretation and the life-world were to exist through satisfaction of the criterion of adequacy, there would still be considerable problems involved in showing the relevance of interpretations to commonsense activities. At the most general level the problems stem from two related aspects of social-scientific explanations; first, their detachment from the lived-world, for they are retrospective reflections from within the scientific attitude on a world which is prospective in character; and second, the fact that they are expressed in typifications; their second-order constructs refer to the socially

---

[50] This is reflected in the growth of that contradiction in terms, "applied sociology": see, for example, Gouldner and Miller, (1965) and Zetterburg (1962).

typical while practical decision-making is carried through by actual individuals in actual situations. Two particular problems stem from this. First, there is the sociological problem of how sociological interpretations framed in terms of *typical* courses of action can clarify the understanding of *particular* courses of action of actual individuals in unique social settings; second, there is the practical problem of how interpretations expressed in second-order typifications can be made sense of and made relevant to actual courses of action by men in their practical activities.

When the range of perspectives in sociology, each of which imputes different meanings to the social process, is examined, it is clear that the problem of transforming them, without losing their meaning, into commonsense terms so that they make sense for members is considerable. Translating explanations made from within conventional sociological perspectives into commonsense terms is problematic because they have not satisfied the criterion of adequacy; there are only tenuous links between concepts and members' experiences. They are imposed after the fact, and often arbitrarily. The ideological content of sociological explanation, that which enters as a result of their distance from intentionality, is unrecognized by sociologists, who consider their explanations to be objectively documenting the "underlying patterns" of "what happened". Even if it is partially recognized, sociologists may have vested interests in concealing their ideology under the veneer of their claims to objectivity. Practical men who wish to make some kind of use of sociology increasingly take-for-granted its scientific status and are obviously neither conversant with nor interested in the internal disagreements in sociology which would call into question the validity of much sociological interpretation and data. Their interest is in establishing whether the sociologist can provide them with data or ideas which they can use to justify a practical course of action.[51] Practical men will judge the data pragmatically so the data have to be presented in terms which "make sense" for them; but translation into terms which "make sense" for the practical decision-maker can only be achieved, for most sociological explanation, by the sociological translator imposing his own commonsense on the explanation, thereby transforming it.

This is necessary because the content of most sociological explanations typically has few links with the constitutive commonsense activities of the members it refers to. In transforming a conventional sociological interpretation into terms comprehensible to practical men, the sociologist relies on his own commonsense as an unexplicated resource. In this way the practical use which is made of any sociological explanation rests upon at least three layers of ideological

---

[51] See, for example, Chomsky's critique of the role of "liberal" behavioural scientists in supporting the American war effort in Vietnam; he says of the practical use by politicians of the behavioural perspective to justify courses of action: "the 'behavioural persuasion' seems to me to lack merit; it seriously mistakes the method of science and imposes pointless methodological strictures on the study of man and society, but this is another matter entirely. It is, however, fair to enquire to what extent its appeal is based on the ease with which it can be refashioned as a new coercive ideology with a faintly scientific tone" (Chomsky, 1969, pp. 50–1).

glossing; the gloss of the original explanation with its inadequate grasp of intentionality, the gloss of the sociological translator who transforms it into commonsense terms, and the gloss of the practical decision-maker who both imputes certain overall meanings to it, according to his commonsense relevance system and problem at hand, and also selects out some features of it according to his problem's requirements.

Until sociologists recognize the limiting conditions of their discipline and attempt to come to terms with the phenomenological criterion of validity, their explanations will continue to bear unknowable relationships to the experienced realities they are trying to comprehend. Indeed, until they make explicit their relevance systems and taken-for-granted assumptions about the meanings of the projects in which they are involved, it will be very difficult for either the sponsor or other sociologists to establish the meaning of their interpretations; their grounds of inference will remain implicit in their explanations.

Explanations from within any theoretical perspective which rest on data collected through conventional research methods are treated as "objective" and evaluated in commonsense terms by practical decision-makers who wish to use them. The use of sociological explanations would seem to rest to a considerable extent on the increasingly taken-for-granted assumption that they are akin to natural-scientific explanations and that therefore one need no longer question sociology's methods or its assumptions. Political legitimacy is thus granted both to the methods and explanations of sociology as valuable neutral aids to policy making. One result is that those who carry through practical actions which stem from or use sociological explanations and data typically mistake the claimed objectivity of these explanations for validity at the level of meaning; explanations are presumed to be more or less adequate reconstructions of "what happened" rather than a reflection of the structuring principles of their underlying assumptions.

The mystification which surrounds the sociological enterprise encourages this assumption and provides a context in which practical actions are justified on the basis of invalid data. The frequent failure of such actions to achieve their aims must be seen not simply as a result of their unanticipatable consequences, but equally as a demonstration of their invalidity. This problem is well illustrated by the vast amount of practical action which has arisen from sociological research into delinquency. Many practical preventive actions or projects have been developed in response to particular explanations of delinquency in the USA; where evaluation of these actions has been carried out, none of them has been found to have any effect on patterns of delinquency.[52] This stems partly from the fact that most sociological analysis within this area has stayed firmly within the commonsense attitude by accepting and working in terms of society's definition (or rather politicians' definitions) of "the problem". Only with the emergence of the "deviance perspective", which examines rule making and enforcement as

---

[52] See, for example, Kobrin (1959); also see Marris and Rein (1967) for a discussion of a prevention project based on Cloward and Ohlin's hypotheses concerning delinquency and opportunity structures. For a project with similar results, see Miller (1962).

well as rule breaking, has a genuine sociological perspective on the phenomenon arisen; the implications of the deviance perspective for social policy are radically different from the earlier perspectives which studied delinquency from within the commonsense attitude of everyday life.[53] The failure of the practical preventive actions is understandable when it is recognized that these actions rest on limited and ideologically based explanations which fail to meet the postulate of adequacy.

One problem of developing a dynamic sociology which tries to establish validity by taking its explanations back into the world and to members themselves is that the very process of validation may itself produce changes in the phenomena being studied; these changes would by definition invalidate the original explanation and require a new interpretation. In this way sociological interpretations and theories would always remain open and subject to a continuous process of modification. Thus validation at the level of meaning might lead not only to a modification of the sociological interpretation but also to an alteration of the very situation which had been interpreted. The sociological interpretations presented to members of a society are interpreted by them according to their background relevancies in their natural commonsense attitudes, and may thereby be taken into account in members' subsequent actions. The commonsense new meanings which may be created from the practical use of sociological interpretations require sociological modifications of the very constructs which the sociologist has fed into the commonsense world. The ways in which sociological interpretations and data are selectively taken over by members in their commonsense attitudes present problems for these same interpretations.

Thus at the point where sociological explanation and commonsense intentionality meet one finds a central paradox for sociology; the very process of validating an explanation at the level of intentionality may create new understandings among members which in themselves require fresh interpretation and appropriate validation by the sociologist. The effect of sociologists' retrospective reflections on the prospective action of members of a society requires constant reinterpretations and validations; this process is infinite. An empirical example may illustrate the problem.

A study of delinquency in a London borough showed large and consistent differences in the official delinquency rates of similar secondary schools; it was established that these rates were not merely reflections of the delinquency rates of the schools' catchment areas. Some schools seemed to protect from delinquency while others seemed to facilitate the drift into delinquency. Observation in the schools suggested a number of areas of experience within these schools the clarification of which might have illuminated the differences in their delinquency rates.[54] However, in order to clarify these observations by more detailed study of the different meanings attached to experiences in these schools, access to the schools was required. This could be obtained only by declaring the researchers' interests and initial findings to those who could provide access,

---

[53] See Phillipson (1971b, especially Chapter 6) for a more detailed discussion of these issues.
[54] See Phillipson (1971a).

namely the local education authority and the schools' head teachers. The effects of applying for such access were dramatic; the local authority members and the headmasters, who had been unaware of the rate differences, immediately, and perhaps understandably, became highly defensive and refused access to any of the required data. Some heads even rejected the initial findings of different official rates between schools claiming that they knew their schools and pupils far better than any outside observers.

But the point to be drawn from this example is not contingent on the refusal of access. Even if complete access had been granted, making public the original finding in order to gain access would have changed the situation in ways unknowable to the observer. In other words the initial observations and ideas concerning the sources and meanings of the differences in delinquency rates could not be investigated without acknowledging that the meanings attached by local authority officials, heads or teachers to their experiences were likely to have been changed in unknown ways as a result of informing them of the initial findings. Making public sociological data had changed the situation in unassessable ways, thereby calling into question the continued relevance of the original observations to the new situation. Any future investigation of differences between schools would somehow have to take into account the fact that the meanings which had produced the initially established differences were present only in modified forms; redefinitions of the situation must have occurred.

One neglected way of handling this kind of problem, which all field research faces in some form, that of negotiating the right to do the research, is to treat the processes of negotiation as important data *in themselves*. Thus reactions to the study, both before, during and after it, become a crucial resource for the observer. Everything which impinges on what the researcher does provides relevant data in the phenomenological perspective; in this sense no meaningful distinction can be made between the so-called "fieldwork" and "non-fieldwork" stages which characterize conventional methodology.

The import of my argument is that the limited "truth" of any social scientific interpretation can be established only by locating the interpretations in the world of practical activity, for it is the everyday constitutive processes of action which social scientific reflection is trying to clarify:

> The historical world of doing is thus the human world with which any human science must come to terms and against which its understanding is to be checked (Winter, 1966, pp. 57–8).

The lived-world is thus the starting point and ending point for any social scientific interpretation; taking the interpretation back into the world for validation (thereby making it public knowledge) contributes to, and in so doing changes, the very realities retrospectively clarified. As Winter says:

> The human sciences are engaged in the social processes which they explore. Their very existence alters that process, and each of their publications, if it gains attention, alters the process further. Moreover each significant change in that social process will in turn have its effects on the total project of human science (ibid., p. 51).

CONCLUDING REMARKS

I have attempted to delineate in this chapter some of the ways phenomenological philosophy can provide a valuable resource for sociological analysis. The full import of the phenomenological imperatives of description and constitution is to require a radical reorientation of both sociological methodology and sub-stantive investigation. Phenomenology redirects sociology away from the blind alleys of natural scientific models of investigation onto the paths of a specifically *human* science which takes meaning and men's consciousness of themselves and the social world as its central focus. Removal of the natural-science model requires a new human criterion of validation and phenomenological sociology attempts to establish the adequacy of its interpretations by taking them back into the social world from which they were derived. Intentionality becomes both the prescription for the proper area of sociological analysis and the criterion for evaluating its interpretations.

Phenomenological sociology qualitatively changes the sociological tradition in two ways. First, it asks a series of new questions and draws attention to new problems for sociology; and second, by focusing on these new problems, it requires sociologists to reformulate the problems and questions which have traditionally formed their central concerns. In this way it both expands and changes what sociology is, or should be, about. Traditional sociology provides a series of alternative commonsense accounts of the social world which bear unknown relationships to that world; phenomenological sociology *inquires into* members' and sociologists' commonsense constructions of the social world while at the same time attempting to make explicit its own ultimate reliance on the resource of commonsense.

A common but mistaken view of phenomenological sociology is to see and treat it as a "micro-sociology", limited to studying "face-to-face" interaction whilst ignoring the traditional sociological problems connected with the concept of "social structure". If by "micro" is meant the study of the way particular men in particular social contexts together construct their social worlds then the label is appropriate; but of course the label is intended to mean more than this. "Micro" is meant to imply narrow concerns and the study of "small" issues. The label provides a way of classifying phenomenological sociology as a kind of off-shoot of social psychology, or the study of small groups, and hence of neutralizing its threat to the vested interests of the sociological tradition.

From the viewpoint of phenomenological sociology it is hard to see how its concern with the intersubjective constitution, sustenance, accomplishment and acquisition of a sense of "social structure" is anything other than central to sociology. The field of sociological analysis is anywhere the sociologist can obtain access and can examine the way the "social structure" is a meaningful ongoing accomplishment of members. As meaning is present wherever there are members or sociologists, the only limits on sociological analysis are those which either arise from the interests and ingenuities of sociologists themselves or are imposed on sociologists by members for political reasons. These are the only limits on the subject matter of an empirical sociology concerned with meaning. However, by stressing the empirical character of sociological analysis the phenomenological perspective emphasizes that if you cannot obtain data, if you cannot obtain access, if you cannot examine the construction of meaning and therefore offer a reconstruction, then there is not much you can say. Interpretations under these conditions will remain commonsense speculations.

SUGGESTIONS FOR FURTHER READING

The clearest introduction to Husserl's ideas is his own article in the *Encyclopaedia Britannica* ("Phenomenology"). A series of Merleau-Ponty's essays, including one on phenomenology and the social sciences, is brought together in *The Primacy of Perception* (1964b)—available in a paperback edition. Of the work of Schutz, the first selection in Vol. 1 of his *Collected Papers* (1962) contains a concise presentation of his clarification of sociological analysis, whilst the papers in Douglas (1970b) illustrate the directions of empirical work grounded in the phenomenological critique.

Ironically, the objections made by traditional sociologists with regard to ethnomethodology, namely that it is both commonsensical and intuitive, fail to grasp how that is a precise characterization of traditional sociology itself. In this sense, it is traditional sociology by virtue of its reliance on everyday commonsense views of social order and its reification of the social world that may be appropriately labelled as "folk sociology". Moreover, as Silverman demonstrates, the traditional objections to ethnomethodology fundamentally misconceive the nature of the approach itself.

Developing the ethnomethodological position of man as a practical theoretician and social order as the outcome of everyday interpretive work, Silverman goes on to explore the analytical consequences of such a position for the study of two areas of social reality, namely, social organizations and natural language. The fundamental importance of the latter area is constrasted with its almost total neglect in traditional sociology.

SEVEN

Some Neglected Questions About Social Reality[1]

DAVID SILVERMAN

It has been my experience that people generally find it rather difficult to understand both phenomenology and its more specific applications to the study of social reality. Quite often, indeed, they present a picture of the approach which, at one and the same time, is simple, open to fairly obvious objections and completely inaccurate. It is only fair to add that this situation, unfortunately, is not totally unrelated to the apparent difficulties that many writers in the field—but most notably the ethnomethodologists—have in setting out their ideas clearly and intelligibly. In this chapter I want to examine briefly some of the assumptions that phenomenologists make about social reality and to illustrate the potentialities of their approach by posing what I take to be neglected questions about the interpretive "work" that constitutes the everyday world. In the course of this discussion, I shall have occasion to comment upon one or two misleading views about the approach—in other words, I shall try to outline "what phenomenology is not".

SOME BASIC ASSUMPTIONS

Phenomenology, almost uniquely among philosophies of science, is committed to an exploration of the obvious. Paradoxically, it is this very concern which, I believe, has made the approach so difficult to comprehend. The obvious is necessarily taken for granted; by suspending our doubts about certain aspects of our universe we are able to conduct without undue reflection our daily lives and, indeed, many scientific enterprises. Any approach, therefore, which

[1] I am grateful for comments made on this chapter by Aaron Cicourel, Roy Turner and Ian Hextall.

calls into question the obvious runs the risk of being misunderstood if for no other reason than that it offends our sensibilities. And this is true both for the proverbial man in the street and the scientist who is required to question his preconceptions about the universe of objects (or people) that he studies. What, then, does phenomenology tell those of us who study social reality?

We are enjoined, in the first place, to pay due attention to the *human* character of the word with which we are concerned. Human actions have a meaningful character; that is to say, our actions are *purposive* and we respond not to the activities of others but to their presumed *intentions*. The social objects (institutions, organizations) that people create not only have specific meanings to their founders but, more importantly, are sustained and changed by the manner in which programmes of action are interpreted by the present participants in the context of social scenes. It becomes necessary for the observer, therefore, to avoid a bias in favour of his own commonsense interpretations and to seek to understand, as far as possible, the meaning(s) of the interaction to those concerned and the manner in which everyday reality is routinely accomplished as a natural state of affairs.

Now it is clear that the full richness of an experience is available only to the particular individual who experiences it—to put it crudely, we cannot, at least for this purpose, get inside people's heads. If we want to depict *individual* experience we would do best to let people speak for themselves. To the extent that there is a role for science and an observer,[2] it must be to move beyond the experience of any one person in order to reveal shared assumptions about social reality (and the activities associated with them) which generate and sustain such experiences—it must seek to understand the *process* of experiencing.

To take some examples from everyday life, I normally do not question the impression someone gives because I suspend doubt about his sincerity—provided his appearance in the context of a particular social scene is predictable or, at least, makes sense to me. Alternatively, a person of the same sex who moves closer and closer to me during the course of a conversation is experienced as threatening because I make certain assumptions about social space. Both cases are instances of the operation of background expectancies used to make experiences intelligible. Such expectancies are necessary because social life proceeds by making inferences about unknown parts of others' motives; even in face-to-face relationships, in which the other individual's experiences can be made rather more accessible to me, I have to assume that the other "knows" as I "know".

We organize our everyday lives in a way which allows us to be unreflective. Even experiences which potentially challenge our commonsense knowledge of the world can usually be incorporated into our routine existence.[3] As a "presuppositionless philosophy" (Husserl), phenomenology must seek not only to comprehend the unreflective process of experiencing but to put on one side,

---

[2] I have in mind here a *sociology* which takes account of the insights of phenomenology.

[3] Indeed, language provides us with useful categories, for this routinizing "work"—"mystical", "dream-like" or "sacred" are all adjectives which take the sting out of "unusual" experiences.

bracket as it were, commonsense and even traditional "scientific" views about this process.[4] This has led to three major contributions to the study of social life;

1. The analysis of the properties of commonsense thought and action, most notably expressed in the works of Alfred Schutz, is perhaps the most important achievement of a sociology in this tradition. Our everyday world possesses a "paramount reality" for us, according to Schutz. While we regularly engage in dreams and sometimes in religious or mystical experiences, these take place in the context of an almost unshakable faith in the facticity of everyday life. This is well expressed in our sense of shock when, on awakening from a particularly vivid dream, we realize that things are "really" the same as they always were. In this everyday world, men are pragmatically motivated, seeking not the whole truth but merely "cook-book" knowledge sufficient to give them practical mastery of the immediate activities in which they are involved. Their "knowledge" is expressed in the form of typifications, language-categories which define their universe, both symbolic (law, good, bad, fate) and human (relative, friend, policeman), and of recipes for social success in the known world—most obvious as proverbs but including a vast array of unacknowledged background expectancies which usually ensure that everyday life is experienced as commonplace. When potentially disturbing events occur, cook-book knowledge allows us to take their sting away with a label (a dream, a hallucination) or with a recognition that, while we may not be able to understand the experience, nevertheless there are experts (doctors, scientists, priests) with the knowledge to transform the problematic into the routine. In this world, then, we are rational but only in the sense of being concerned with the *practical* adequacy of our actions—that is, their adequacy in attaining our everyday interests.

2. It is arguable that sociologists have been unable satisfactorily to relate their contention about the existence of an objective world of social structures, institutions and roles, in which impersonal forces operate, to the reality and immediacy of personal experience. Usually, we just have to put up with an implicit dichotomy between objective "facts" and subjective "experiences", with an all-too-clear assumption about the causal superiority of the former.[5] It has become a distinguishing mark of sociological research, for instance, to be concerned with a search for objective social forces which may account for subjective experience, while the theory of socialization often seems to depict the passage of a recalcitrant individual into the "real" world.[6] Typically, then, the sociologist uses what Natanson (1965) has described as a model "of a container

---

[4] Its dependence on language makes the attempt at "presuppositionless philosophy" ultimately unattainable.

[5] These "objective facts" arise in the observer's use of his commonsense knowledge in analysing data (for example, the "fact" of suicide is established by the way in which the observer makes sense of official statistics and other accounts).

[6] The justified revival of a "social action" approach in British sociology is threatened by such an attachment to objective forces.

with an 'inside' (personal experience), and an 'outside' hooked up by wires to receive messages from the 'real' world" (p. 231). What is missing from this conventional account is the processual relationship between subject and object in the social world, i.e. an acknowledgment of the *intersubjective* character of social life. The reality of my subjective world is based upon the recurrent activities of others and my imputations about their motives; the other's reaction to my acts shapes my ends (Schutz's "in-order-to" motives) and my view of myself ("because-of" motives) and confirms my view of reality. At the same time, the objectivity of the social world is sustained by ongoing interaction and compliance with symbols of legitimate authority. History may have defined the characters and the lines but nonetheless the parts have to be played and the plot to be taken seriously if the drama is to continue. In this mesh of definition and redefinition of reality, it becomes clear that men and society are linked dialectically.[7]

It follows from this discussion that the defining processes of social life make *social* objects and forces different in kind from *physical* objects and forces. It would, indeed, be absurd if it were not so commonplace to treat the relations between social institutions and human behaviour in the same way as the relations between a magnet and iron filings. The reification of social phenomena—their treatment as objects—is part of the "natural" attitude of everyday life in which the world appears as a collection of objectified typifications both solid and real. A phenomenological consciousness leads to a suspension of belief in the reality of these objects and an analysis of the social processes through which human definitions are objectivated by members.[8] A profession, an organization or an ability range, to take three examples, are no longer treated as "real" things, or as objects which (in the case of the first two) take actions to meet their needs; they are viewed instead as labels which members use to make sense of their activities and as ideologies used to defend these activities to others.

3. It is a conventional wisdom of sociological theorists, maintained by the classical writers and sustained in a recent work (P. Cohen, 1968), that social order is the primary concern of the discipline. It is unfortunately true, however, that almost all empirical researchers have left the issue of order to the theoreticians or have assumed that by referring to the "macro" concepts of "culture" or "social structure" they were absolved from a consideration of order at the "micro" level. The dependence on others for the theory will clearly not do, but neither will a reliance on sociological jargon referring to the objective world "out there". Cultural roles, for instance, necessarily contained "et cetera clauses" (Garfinkel, 1967) because of the complexities of possible experience. They must

---

[7] In the work of G. H. Mead, intersubjectivity is firmly rooted in the act of role-taking; only by putting oneself in the role of another is social action possible. At the same time, Mead fails to describe the commonsense knowledge presupposed in the act of role-taking.

[8] "We come to the conclusion that social things are only understandable if they can be reduced to human activities, and human activities are only made understandable by showing their in-order-to and because motives", Schutz (1964, p. 13). I am not suggesting, however, that people are "wrong" in treating the world as real. The subsequent analysis, then, does not seek to *remedy* this view but to see how it is sustained and the "*work*" that it does.

also be interpreted and implemented by members in the context of unfolding social scenes. It becomes clear, then, that social order owes a great deal to the practical theories, working categories and acts of decision-making of members themselves. In many respects it is a negotiated order in which definitions of situations emerge out of bargaining and expediency.[9] Once again, the insights of phenomenology compel us to investigate the generation of that order, rather than to assume it and happily to relate *A* to *B*.

OBJECTIONS TO PHENOMENOLOGY

In this section I want to deal with some fairly common objections to pheno-menology as applied to the study of social life. These are the objections that phenomenology is a philosophy which it is inappropriate or impossible to apply in sociology; that it is little more than commonsense; that it relies on intuitive methods which put it outside the bounds of a scientific discipline; or that it is psychologistic, being mainly concerned with the character of personal experience. I believe that none of these objections ought to be taken too seriously since, as will be seen, they rely upon a misinterpretation of the approach. At the same time, the fact that these objections are put rather weakly and that many socio-logists, wedded to variable analysis, are prepared to accept the weight of argument favourable to a phenomenological position with implications quite opposed to that which underlies their own work, reflects the malaise which currently affects sociology. I want now to examine each criticism in turn.

It is sometimes argued (or implied) that phenomenology is best left to the philosophers for, while it may have interesting things to say in its own field, the appropriate path for sociological investigation is now pretty well mapped out, and it only requires more work in the existing tradition for further progress to be made. In addition, it is pointed out that to suspend belief in all the objects of social reality at the same time is to reduce things to a perpetual state of flux, if not chaos, where it becomes impossible to carry out systematic research—in which it is always necessary to make certain limiting assumptions.

The obvious response to this line of criticism is that *any* scientific investiga-tion is based upon a "paradigm" (Kuhn, 1970a), involving a set of metaphysical assumptions about the nature of the reality being investigated. One simply does not escape the problem by hiding behind the skirts of the "scientific method" which presumably underlies our work.[10] It is clear, then, that an approach which seeks to raise such submerged assumptions to the level of discussion is usually to be preferred to one which grounds its analysis in a non-problematic universe. Further, social phenomenology does not question everything at the same time; it merely places *brackets* around many of the assumptions both of commonsense and of social science in order to see what may be revealed by its own particular

---

[9] Cicourel (1968) puts a similar stress on *negotiated* orders. I do not deny the relevance of antecedent factors (biography, past exchange and so on) but these do not absolve us from exploring interaction to discover how these are called upon, interpreted and redefined.

[10] The research process is discussed in Chapter 8 in greater detail.

insights. For instance, a suspension of belief in the reality, as social facts, of criminal statistics may be the first step away from the apparently arid macrosociology in the area of deviant behaviour.

The charge of commonsense, of "telling us what we already know but in more impressive language", manages the art of standing phenomenology on its head. Phenomenologists certainly seek to *understand* commonsense interpretations of social reality but they do so in order to stand outside them more completely. They argue that only by questioning taken-for-granted assumptions about reality (phenomenological reduction) is it possible to surpass commonsense. The social world is a *topic* for study but the assumptions and processes of reasoning of its members must not be used as an unexplicated *resource* by the observer (Zimmerman and Pollner, 1971). We need, in other words, not a commonsense sociology but a sociology of commonsense. People who argue that phenomenologists are not the only ones who have been concerned with subjective meaning and experience are undoubtedly right. At the same time, it is surprising that, if phenomenology is really only telling us what we already know, sociologists are still treading familiar paths and, as a consequence, able to produce an unreflective "folk" discipline.[11]

The feeling that phenomenology is associated with an intuitive approach stems from the apparent distance which it travels from those canons of the "scientific method" which are taken to imply that technique is all. Even when people are prepared to accept its insights, they remain troubled about how the data it requires are to be gathered and through what means they can be validated. This involves a discussion of the methodology of a phenomenologically oriented sociology which is the subject of the whole of the next paper. One immediate way of responding to fears of this nature, however, is to point out the unstated intuitive methods of accepted scientific research. For instance, in decisions about the coding of responses gathered from interviews and questionnaires, the "real" meaning of a response and the appropriate label to attach to it are based on recipes for adequacy which reflect the researcher's (but not the respondents') commonsense.

As to the concern about the basis of choice between different interpretations of social phenomena, one should refer to the multiple ways in which scientists check their hypotheses. If, as seems likely, one of these ways is to see how far their knowledge fits with what they know about the experience of those concerned, then phenomenology is on firmer ground than many other approaches. By focusing on the process of experiencing, it is far more likely to be able to validate its findings by this means than is a purely structural sociology.

The view that phenomenology is inextricably linked to intuitive methods is associated with the criticism that, by taking us back to a concentration upon individual experience, it simply presents us with yet another version of the

---

[11] This is not to deny that interpretation of social life ultimately derives from members' knowledge —the issue remains whether such knowledge is utilized in a taken-for-granted manner (see Chapter 1 on the problem of "indefinite triangulation").

discredited nineteenth-century variety of intuitive or interpretive sociology. Following Dilthey, this approach sought an empathic understanding of the motives of others, more especially those engaged in great historical events. If indeed this was all one was being offered, then there would be no case to answer, but, as should already be clear from the preceding discussion, there is no substance to this criticism. Phenomenology directs our attention less to unique experience, which one can never fully grasp,[12] than to the *logic* that underlies social experience as a whole. To use an imperfect analogy, it is not so much concerned with the *words* of any one individual as with the social *language* which gives meaning to his interactions. It seeks to grasp not the idiosyncratic meaning of the other, but the emergent rules which actors negotiate in order to invest experience with meaning—often after the event so as to justify a past action.

Schutz distinguishes between the categories of members (first-order constructs) and the idealized and formalized categories of the sociologist (second-order constructs). The sociologist's categories are thus constructs of the constructs of everyday life.[13] He examined motives and assumptions in order to build models of social games played by puppets. In doing so, he necessarily loses some of the richness of lived experience—but this is a rather different objection to the one with which this discussion was begun. It is, perhaps, somewhat curious that an approach that lays such stress on the intersubjective character of social reality should be accused of psychological reductionism.

A potentially more powerful objection than those so far examined is that a phenomenologically orientated sociology has yet to prove, by the weight of empirical studies, that its insights can be translated into worthwhile research— it has yet, as it were, to deliver the goods. While there is a growing amount of work in this tradition, it must be conceded that such an observation cannot yet be refuted. It is necessary to add, however, that the defenders of more conventional sociology would be hard-pressed to argue that their approach, while it has produced mountains of research, is anywhere nearer to putting the pieces together, so as to produce a coherent whole out of fragmented items of research. They seems to have little more to fall back upon than the "young science" argument (only three thousand years, after all) and the perpetual claim of abstracted empiricists that "one more push" will unite the disparate threads into a rich tapestry. And, even they, I suspect, would not deny the impasse that has developed as sociological theory has become ever more obsessed with analogies

---

[12] "There are a variety of reasons why the ego cannot seize the living actuality of the Other's experience: his Here and Now is unique, his stock of knowledge is built up and utilized from his perspective and by his choice, and he alone knows when his project begins and ends. . . . Even in the immediacies (of personal interaction), I do not 'become' the Other, nor do I enter mysteriously into his lived experience." (Natanson, 1965, p. 233). Roy Turner, however, has justifiably pointed out that, while we don't have access to the other's "internal states", we can at least be sure that they are made up of the same raw materials as our own (most notably language-forms).

[13] The issue is, in fact, rather more complex. The vocabularies of *both* participant and observer reflect attempts to make experience meaningful and accountable—they are both, in this sense, practical accomplishments designed to remedy the uniqueness of experience. In this sense, it is doubtful whether there are "first-order" constructs.

of organisms and computers, while sociological research has the most tenuous links with theory-construction.

A REDEFINITION OF PROBLEMS

If the analysis so far has been valid, then traditional sociology can be accused of having dealt for decades with what in many senses are "non-problems". This can be illustrated by examining some of the topics currently discussed in the learned journals. I will concentrate upon the area of the sociology of organizations both because it is the substantive area with which I am most fully conversant and because, perhaps more than any other branch of sociology, it seems to testify to the belief that, by relating variables which, however loosely, one can define as social facts, one thereby produces sociology.[14]

A few examples of current research topics will suffice for my present purpose. Organizational "effectiveness" is a concept which is regularly discussed. Should organizations be considered effective if they attain their stated goals, or if they adapt well to their environment, or if they have a contented labour force or, perhaps, only if all three conditions are present? Sometimes the search is for a truly "objective" measure of effectiveness, sometimes the writer merely seeks a manageable operational definition of the concept. Always, however, it seems that "effectiveness" is a property "out there" in the real world, albeit one which needs very precise instruments to be measured accurately. In the same way, studies of "work satisfaction", "union democracy" and of comparative strike statistics all assume pre-given categories in the social world. Just as objects such as atoms and molecules exist in the physical world, so, it is implied, do natural objects arise in social reality. The role of the observer then becomes that of the refiner of research instruments so as to "tap" more precisely the orderly, given properties of social structure.

A choice of problems of the nature just discussed reflects an unanalysed attachment on the part of the observer to the attitude of everyday life—the "natural attitude". For what such problems have in common is that they reflect the practical concerns of members—or, more accurately, of vested interests—who, no doubt, are greatly troubled by the "issues" of effectiveness, work satisfaction and union democracy. The sociologist who concentrates on such problems takes-for-granted a social order without questioning how that order is produced. As this is also the attitude of everyday life, his work provides a contribution only to an uncritical "folk" sociology.[15] The subjective categories of experience of all

---

[14] I am reminded of a recent book review which spoke of two kinds of research: one that dealt with *A*'s effect on *B*, and good research.

[15] Again this simplifies the issue. Sociology is necessarily a "folk" discipline inasmuch as its "discoveries" are necessarily made from *within* society. In the act of analysis, we are forced to assume some features of an order "out there" and thus to draw upon our commonsense knowledge of social structure. "All inquiry", argues Pollner, "has a domain which is presumptively *independent* of its being taken up in concern. Indeed, without the presumption of an essentially objective world, inquiry loses its sense as inquiry. *All inquiry is mundane inquiry*" (1970, p. 53, my emphasis). One objects to much sociology, then, *not* because it draws upon commonsense knowledge, but because it fails to examine how commonsense practices are used as a resource by participants *and* observer.

the participants and the patterns of interaction which sustain and are sustained by these categories are typically ignored by this type of analysis. In the case of effectiveness, for instance, the extent to which different actors call upon this term, the meaning that they assign to it and the use to which they put it (for example, as an ideological ploy in order to attack another clique), become non-problems as the sociologist seeks an "objective" or sociologically "useful" meaning by reflection (in his armchair) or by examining organizationally produced statistics.

In such an approach, to take another example, "job satisfaction" becomes a problem merely because it appears to trouble personnel managers.[16] "Rates" of job satisfaction are presumed to exist in the social world and, it is assumed, all that is required is to design the appropriate questionnaire in order to bring in the data which is, as it were, ready and waiting. Whether the workers concerned are troubled by work satisfaction or whether, indeed, it is in their vocabulary or refers in some meaningful way to their sense of social structure, are all rejected a priori as worthwhile questions.[17]

In the "natural attitude", the world is perceived as a set of unchanging properties in an invariant relationship with one another. In the variety of sociology just described, which here too takes its cue from commonsense, *givenness* replaces *process*.[18] This is well illustrated in Cicourel's (1968) discussion of juvenile delinquency. Ordinary people see delinquents as a "type"—a bearer of attributes—while sociologists are inclined to view delinquency as a product of social structures. The surface differences between these two perspectives become lessened when one observes that both views take delinquency as a given. Process can only be introduced, Cicourel argues, by viewing the delinquent as *generated* by acts of practical decision-making and labelling by members of custodial and welfare agencies.[19] Typing "delinquents" is literally social *work*: it is the practical accomplishment of certain agencies which both reflects and sustains their members' sense of social structure.

The introduction of process into the analysis necessarily (and rightly) makes "delinquency" into a problematic category. To relate organizationally generated statistics of "objective" delinquency to "social forces" (broken homes and so on) is once again merely unreflective "folk" sociology. The issue of order (as it is constituted by both participants' and observers' accounts) reasserts itself continually and cannot be escaped.[20]

---

[16] It may also be a problem if one is prepared to make the assumption that men bring to work a set of personality needs, one of which is the need for self-actualization (see, for example, Agyris, 1964). Whether this is more of a liberal ideology than a serious research tool is considered in Silverman (1970, Chapter 4).

[17] Of course this approach is self-confirming: if questions are asked then rates of job satisfaction will be produced.

[18] Compare the view of givenness in studies of technology and work satisfaction (for example, Blauner, 1964), with the consideration of process in some material on organizational careers (for example, Goffman, 1968).

[19] "The delinquent is an *emergent* product transformed over time according to a series of encounters, oral and written reports, prospective and retrospective readings of what will happen (has happened), and the practical circumstances of settling everyday agency business "(Cicourel, 1968, p. 333).

[20] This refers to Garfinkel"'s (1967) description of the reflexivity of accounts. See Chapter 9 for a fuller explanation.

SOME PROPERTIES OF NATURAL LANGUAGE

The discussion of what are taken to be "problems" in sociological analysis referred to the "vocabulary" of actors. Yet, although it is accepted that language is fundamental to social order, very little attention has been paid by sociologists to empirical studies or theoretical elaborations of what language consists of and *how* language comes to be so central to the study of social structure.[21]

One view of language has been developed in transformational linguists' theories of the "deep structure" which underlies language use. In particular, they have described language as various phonological and syntactic rules which enable us to produce an infinity of sentences and yet to distinguish "improper" usage. The child, for instance, is able to generate sentences that he has never heard used before and to reject certain sentence constructions even though they break no formal grammatical rule.[22] Now, while such work is a notable advance on simplistic notions of language-acquisition through the mechanical means of stimulus-response, a concentration on language itself fails to do justice to the socially derived (and transformed) meanings of specific language use.

The complexities involved in the social location of language can be illustrated by the manner in which the hearer (participant or sociologist) interprets the meaning of the speaker. It becomes clear that the sentence itself is not enough to convey the meaning—attention must also be paid to the intonation, gestures and facial expression of the speaker and to the cues to be taken from the participants' sense of the nature of the social scene. Furthermore, the meaning of a statement cannot be divorced from what has been said earlier and what will be said shortly. From the point of view of all concerned, the sense of "what is going on" emerges in (and after) the course of interaction. To put it another way, the definition of the past, present or future is always made with reference to the other two time periods.

Cicourel (1969) has pursued very much the same argument. Linguistic theories of sets of rules which can generate sentences fail to pay attention to paralinguistic expressions (gestures and so on), imperfect sentences and the variety of relevancies brought to play in an everyday conversation. He adds that, as a consequence, such theories cannot account "for the emergent, negotiated nature of meaning over the course of social interaction" (p. 13). Necessarily, then, the observer cannot escape using his tacit knowledge of the world (his background expectancies) to round out the limited picture provided by analysis in terms of linguistic rules. And, furthermore, this reflects members' tacit knowledge as it is used to "bring off" an adequate conversation—for instance the manner in which they *apply* a rule and their recipes for success in interactions.[23]

---

[21] This has not prevented them from using natural language to define their problems and as a basis for assuming that they "know" what people mean when answering interview items.

[22] See Chomsky's (1965) discussion of generative-transformational grammar.

[23] "Our 'check-out' of others' use of standardized sign-vehicles does not consist of interrogation or pulling a dictionary out of our pockets or purses, but of (often unwittingly) processing the surface signs against a wider horizon of assumed social meanings ('an oral dictionary') invoked for the occasion" (Cicourel, 1969, p. 36).

Cicourel is implying that what should interest the sociologist is the way in which conversation is produced, exhibited and recognized by members as being "in accord with a rule". Rather than seeking to develop a set of formal rules capable of producing an infinity of sentences, he should examine what, for all practical purposes, counts for a rule in members' exchanges and how the orderly appearance of conversation is routinely demonstrated. We could then begin to develop a "generative semantics" which would analyse members' use of rules and their procedures for assigning meanings to interaction.[24] The term "generative" is appropriate because:

> Everyday meanings are generative in the sense that interpretive procedures and the indexical properties[25] governing oral and non-oral signs rely on a common body of unstated knowledge that is socially distributed and which participants depend on for recalling, imagining or inventing ethnographic particulars for locating the sanctionable normative character of their experiences (Cicourel, 1969, p. 38).

This knowledge is necessary for understanding conversation which is composed of "indexical expressions"—that is statements, phrases and utterances which imply a set of proposed properties of the social scene.

A focus of attention on the properties of natural language has been a distinguishing feature of ethnomethodology. Thus Garfinkel and Sacks (1970) consider what they call "practical sociological reasoning" where the choice of problems and the availability of resources to resolve them is defined by natural language. Often such work seeks implicitly to reveal the "one-sidedness" or "bias" of popular views of social order, substituting "objective" factors (class, ethnicity, demographic material) for members' accounts of their activities. This form of reasoning (later termed "constructive analysis") engages, then, in "remedial practices" to reveal the objective world of social facts which is presumed by its practitioners to underlie social action. Ethnomethodology, on the contrary, seeks to show:

1. How indexical expressions have ordered properties—that is, they demonstrate the social organization of members' accounts whose conversation reflect an order.
2. That this order and orderliness is accomplished—that is, it involves interpretive "work".[26]

Garfinkel and Sacks reject the view of man as a "cultural dope", socialized into conforming to a predefined order, and begin from the notion of "member"—an actor with a mastery of natural language in a certain social setting. Language is

---

[24] Basic to the idea of a generative semantics is the necessity of a theory that would incorporate members' use of interpretive procedures for assigning a negotiated sense of meaning that become concretized appearances during specific exchanges (ibid., p. 33).

[25] The nature of indexical properties and expressions is examined shortly.

[26] "That they [indexical expressions] are ordered properties is an ongoing practical accomplishment of every actual occasion of commonplace speech and conduct" (Garfinkel and Sacks, 1970, p. 341). This, of course, is equally true of practical sociological reasoning. Its orderliness derives from members' methods for assembling sets of alternatives, ensuring consistency, validity and so on.

central to their analysis since its use in social scenes make these accountable (that is, "observable-reportable"). Orderliness is conveyed, they argue, by members implying many things in a few words. The work of producing order "is done as assemblages of practices whereby speakers in the situated particulars of speech mean something different from what they can say in just so many words, that is, as 'glossing practices' " (1970, p. 342, my emphasis). People accomplish "acceptable" conversations by referring to only narrow parts of what is taken to be the nature of the scene (that is, they "gloss over" many aspects). Furthermore, to ask them to fill in the missing elements is necessarily to destroy the sense of what they are saying—for instance the fact that somebody is speaking and that another can hear and understand him are not matters for competent remarks in everyday conversations. Indeed, the sense of what they are saying is continually evolving in the course of the conversation—people find out by the replies to their statements what they were taken to be talking about in the first place.[27]

Given the necessary indefiniteness of conversation, people often treat part of their exchanges as an occasion to describe that conversation. An example of this is offered by Garfinkel and Sacks (1970, p. 350):

JH: Isn't it nice that there's such a crowd of you in the office?
SM: (You're asking us to leave, not telling us to leave, right?)!

The "formulating practice" noted in the brackets seeks to remedy the indefinite qualities of indexical expressions. Yet formulations never do the work of the original indexical expressions. They are themselves produced in terms of natural language and thus, necessarily, consist of glosses—they represent members' view that their conversation is accountably rational but they are not the definitive means whereby that rationality is established. Thus formulations (whether lay or professional) do not resolve the issue of social order.

The role of the sociologist, according to Garfinkel and Sacks, then becomes that of the analyst of the invariant practices (unavoidably used methods) of members in their work of decoding and encoding indexical expressions. Yet the formal structures of practical actions generated by these practices are unavailable for study in "constructive analysis". It is not that conventional sociology has so far been unable to deal with formal structures but that its methods, because they reflect the "remedial practices" of members in substituting objective for indexical expressions, *exclude* such analyses.

The task of the ethnomethodologist now becomes clearer. It is to make these invariant practices *visible*. As Cicourel (1969) notes, two procedures are possible: (1) experiments with everyday speech exchanges; (2) the use of field settings that will reveal the principles of interpretation during routine encounters. A laboratory study that he conducted with Ken and Sybillyn Jennings

---

[27] They give the example of somebody saying on a visit to a strange town: "It certainly has changed". The possible reply: "It was ten years before they rebuilt the block after the fire", gives the original statement its meaning. As the authors put it, "the definiteness of circumstantial particulars *consists of* their consequences" (ibid., p. 366).

involved giving various sentences in active and passive voice (with direct and indirect object construction) to children. Some were "proper" and some would not seem to be "natural" (for example, instead of saying "Give the ball to the boy", one might say "The ball, the boy, to give"). Yet the task was nearly always accomplished in the appropriate way.[28] The sense of the instruction, it seemed, arose not in the child's expectancies of sentence construction but in the cues he took from the setting or from past experiences which he took to be relevant. An analysis of the language alone would not convey the social setting which gave it its meaning.

Roy Turner (forthcoming) has used conversations arising in a group-therapy setting to illustrate how the use of certain language conveys a definition of a scene. When people assemble prior to a formal gathering, it is possible for an entering person to tell right away that they have not yet "started". This is because members engage in distinctive activities to display that they are *doing* waiting. For instance, they may chat to one another, arrange their coats and other possessions in their appropriate places or even sit with a vacant expression on their faces. Even when the person responsible for directing the occasion enters, the activity itself is avoided until after some "proper" beginning—the interval between his arrival and "beginning" may be filled in by a discussion of arrangements for future meetings. The meeting only "begins" when standard boundary markers are employed for doing and recognizing "beginning". A long silence may be allowed to elapse to signify that no more pre-meeting talk would be appropriate, or the therapist (or other director) may remark on absences and this, by making absences accountable, serves the purpose of "doing the work of providing an account of how presently assembled participants stand with respect to beginning the session". A therapist's statement: "Well, we might as well begin", is not the same, Turner notes, as a physical occurrence (a bell ringing, for instance). It reflects his recognition of a social setting in which the assembled audience is aware that not everybody is present and expects this to be made accountable before their waiting activity is over. Once an appropriate account has been offered, the session "begins" and waiting talk, actions and facial expressions become sanctionable.

The work of the ethnomethodologists implies the direction in which a re-definition of sociological problems might follow. Instead of using "adequate" or "appropriate" operational definitions of aspects of social life, one seeks to understand members' sense of adequacy and appropriateness in interaction. Further,

---

[28] This study was related by Cicourel in a seminar at the Institute of Education, London, in October 1970. The centrality of the interpretive work of members to an understanding of meaning is presented very clearly in the following passage from a recent paper:
"If we hope to construct a theory of meaning that enables us to understand how we assign sense to our everyday worlds and establish reference, then we *cannot* assume that oral language syntax is the *basic* ingredient of a theory of meaning. The *interactional context*, as reflexively experienced over an exchange, or as imagined or invented when the scene is displaced . . . remains the heart of a general theory of meaning (Cicourel, forthcoming, p. 71).
The interpretive work, then, constitutes the context within which the meaning of language and action is understood.

instead of regarding the features of interaction as a reflection of culture (a natural fact of life), one examines how the properties of interaction are produced, displayed and observed by the practical activities (the "work") of members. For performing "adequately" within a culture is not simply a matter of *learning* a language or a culture but of what Turner calls "interactional competence"—that is, "bringing off" an act or an account as an observable-reportable phenomenon.[29]

THE CASE OF ORGANIZATIONS

I am going to conclude this chapter by examining the ways in which the insights discussed earlier can help in the analysis of organizational behaviour. Since the last thing that I want to do is to reify a label, it would be as well to recognize from the outset the problematic elements in the concept of "organization". Schools, hospitals, business enterprises and so on ("formal organizations") are often distinguished by sociologists from families, friendship groups and communities ("social organization") by referring to the supposedly "clear-cut" goals and the formality of social relations to be found in the former type. This distinction is usually made on purely analytic grounds—that is, without any reference to the orientations and experiences of the participants themselves. It remains as an unexplored issue whether members *do* orient themselves towards specific goals (and, if so, of what nature) and *do* experience rules as predesigned and given in their relations with each other. What I am arguing, in other words, is that analytical distinctions which do not take account of commonsense interpretations of social reality (but instead use simply what is accepted as commonsense in sociology) are generally misleading.

As I have sought to imply, one of the recurring weaknesses of sociological analysis has been to reify human institutions—that is, to treat them commonsensically as facts, objects and things. This practice avoids the issue of social order by failing to consider the manner in which institutions come to be regarded by members as "facts", "objects" and things". As a consequence, such analysis lapses into an empty determinism in which "cultural dopes" comply more or less happily with what the sociologist views as the real needs of an impersonal system. In studies of organizations, this has been reflected in a common distinction between the "formal structure" (specialization, size and hierarchy) and the activity

---

[29] This is not the point to consider at length how such a sociology might validate its propositions. As argued in the next chapter, at least one thing is clear, however: the "scientific method" is no guarantee of validity. Nevertheless, the question remains whether even this type of sociology can be distinguished from commonsense. Turner (1970) implies that the ethnomethodologist cannot escape using his folk knowledge as a resource—for instance in how he recognizes the "same" activity at different points. Like Cicourel, he argues that a safeguard is that such a sociology is directed to identifying the background expectancies of both observed *and* observer: "The sociologist, having made his first-level decisions on the basis of members' knowledge, must then pose as problematic how utterances come off as recognizable unit activities. . . . At every step of the way, inevitably, the sociologist will continue to employ his socialized competence, while continuing to make explicit what these resources are and how he employs them. . . . In short, sociological discoveries are ineluctably discoveries *from within society*" (pp. 16–17).

of the participants. Furthermore, it is only too clear that the former is to be assigned causal supremacy and, indeed, constitutes "organizational analysis proper" (Blau, 1968).[30]

If one suspends belief in organizational structures as "real things", it becomes possible to develop an alternative posture concerned with the manner in which members *use* rules to do the work of defining and interpreting actions. Treating the facticity of rules as residing in convincing explanations of action, Bittner (1965) has outlined some neglected areas of research. Studies might focus, he suggests, on: (1) the manner in which the concept of organization is invoked by members to solve particular problems; (2) the meanings that problems acquire through being referred to the generalized formula of action and meaning that actors refer to as "the organization"; and (3) how behaviour is presented as "being in accord with a rule".[31] I can now examine some studies which have taken up some of Bittner's research imperatives.

Zimmerman (1971) has examined the activities of personnel who deal with social security claims in a district of the American Bureau of Public Assistance. He introduces his account by referring to an anecdote told by an intake case-worker. Apparently, an applicant could not find the official records giving her age and thus establishing her eligibility for assistance. She did say, however, that she had, at a previous date, copied her date of birth onto a piece of paper which she had given to the worker. The other caseworkers, Zimmerman notes, found this story highly amusing. Clearly, while paper records are important to the caseworker, not any piece of paper will do. Only "official" records are treated as "plain facts"—as from the outset reliable. Applicants' accounts are to be viewed with scepticism—from the outset open to doubt. Workers accomplish the adequacy of official records by taking for granted that people in bureaucracies follow rules and necessarily record "objectively" what happens. That is to say, they assume motives among bureaucrats and standardized procedures in bureaucracies.

Official records, of course, by no means tell all (or anything) of "what happened". Zimmerman notes a case, for instance, where a firm may have no record of an unsuccessful interview for employment. Yet even where official records are questionable (and in this case the "proof" of an applicant's claim to have diligently sought work was in the balance), workers are reluctant to see them as anything other than faithful reflections of real events. Bureaucratic procedures in the agency depend on the "verification" of clients' claims. To cast doubt on the validity of official records is, therefore, to question the basis of normal procedures. Further, if the records are not allowed "to speak for themselves", delay is generally engendered. The required limit of thirty days for the

---

[30] Blau (1968) distinguishes "three foci" in the study of organizations: "role analysis" and "group analysis", concerned with the social relations of individuals and groups (hence human action) are treated as something separate from, and at a less general level than "organizational analysis".

[31] An example of (1) can be found in Burns's (1961) account of the use of the symbol of the organizational "goal" as a means of legitimating actions for private purposes; (2) and (3) are reflected in Cicourel (1968)—discussed in the next chapter—and in the examples below.

"normal" case produces a constant pressure for quick decisions. Thus "strong organizational reasons can be found for protecting the determinateness of such procedures" (Zimmerman, p. 46), and agents are inclined to fashion accounts to support the reliability of official records. The outcome of this work is a product that appears non-problematic both to the agents and to sociologists who base their studies on official records. "The end result", Zimmerman notes, "is a 'documented' case that both indicates the approved or disapproved status of the applicant, and provides a record or justification for the action taken, i.e. its accountably rational character" (ibid., p. 52). Yet this outcome is a product of the participants' acts of practical decision-making and their commonsense typifications and background expectancies.[32] The nature of the resolution of a "case" lies not in a pre-given social structure but in members' sense of social structure and in their activities which embody this sense (and produce a "real" society).

Sudnow's (1968b) study of the commonsense practices of public defenders in United States courts provides a related example of the negotiation of reality. It is well known that the majority of criminal cases never "go to trial" because the defendant pleads guilty. The guilty plea appears as a non-problematic outcome of a system where the police only press charges where they are convinced that the defendant has committed a crime. Yet Sudnow notes that a plea of "guilty" is usually the outcome of a bargaining process between public defender and client in which the latter is promised a lighter sentence if he will agree to facilitate the course of justice and plead guilty to a lesser offence. Now in principle it might seem that this "instant reduction" of the charge is clearly provided for in legal statutes. Lesser offences may be charged, according to the law, if they are either "necessarily included" (murder necessarily includes the lesser offence of homicide) or "situationally included" (petty theft may be situationally included in the features of a particular burglary but not necessarily so). Typically, however, the public defender bases his offer to his client on what he takes to be the normal features of "crimes of this nature"—that is, he refers not to the legal concept of a crime but to his view of "normal crimes".

"Normal crimes" involve typifications of different offences and offenders, of the features of the settings in which offences occur and of the usual victims involved. The public defender, drawing on his knowledge of the local community, can then ask: "Is this a burglary (rape, drug offence) like any other?" His competence is judged in terms of his ability to "draw out" the typical features of an offence and an offender in order to settle the matter as soon as possible with a "proper" conviction. In bargaining with his client about the outcome of his case, he utilizes the concept of a "normal crime" by: (1) taking into account the personal and social characteristics of the defendant and the mode of operation used; (2) assuming typically that persons who come before the courts are guilty

---

[32] In this case, because the agents are predominantly concerned with the "verification" of claims, they (1) evoke the features of a setting which are investigatable matters (can be settled by a document); (2) use typifications of actors to pick holes in applicants' accounts (they ask: "Is that what you would reasonably expect a person needing help to to do (have done)?").

of crimes and to be treated accordingly;[33] and (3) using "recipes" for replacing the original charge with a lesser offence based upon what is "reasonable" inasmuch as it will get the defendant to plead guilty, while ensuring that he "gets his due". As a consequence, the charge on which the defendant pleads guilty and is convicted is related to the original offence only in so far as it is a typical reduction formulated for handling a "normal crime".

The studies of Zimmerman and Sudnow illustrate how behaviour is not a simple outcome of a "formal" structure.[34] Enacted rules operate in social situations only by continual interpretation of their "meaning" in the context of commonsense decision-making. Activities that appear to be in accord with a rule (the "proper" processing of welfare applicants and criminal defendants) are an ongoing practical accomplishment of members who succeed in demonstrating (if only retrospectively) that they are doing (have done) things "according to the book".[35]

SUGGESTIONS FOR FURTHER READING

Kockelmans (1967) provides, in a paperback edition, a valuable introduction to the work of Husserl together with some material on Merleau-Ponty and Sartre. Wagner (1971) contains much useful material from Schutz, while two of Schutz's papers may be found in the far cheaper MacIntyre and Emmett (1970). An extended look at a piece of ethno-methodological research (discussed in this chapter and the next) is provided by Cicourel (1968). For more recent examples see Silverman and Jones (forthcoming) and Silverman (forthcoming).

---

[33] As Sudnow remarks: "This presupposition makes such first questions as, 'Why don't you start by telling me where this place was . . .', reasonable questions. When the answer comes: 'What place? I don't know what you are talking about', the defendant is taken to be a phony, making an 'innocent pitch'. The conceivable first question: 'Did you do it?' is not asked because it is felt that this gives the defendant the notion that he can try an 'innocent pitch' " (1968b, p. 167).

[34] Bittner (1964) argues that "the formal organizational designs are schemes of interpretation that competent and entitled users can invoke in *yet unknown ways* whenever it suits their purposes" (pp. 249–50).

[35] For a more extended examination of organizational analysis in these terms, see Silverman (forthcoming).

Chapter 8 continues the critique developed in Chapter 7 into a more specific examination of the methodological problems associated with traditional sociological analysis by way of a distinction drawn between the social world as a topic for study and as a resource for explanations. Particular attention is paid to the inevitable split that emerges within traditional sociology between theory and method as a consequence of the interpretive activity in which it engages and the metatheoretical assumptions in which such activity is grounded.

The second half of the chapter concentrates on building an alternative methodology grounded in the phenomenological position.

EIGHT

Methodology and Meaning[1]

DAVID SILVERMAN

I

The distinction between theory and method is one of the more curious features of the social sciences. On the one hand, according to the structure of many undergraduate courses, there are the theories; on the other hand, the methods. And in practice, despite pious words to the contrary, the two never formally meet. Of course any formal distinction cannot escape the essential unity of theory and method. Both theories and methods necessarily operate within a universe with certain assumed characteristics; both imply a metatheory and a methodology. I cannot assert that A determines B or make use of multiple-choice questionnaires without taking a position about the nature of the reality which I am studying and the kind of problematic areas to be found within it. If, however, there can be no real dichotomy between theory and method, formal distinctions have served to confuse the issue, making researchers miss the theoretical implications of their work and encouraging theoreticians to work on a level of abstraction which seems dangerously far from the everyday social world. In this chapter I want to draw out some of the methodological implications of a phenomeno-logically orientated sociology.[2] In doing so, I seek to offer a somewhat simplified analysis of the main features of sociological research and to present an alternative and, in my view, more fruitful perspective.

Basic to my argument is the view that social scientists have drawn far too readily on what they have understood as the scientific method. Usually this has meant little more than copying what is presumed to be the frame of inquiry

---

[1] I am grateful for the comments of Aaron Cicourel on this chapter. I alone am responsible for its content.
[2] Following Phillipson (Chapter 5), I understand by a methodology a means of generating abstract views of social scenes.

used by natural scientists. Whether or not the methodology of natural science has been fully comprehended—even writers like Popper have doubts—the question of the *appropriateness* of such methods has generally been pre-empted in the rush to be as "scientific" about society as about organisms and matter. It remains as a largely unexplored area whether the particular qualities of social order, as distinct from the natural and physical orders, create a different problematic and demand an entirely separate approach (see Chapter 2). To resolve such issues requires a fundamental reappraisal of the tasks of the social sciences. Rather than restating the phenomenological position (which is dealt with at length in other parts of this volume), I want to consider how two writers, one a philosopher (Husserl) the other a sociologist (Blumer), whose work is separated by almost fifty years, have framed their replies to such problems.

Edmund Husserl, in a paper called "Philosophy as Rigorous Science", has argued that the subject-matter of a discipline should determine its method of study: "The true method", he writes, "follows the nature of things to be investigated and not our prejudices and preconceptions" (1965, p. 102). In the context of an appeal for the restructuring of psychology on the basis of a systematic phenomenology, he points out that the meaningful nature of human experience creates problems of a different order than are confronted in the natural sciences. To comprehend human activity one must first understand the experience of those studied; matter, on the other hand, has no meaning for itself. The predominant naturalistic bias of psychology, he concludes, is fundamentally misleading since it equates human experience with the processes of the natural world—it confuses the psychical with the physical.[3]

The issue of the two types of order is avoided by the use of operationally defined variables which are then related together. The statistical correlations that are provided give the illusion of having established the characteristics of an ordered universe but, since its concepts do not relate to human experience, it is an imposed order. Husserl wonders: "How could psychology fail to see that in its purely psychological concepts, with which it now cannot at all dispense, it necessarily *gives* a content that is simply not taken from what is actually given in experience but is *applied* to the latter?" (ibid, p. 101, my emphasis).[4]

As a consequence, the psychology of his time, Husserl argues, has turned human processes into objects. In relating its concepts to one another, it has *produced* a natural order of non-problematic objects, causally related together and subject to objective forces of change. Psychology must be reformulated on the basis of a concern with phenomena rather than nature; while nature has its own

---

[3] Such an approach, "places analysis realized in empathetic understanding of others' experience and, likewise, analysis on the basis of one's own mental processes that were unobserved at the time, on the same level with an analysis of experience (even though indirect) proper to physical science, believing that in this way it is an experimental science of the psychical in fundamentally the same sense as physical science is an experimental science of the physical" (Husserl, 1965, p. 97).

[4] The avoidance of a consideration of the meaning of experience is noted by Husserl. Psychology "has neglected to consider to what extent the psychical, rather than being the presentation of a nature, has an essence proper to itself to be rigorously investigated prior to any psychophysics" (ibid., p. 102).

reality, phenomena are real to the extent that we take them to be real. "A phenomenon", Husserl points out,

> is no "substantial" unity; it has no "real properties", it knows no real parts, no real changes, and no causality. . . . To attribute a nature to phenomena, to investigate their real component parts, their causal connections—that is pure *absurdity*, no better than if one wanted to ask about the causal properties, connections, etc. of numbers (ibid., pp. 106–7, my emphasis).

Husserl's case against social science clearly involves more than a philosophical quibble. Furthermore, his intention is fundamentally constructive—he does not wish to crush the idea of a rigorous study of human activities but to offer, through a reorientation of approach, a potentially fruitful path for analysis. Once the social sciences rid themselves of their naturalistic bias, a rich array of human experience will be available for investigation. Only the temptation to reify human processes—to treat them as concrete objects with real relations and needs—stands in the way.[5]

More than a generation after Husserl, his structures are still almost unnoticed among social scientists. The dominant mode of analysis directs our attention simply to *A*'s effect on *B*—where *A* and *B* might equally refer to atoms or viruses rather than aspects of social life. In such a context, methodology has come to mean little more than precise statistical techniques for handling quantitative data, while "grand" theory seems more suitable for the armchair than the research process.[6]

In a paper a generation later, Herbert Blumer, a sociologist, returned to a critique of the underlying assumptions of contemporary social science.[7] Studies that relate *A* to *B*, he argues, do not tell us the meaning that the relation in question has for the participants or how it bears on their other experience. For example, a work which relates "job satisfaction" to empirical indicators of the structure of the host organization fails to consider the *meaning* of job satisfaction (if any) to the participants and their experience of organizational structure. Neither are we informed about the relation of feelings about work to experience in the wider society or about the processes of change in such orientations. We have, to put it bluntly, very little more than a snapshot taken from a misleading angle and frozen in time. Variable analysis, then, has left out "the process of interpretation or definition that goes on in human groups" (Blumer, 1967, p. 68). In its search for clear-cut unitary variables which will lend themselves to complex

---

[5] Reification of human phenomena reflects the use of the social world as a *resource* as well as a *topic* for study (see Zimmerman and Pollner, 1971). It is a characteristic of commonsense thinking to treat socially sustained categories as objects which are "out there" in the same way as physical objects.

[6] I am reminded of a gathering of sociologists who felt obliged to acknowledge the need to be "more theoretical" in their treatment of empirical work; when asked, however, to name one theory which could make sense of that work, an unbroken silence developed.

[7] "Variable analysis" (the subject of Blumer's paper) is discussed also, with examples, in Chapter 3.

statistical analysis, givenness has replaced process—except where that process is imposed on the material by an observer. [8]

The usual reply to criticisms such as Blumer's is that current research is rarely so naïve as simply to relate A to B. What generally happens is that a third variable is introduced which often relates to the experiences of the participants. This "intervening variable", it is suggested, *limits* the effect of A upon B. [9] Blumer, however, will have none of this. [10] According to such a perspective, he argues, both A and B remain "out there" as objective social facts separate from the defining activities of actors. The creative process through which the character of social objects is constructed and sustained by acts of interpretation remains an ignored issue. As a consequence, we must seek to be more radical and, by beginning from an analysis of the experiences and meanings of the actors themselves, focus on the processes through which social definitions arise, are sustained and change. Before I go on to outline such an alternative, however, I want to draw the threads together and to attempt a brief characterization of what seem to be the dominant features of contemporary sociological research. More specifically, I will consider the metatheory that underlies it, the bases on which it defines its problems, its methods of study and its view of the research process in relation to sociological theory. [11]

The set of assumptions about the universe of objects it studies (metatheory) is predominantly mechanistic in nature. A social system is presumed to exist in which social forces operate to shape our lives. In equal measure, then, the conceptual apparatus of much sociological research draws upon the concept of order proposed by the system theorists and upon Durkheim's notion of social facts. Within such a universe, it would not seem to matter where one begins. Since everything is related to everything else and to the whole by inexorable social forces, any one aspect of the order will necessarily lead one to the central characteristics of the system. In their choice of problems to study, however, it does not seem that the behaviour of sociologists has been as random as this would suggest. Any consideration of a sociological journal would reveal two recurrent characteristics of the problems chosen for study. On the one hand, they reflect what the man in the street (or, more normally, the administrator) takes to be problematic areas—what, for instance, influences the level of crime among different parts of the population, strike-levels in different societies or the effectiveness of formal organizations? On the other hand, such problems reveal

---

[8] For instance, by inferring a process from the results of two questionnaires offered to the same respondents at different times.

[9] I have in mind here a study which discovered that the effects of "objective" aspects of job structure were limited by the social values and religious orientations of the workers concerned (Turner and Lawrence, 1965).

[10] Although it should be pointed out that Blumer is very imprecise when it comes to prescribing alternative research postures. Like many symbolic interactionists, his analysis of meaning fails to analyse the properties of commonsense thought (see Schutz, 1962) and of language (see Cicourel, 1969).

[11] I should point out that I am presenting only what I take to be an ideal type of sociological research as currently practised. I do not deny that there is some work to which this picture does not apply.

a preference for variables that are amenable to statistical test and for data which, therefore, can be readily passed over to the computer for analysis.

The methods of study, the techniques of research, are also surprisingly uniform. One begins with a recognition that the commonsense meanings of terms are imprecise and that the richness of experience must necessarily be sacrificed in favour of clear-cut concepts. The first step, then, is to construct from the armchair "operational definitions" of the variables that come within the scope of the chosen problem. "Effectiveness", for instance, may be defined for the purposes of the study as the number of cases dealt with (in the case of an administrative organization) or as return on capital invested (in the case of an economic enterprise); "crime" will generally be defined as that which is recorded in official criminal statistics. Using these operational definitions, one goes on to formulate hypotheses, usually couched in a form capable of statistical test (for example, high effectiveness, low bureaucratization; high rate of juvenile delinquency, high rate of broken homes). Until this stage has been passed, it is important to note, the researcher rarely has come into contact with the objects of his research—he has not "entered the field". Research typically functions, then, on the basis of a priori problems, concepts and hypotheses.[12]

At some point, clearly, the data must be gathered in. Sometimes this need only involve the collation of official statistics. More frequently, however, precoded questionnaires and interview schedules are mobilized in order to gather the responses of the sample to the questions that are asked of them. More unstructured methods, such as participant-observation and even open-ended questions, are sometimes used but there are doubts expressed about their objectivity (as compared with other techniques) and their users are unnaturally self-conscious about the dangers of departing from the precise scientific method.

With his data gathered in, the researcher proceeds to analyse it. When dealing with precoded answers no problems arise—the data almost jumps from the sheet of paper onto the punched card. Open-ended questions provide more complex answers which need to be coded into "scientific" categories before analysis can proceed. Usually, almost unreflectively, the researcher will pass this tedious task on to graduate students who may have only a vague idea of what the study intends to examine. Statistical tests of significance may now be readily used to establish whether or not the predesigned hypotheses can be refuted.

If the scientific pretensions of sociology are to mean anything, research should not be an end in itself (however essential for the promotion of the researcher), but should generate a growing corpus of knowledge expressed in sociological theories. The conventional view of the research process is that of the testing of theory. Theory arises and then we must go out into the field to see whether or not it works. This "rhetoric of verification", however, notably fails to specify how theory is to be generated—except by abstract contemplation. All that we are offered is that occasionally, the serendipity principle (discovering

---

[12] Pilot studies are sometimes used but seldom for clarifying the commonsense world of the participants (and the observer).

things by accident) may allow us to find implications in our data which, by chance, make it possible to postulate a new theory (see Merton, 1949).

If empirical research bases itself on the role of testing theory, it also works within an assumed order which is not itself problematic. The function of research then becomes to examine in intricate detail the relations between the given parts of this order. As already noted, the order presumed to exist is assigned the properties of the natural world—objective reality, necessary causal connections—and no serious attention is paid to how a distinctively *social* order is produced. Implicitly, the researcher works with concepts, such as social structure and culture, which, for him, satisfactorily define and sustain the existence of that order. For instance, when his participants act in a certain manner, he has no trouble in conjuring up a cultural rule (for example, an emphasis on universalistic criteria of evaluation in formal organizations) which determines that action.

This typification of a dominant view of the research process underlines the *reflexive* character of contemporary accounts of social phenomena. In many senses, such research generates accounts which produce a real world, with orderly properties, by calling upon the language of sociology. Such a process is difficult to distinguish from the manner in which we objectify the character of the everyday world in conversation and interaction by paying attention to certain presumed properties of the situation and ignoring others in our use of language. Accounts are reflexive, then, since, in the manner of a self-confirming prophecy, they reflect the order which they purport to describe.

To interpret the features of a social setting, such as the statuses of the participants and the expectations attached to their activities, as objective and pre-given is to follow the attitude of everyday life in which such features are "normal, natural facts of life" (Zimmerman and Pollner, 1971).[13] Such an interpretation completely misses the manner in which the definition of social scenes is a practical accomplishment of the participants. While members make use of a common social stock of knowledge ("culture"), the presentation of their behaviour as being in accord with a rule and its interpretation as such by others is an outcome of their own social "work". The features of a setting, then, are an "occasioned corpus"; the order that arises is accomplished and not simply pre-given.[14]

II

The outlines of an alternative view of the research process are now becoming clear. Beginning from a metatheory which stresses the uniquely meaningful character of social process, its first task must be to uncover the participants'

---

[13] Under the attitude of everyday life, these features are objective conditions of action that, although participants have had a hand in bringing about and sustaining them, are essentially independent of any one's or anyone's doings (Zimmerman and Pollner, 1971).

[14] "By the use of the term, *occasioned* corpus, we wish to emphasize that the features of socially organized activities are particular, contingent accomplishments of the production and recognition work of parties to the activity" (ibid.).

rules for applying the meanings, labels and understandings that constitute for them an undoubted reality. Before the imagined procedures of the natural sciences are imposed on social reality, concern must be shown, therefore, for their appropriateness to the task in hand. Cicourel and Kitsuse (1963a) are not alone, for instance, in wondering whether quantitative data derived from multiple-choice questionnaires—based upon the distinction of attitudes into discrete categories—does in any sense reflect the manner in which people in everyday life generally conceive of objects and events. The concern, however, must be to *understand* members' ordering of experience in order to *step outside it* so as to understand the human processes through which activities are assigned meanings.[15] In this way, by seeking to grasp the logic of social life, the unseen assumptions that are used to label phenomena and make decisions about the normality of an experience, a phenomenological consciousness reasserts the issue of order as central to the research process.

Given the importance attached to comprehending the actors' views of reality, it follows that the attachment of many researchers to a priori definitions and hypotheses must also be brought into question. Such a procedure usually serves only to enable the observer to avoid coming to grips systematically with the constructs of the people he is studying. It arises because the dominant view of the research process stresses its role of *testing* theory and hence demands initially clearly-defined concepts. If, on the other hand, we use research to *generate* theory, then we are under no such restrictions. "Grounded" theories can emerge which, instead of forcing data into a preconceived "objective" reality, seek to mobilize as a research tool the categories which the participants themselves use to order their experience (see Glaser and Strauss, 1968).[16] If this seems to suggest primarily an exploratory role for sociological research, then so much the better. For, to the extent that there is any validity in the critique of the dominant approach that has been offered, it is unfortunately necessary to assume that we know very little, despite decades of sociological research, about the *social* construction of reality.

In the context of the suggested redefinition of the subject-matter of sociology, the narrow discussion of the reliability of techniques for gathering data—which sometimes passes for methodology—appears less significant. It is true also that the inherent advantages of any particular technique are often less important than the degree of sophistication with which the technique is applied. Nevertheless, any discussion of methodology which did not contain an examination of the various means of gathering data would be incomplete.

---

[15] "For the member the corpus of setting features presents itself as a product, as objective and independent scenic features. For the analyst the corpus *is* the family of practices employed by members to assemble, recognize and realize the corpus-as-a-product" (ibid.).

[16] In this respect, I rather like Northrop's (1947) view that, "a subject becomes scientific not by beginning with facts, with hypotheses, or with some pet theory brought in a priori, but by beginning with the peculiar character of its particular problems" (p. 274; quoted by Dalton, 1959). On the other hand, the process through which (according to Glaser and Strauss) one moves from substantive to formal theories suggests an attempt to remedy members' accounts rather than to understand the "work" that they accomplish (see Garfinkel, 1967).

Typically the basis for choosing between research techniques has been in terms of their relative capacity to provide objective, preferably quantified data. Sometimes the tail has even wagged the dog—problems being chosen on the grounds of their suitability for the employment of a particularly favoured method. Our previous analysis, however, gives us an alternative criterion of choice: to what extent does any research technique allow us to pay attention to the unique character of social life, in particular the human activities of labelling and decision-making which define its nature?[17] By posing this question, three methods—participant-observation, laboratory studies and tape-recorded discussions—are presented as holding, at the present time, the greatest potential. It cannot be stressed too strongly, however, that the problem should come *before* the technique and that the use of any particular method by no means guarantees valid research—indeed, some of the more positivistic social-science research has stemmed from the use of the laboratory method.

III

Participant-observation has a long and distinguished history in social science. At one and the same time, it is probably the most rewarding and dangerous research technique. In unsophisticated hands, its results reflect an ethnocentrism which simply confirms the preconceptions of the observer. At the other extreme, the pioneering work of William F. Whyte (1943) on clique activities among gangs of young slum-dwellers is still noted as a classic. As Dalton (1959) also showed, participant-observation comes into its own in describing the unofficial practices and codes which are generally more significant in the lives of people than formal rules and constitutions. Its great advantage is that it can give the good researcher a "feel" of the situation and help to generate hypotheses which can be revised as his knowledge increases. Quantitative data gathered from questionnaires and interviews can create a chasm between the investigator and his material: "Studying them (informal relations) at a distance", Dalton observes, "the investigator may be so 'objective' that he misses his subject matter and cannot say just what it is that he is objective about" (ibid.). A recent work by Severyn Bruyn (1966) has developed in a more extended discussion the nature of the questions that participant-observation can appropriately be used to answer.

Bruyn begins by arguing for the use of research techniques which illustrate the social drama as it appears to the actors—their view of their parts in the drama and their assumptions about the unfolding plot.[18] In particular, we should seek to understand the actors' subjective categories for ordering their experience. These "concrete concepts" take the place of operational definitions constructed by

---

[17] The question of validity is discussed at the end of this chapter.

[18] "The method of the social scientist, we are saying, must take dramatic account of the socio-cultural world—the complex of actors and their plots as they live and dream on the stage of society—as a breathing part of his theoretical design" (Bruyn, 1966, p. xiv). As will become clearer later, I find important deficiencies in much participant-observation work.

the observer. They lead us on to search for socially shared categories or "concrete universals" and help in understanding the participants' explanations of phenomena in their social universe.

Now any attempt to grasp the meanings embodied in action—the "in-order-to" and "because-of" motives of the actor—might seem to be threatened by the taken-for-granted character of the assumptions of social life.[19] Even Weber, whose sociology was based around the analysis of meaningful social action, noted that usually, "actual action goes on in a state of inarticulate half-consciousness or actual unconsciousness of its subjective meaning" (1964, p. 111). Nevertheless, the fact that alter is able to comprehend at least some of the purposes of ego is

FIGURE 3: BRUYN'S ANALYSIS OF MEANING[20]

	Time	Place	Circumstance	Language	Intimacy	Consensus
			DIMENSIONS OF DATA			
Cognition (how meaning made intelligible)	When did meaning arise?	Where does it arise?	Among what actors?	Conveyed through what language?	Is it expressed in private?	How is it confirmed?
Cathexis (quality of feeling linked to meaning)	When did sentiment arise?	Where?	Does sentiment vary from role to role?	Conveyed by . . . ?	Public or private?	How confirmed?
Conduct (action accompanying meaning)	When did action arise?	Where?	Which people involved?	What actions conveyed it?	Public or private?	How confirmed?

reflected continually in the non-problematic, routine nature of our everyday existence. The *intersubjectivity* of the social world is a guarantee that the meanings of others can be comprehended. It provides a basis for Bruyn to set out a series of questions designed to sensitize the participant-observer to the meaning-structures be will encounter. How is the meaning made intelligible to others? What quality of feeling is associated with the meaning? What action accompanies the meaning? And at what times, in what places, in what circumstances, and through what language is the meaning conveyed? Bruyn presents a table representing these series of questions and, in a modified form, it is set out in Figure 3.

Bruyn is content to describe the subjective world as it appears to the participants. This world, he rightly argues, is capable of being explained in terms of itself alone—that is, without reference to the constructs of the observer. The world of commonsense is complete in itself; any analysis or search for objective causes necessarily does an injustice to the genuine reality which it possesses for all of us. If, however, we do not wish to go beyond lived experience, we would

---

19 See Chapter 6 for an account of Schutz's analysis of motives.

20 Drawn from a table in Bruyn (1966, p. 261). The question still arises: how does he (the participant-observer) claim to know that he knows what the member knows? Work in this tradition has notably avoided the issue of the use (by participants *and* observer) of commonsense knowledge as a resource in making assumptions about social structure.

do best to rely upon what a person has to say for himself or, although this is clearly dangerous, a sophisticated journalist. The role of sociology must be to go beyond this position in order to understand the logic that underlies it. While the sociologist must *begin* from the first-order constructs of the participants themselves, his work necessarily involves a distortion of their experience as he seeks to idealize and formalize, to talk about the typical where there is ultimately a number of unique cases. Even the work of Bruyn plainly involves a level of abstraction away from immediate experience but his analysis retains its usefulness as an indicator of what may be the necessary first stage in the resolution of many sociological problems.

IV

A concern to discover the order underlying the flux has been the typifying feature of the work of the Californian ethnomethodologists, notably Harold Garfinkel (1967), Aaron Cicourel (1964 and 1968) and Harvey Sacks. Somewhat misleading, "ethnomethods", while incorporating a study of the approaches used by social scientists, refer to the practical activities and accounts of people in society. Ethnomethodology, therefore, does not relate directly to a method of sociological research but to a probing examination of the nature of social action and of accounts (both lay and professional) of social process.

One of the paradoxes of participant-observation is its combination of an extreme diffidence about generalization (the writer being content to "let the data speak for themselves"—Cicourel, 1968, p. 12) with a sufficient measure of abstraction to escape the charge of mere journalism. As a consequence, the unstated assumptions, concepts and theories of the observer may be substituted for an analysis of the practical theories of the participants. A social order is thereby *imposed* upon the situation and the central problematic of the actors' construction and maintenance of a meaningful universe of beliefs and activities becomes a non-issue, resolved *a priori*. Garfinkel's approach replaces this imposed, mechanistic order with a directive which reasserts the problematic. Social life proceeds routinely in what we take to be an objective universe of taken-for-granted events and ideas. It is only able to do so, Garfinkel suggests, because of commonsense ideas about the appropriate components of social scenes and the "rationality" of certain ways of acting and making decisions. These ideas or background expectancies exist not simply in the mind of any one individual but are sustained and indeed originate in social action. In our intersubjective universe, the "rationality" of our actions and the "non-problematic" nature of situations is a continual accomplishment of social action. Conversely, shared assumptions about reality become taken-for-granted and, like a self-fulfilling prophecy, create "objective" situations which exert constraint upon us.[21]

If social reality is the outcome of interpretive "work"—that is the practical accomplishment of members using commonsense schemes of interpretation—it

---

[21] See also the work of Zimmerman and Sudnow referred to in the previous chapter.

follows that means of research which avoid the everyday world (demographic analysis, multiple-choice questionnaires, behaviourist laboratory studies) are sociologically of limited value. Garfinkel's own studies suggest two alternatives. First, an analysis of discussions between participants to reveal the nature of the language used to type actions and people and the manner of decision-making in the context of organizational rules. We learn through such means how attribution to a subject of a particular form of mental illness fits the practical requirements of a bureaucratized hospital service and how even sexual identity is not simply pre-given but accomplished (see the case of the transvestite, Agnes, in Garfinkel, 1967).[22] Second, Garfinkel sets about creating disturbances in accepted settings in order to reveal the assumptions about "normality", "routineness" and "rationality" which sustain the "objective" character of the social world for members. Since background expectancies are by their nature taken-for-granted— that is, accepted on a preconscious level, it is arguable that only by making trouble in presumptively non-problematic social scenes can implicit typifications and expectations be brought to the fore and a worthwhile account of social "work" by members offered. Garfinkel reports the activities of his students told to act as a "lodger" in their own families, to doubt the sincerity of the other or to act illegally in a board-game, thus revealing how order in different social scenes is routinely produced and sustained.[23] Peter McHugh, following this approach, has used the laboratory situation to make his own kind of trouble.

McHugh (1968) invited college students to participate in a series of psychotherapeutic counselling sessions.[24] They were informed that the sessions were designed to assess a new method of counselling in which the counsellor would only answer "Yes" or "No" to questions, thus speeding up the interview. Those willing to participate were asked to present a general statement of their problems to the counsellor and then to ask ten questions. After each question, they should comment on the reply and, at the termination of the session, they were asked to state what, if anything, they felt they had gained from the interview. What the students did not know was that the answer to their question depended on a random-numbers table—the "Yes" or "No" answer given was thus entirely a chance outcome. Furthermore, the "counsellor" was placed in another room, and, without the participants' knowledge, unable to hear the question or the subsequent comments and, perhaps, to be affected by either.

A surprising outcome of the study was the number of participants who were

---

[22] In order to attribute such qualities to people and activities, participants rely on what Garfinkel calls "documentary method of interpretation". That is to say, they accomplish their accounts by reading *underlying patterns* into talk and action.

[23] "Procedurally it is my preference to start with familiar scenes and ask what can be done to make trouble . . . to produce disorganized interaction should tell us something about how the structures of everyday activities are ordinarily and routinely produced and maintained" (1967, pp. 37–8).

[24] His study is a replication of a study presented in Garfinkel (1967). McHugh's study is also discussed as an example of practical reasoning in Filmer's chapter (p. 223–5).

able to maintain their expectation of a counselling relationship. When faced with different answers to a question repeated during the interview, they reconciled the discrepancy on the grounds that the counsellor had now learned more about them and their problems—some were even grateful for the experience and felt "a lot clearer in their minds". However, many were perplexed by the situation as it unfolded, unable to account for what was happening and searching for an appropriate way to redefine the scene and recreate order out of anomie. The precise nature of the findings are probably less important for our present purpose than the theoretical framework which they enlarge.

McHugh takes as his starting point Thomas's argument that defining situations in certain ways produces a real world for participants. The problem is, however, how are men *able* to define and sustain definitions of situations? The answer no doubt lies in the forms of language which men use and the cultural rules which create a measure of interchangeability of perspectives. Such rules, however, do not simply define our actions and assumptions about the intentions of others. Rules are never complete and always contain "et cetera" clauses; we are compelled to draw upon them in particular ways on the basis of often tenuous pieces of evidence. Social "work" is, therefore, required to sustain rules. Furthermore, in such work, rules and the background expectancies attached to their use are frequently changed.

It follows that the meanings of situations are not simply pre-given. On the contrary, in McHugh's terms, they possess the properties of emergence and relativity. That is to say, meanings are never complete (for instance, the meaning of a situation changes when viewed retrospectively) and are relative to certain scenes and to the unique biographies of the participants. Both these properties were apparent as the students in their different ways defined and redefined the counselling situation. But this does not explain the circumstances in which people perceive sufficient disorder in a situation to question their original definition of what has been going on. On this point McHugh argues that an activity is perceived as strange when we cannot apply our background expectancies to it in any intelligible way.[25] More precisely, disorder occurs when an actor believes that the purpose of an interaction is incomprehensible or that no means are available by which any purpose may be attained by the interaction. In the case of the students, an anomic situation was created when their background expectancies of the appropriate purpose of a counsellor/counselled relationship were perceived to be invalid. It was strengthened when many of them were unable to understand either what the counsellor's intentions were or how the situation might be turned to their own advantage. McHugh's manner of making trouble is clearly different from the normal use of the "laboratory" method since it involves an attempt to make members' theories more comprehensible rather than seeking to examine responses, usually as measured in physical acts, to an

---

[25] McHugh argues that "meaning" is not the *content* of the description of an object but the *rule* which is used to assign the experience to a particular category. We perceive disorder, therefore, when we cannot apply any rule to a situation.

"objective" stimulus.[26] The former concern has also been expressed in empirical studies by Cicourel and Kitsuse which have used tape-recorded interviews and discussions as research instruments. I propose to outline very briefly the outcome of these studies, to examine the theoretical apparatus which they develop and to comment on their methodological implications.

V

In their study of an American high school, Cicourel and Kitsuse (1963a) posed themselves two research tasks: (1) the exploration of the vocabulary and syntax of the language used by school personnel to distinguish significant student types; and (2) the consequences of this classification process for the career of students within the high school. Both areas may appear somewhat surprising given the usual assumptions about the predominance in the United States of a "contest" mobility system in which selection is delayed as long as possible so that all students run the same race under the same conditions. Furthermore, it might seem that acts of interpretation by teachers and student counsellors would be severely limited in the American school system where so much attention is paid to "objective" criteria of measuring students' abilities—notably regular IQ tests and a continuing "grade-point" average. Cicourel and Kitsuse, however, introduce a great deal of material which suggests that these conventional wisdoms are somewhat inaccurate.

First, objective records (which also include the expressed intentions of students with reference to entering college) do not necessarily speak for themselves. They must be interpreted by school personnel and never more so than when the records are inconsistent.[27] Second, school personnel are not unaware of (and often support) a national priority in a rapidly changing age to identify and develop talent. This clearly must involve a "sponsorship" element in mobility through which talented students are identified at an early age and given special treatment. Third, a bureaucratized system like the American high school requires a set of labels to be applied to students in order to maximize the opportunity of school personnel to apply their specialized talents where needed. Finally, the professionalization of counselling and the recognition of the social sciences as legitimate disciplines has opened the gate to the use of a wide variety of imponderable personal and social factors (in addition to the "objective" measures of ability) when assessing students' performance and potential.

As a consequence of these conditions, school personnel have developed a variety of labels to be applied to students ranging from "excellent" to "opportunity" (the latter a euphemism for a student who demonstrates neither inherent ability nor satisfactory present performance). Most interesting are the categories "underachiever" and "overachiever" both applied to students with a discrepancy

---

[26] I have in mind behaviourist studies (such as those that measure the blinking of eyes in response to a "threatening" situation or sociable behaviour in response to "praise").

[27] What is a teacher to make of a student with a high IQ but a poor performance in class (or the converse)?

between IQ and GP average—a discrepancy which is uniformly explained by reference to the personal characteristics of the students concerned. Before labels are applied it is clear that acts of interpretation are required from the school personnel about not only the "real" characteristics of a student but also the appropriate distribution of students among the various, organizationally defined categories.[28] Furthermore, in the context of a bureaucracy, the labelling of a student creates for him a certain type of career, with given contingencies and rewards during his stay at the school and a likely direction for further study. The process that emerges is, moreover, clearly likely to be self-confirming in terms of students' self-conceptions as well as of teachers' and counsellors' labels.[29]

Cicourel's (1968) later study of the careers of several young people in the process of becoming "juvenile delinquents" also illustrates the patterns of commonsense reasoning which underlie the production of certain types of career-passages. Very briefly, the policemen in the communities that Cicourel examined were subject to the exigencies of a vast number of rules relating to standardized procedures and reports. Having limited opportunities for mobility and restricted in-group relationships, they developed a police argot to explain in shorthand their common experiences. At the same time, when dealing with offenders they had to work within the confines of the law and (in the case of juveniles) of welfare regulations. When explaining "what happened", for instance in the arrest of a "delinquent", Cicourel found that policemen set about fitting their argot into the official categories. Where an officer was convinced that an offence had been committed, his translation of a commonsense category into a legal framework could be fairly arbitrary.

The significance of all this is that, whether or not court action ensues, a label is applied to a juvenile and the possibility of a particular career is opened. Moreover, policemen themselves use certain assumptions about typical career-passages when dealing with deviants: their accounts are both retrospective ("always been bad", "a born loser") and prospective ("bound for trouble"). Indeed this "creation or generation of history" (Cicourel, 1968, p. 328) goes back to before the police contact with the juvenile since police officers' informal recipes for success include an organization of the city into areas where trouble can be expected and areas where little difficulty should arise and it is necessary to tread carefully if it does since vested interests are likely to be involved.

The generation of delinquent careers cannot be separated, then, from the contingencies of practical decision-making within a bureaucraticized police and legal system. Policemen, probation officers, schoolteachers, lawyers and judges apply a series of typifications and recipes in their dealings with what becomes a juvenile delinquent. Delinquent careers are created by their activities and by their self-confirming ex post facto accounts of what "went on". For instance,

---

[28] Any planning for the future, especially with regard to the hiring of staff, must necessarily depend upon an assumed distribution of any year of students between the various categories.

[29] "The classification of students activates an organizational recording system that has important feedback effects tending progressively to *reinforce* the limitations and opportunities of the students' initial placement" (Cicourel and Kitsuse, 1963a, p. 61).

policemen, like all of us, select propositions in giving their evidence in order to justify their past actions as "normal" and "legitimate". The delinquent emerges as a result of the negotiation of history.[30]

Cicourel's account of the social organization of juvenile justice is to be distinguished from other work in the field by its continual assertion of the centrality of the issue of order to empirical investigation. This becomes clear in Cicourel's avoidance of the use of explanations which rely upon unexamined characteristics attributed to the social structure (for example, social "forces" or "needs" which motivate or structure the entrance into delinquent activity). Such explanations, he argues, *impose* an order instead of considering the social "work" that produces its unique character.[31] Instead of social-structural explanations of an actor's behaviour (as measured by a structural indicator), he calls for an analysis of the *sense* of social structure (what is routine, what is appropriate) that underlies human action. Only in the natural attitude are social structures perceived as "things"; for sociologists, structure must necessarily be viewed as a human product made available by social activities.

If Cicourel's metatheory is different from much conventional sociology, so is his research strategy. The research-worker, he implies, must generate his own data. Official records provide material that is insufficient, not because it is "wrong" or "distorted" but rather because it reflects a series of unknown decisions.[32] Methods must be used which reveal the way in which members' theories combine with formal rules and practices to allow the definition of present and past events ("decoding") and the preparation of the scene for further action ("encoding"). The researcher will thus be less concerned with counting (in terms of his own operational categories or of official statistics) than with understanding how members count (encode) and place interpretations on the counting of others (decode).

Cicourel's manner of gathering his data—participant-observation, tape-recordings of discussions and collation of official reports and court transcripts—is a direct reflection of his theoretical stance. It may seem, however, to follow a fairly traditional path; that of the *qualitative* study recommended by all the conventional texts when the research area seems unsuitable for "counting" and the intention is primarily exploratory. Yet Cicourel's purpose and method is entirely different. The traditional approach makes use of actors' statements and conversations as illustrative of an order to which both the actor *and* the sociologist address themselves. Lay depictions of social order are inserted as anecdotes in research reports as a means of strengthening an argument. What Cicourel is

---

[30] It should be added that the delinquent also participates in this negotiation. Traditional "labelling" theory has sometimes been criticized for paying insufficient attention to the object of the label (and the processes of practical reasoning which allow labelling activity to take place).

[31] Compare, for instance, Cicourel and Kitsuse's account of high-school careers with studies which link educational performance to structural indicators like social class.

[32] "Truncated official records 'freeze' the temporal properties of emergent interaction so that what is 'managed' by the police and probation officers in making decisions—the negotiated and bargaining character of assigning charges and making dispositions—are distorted by a conventional search for 'objective' indicators of delinquency and official actions" (Cicourel, 1968, pp. 103–4).

trying to do, on the other hand, is to reveal how actors' accounts of social process sustain an order which has only the *appearance* of objective facticity, which merely *presents* itself as "an exterior field of events amenable to lawful investigation" (Zimmerman and Pollner, 1971). As a consequence, his very detailed analysis of the language used in conversations and reports serves to point out and to confirm the existence of the background expectancies and folk typifications used in everyday life. Put very simply, actors' theories, in Cicourel's approach, are used as a topic of inquiry but not as a resource to provide a theoretical orientation. We move, in his work, from an understanding of subjective meanings to a conception of social order which is fundamentally different from that found in the natural attitude.[33]

VI

At this point in the paper, the researcher or student may well comment: All very well—but how do you test the assertions drawn from such data? How do you validate a finding that is not and, as you argue, *cannot* be expressed quantitatively?[34]

One way of answering this legitimate question is to point out that the problem of validation revolves around wider issues than simply the proof of an explanation. It is not just a matter of *verifying* a relationship between A and B, we must also be able to convince the reader that both A and B exist. To put it another way—the validation of an empirical finding requires both verification and "objectification". This latter issue is usually a "non-problem" in sociological research. Through his technical skill in creating indices and scales or by reference to official statistics (which may be "partial" or "distorted" but nonetheless reflect the properties of an "objective" order), the sociologist gathers his data. To doubt its reality as a reflection of social process is to criticize the technical competence of the researcher or to indulge in a philosophical quibble. The problem then resolves itself into a statistical test of the relations between non-problematic "variables" and the verification or (if the researcher is a Popperian) the failure to refute a "finding"—an issue considered at length in Chapter 2.

Such research fails at two levels. It fails to objectify its data because its references to attitudes and behaviour pay no attention to the background expectancies and processes of practical reasoning through which members make sense of their environment. It also fails to verify its findings because the researcher

[33] "The crucial task is to specify how the content of messages contained in interviews and official reports provide the [actors] . . . with the basis for deciding 'what happened' and the next course of action. A detailed analysis of the language of conversations and the language of official reports has the methodological significance of not relying upon illustrative quotations examined only by implication and indirectly; the researcher must make explicit remarks as to the meaning of the communication exchanges. Thus a particular case must reveal something of the structure of all social action . . . references to communication content are not intended as anecdotes left for the reader to interpret" (Cicourel, 1968, p. 113).

[34] Quantification fails when it seeks to remedy the sloppiness and incompleteness of the data. This avoids the central issue of how "sloppy" talk and "incomplete" actions routinely produce the features of a "real" social order.

omits to treat his own background expectancies as a topic for study. As a consequence, the natural attitude provides him with an unexplored resource to be used in affixing labels to phenomena in the coding of data, the provision of "reasonable" hypotheses and the avoidance of time-wasting with "unlikely" relationships. Only by attention to the properties of background expectancies can studies of social process be validated.[35] Thus the critique is stood on its head—if we are to look for sociological research conducted on unsure ground, we would do well to pay attention to what is conventionally accepted as legitimate.

A way of responding to the issue of validation which complements Cicourel's analysis has been developed by the American humanistic psychologist, Carl Rogers. According to Rogers (1965), the central problem can be expressed as "how do we know?" Our knowledge is grounded in the way in which we check our hypotheses and both for the sociologist and for man as the practical theoretician in his everyday life there are three ways of knowing:

1. "Subjective" knowing is knowledge which is checked by reference to inner experience—I know that I am in pain even if a doctor can find nothing wrong with me.
2. "Objective" knowing is checked by reference to my peer group and its norms —thus as a scientist I know that the earth travels around the sun rather than vice-versa.
3. "Interpersonal" knowing, or what Rogers calls phenomenological knowledge, is checked by reference to my knowledge of your knowledge—I know that the expression on your face indicates that you are reacting unfavourably to my argument.

Rogers's contention is that methodologists and researchers have paid inordinate attention to the "objective" mode of knowing, generally without recognizing that the other types of knowledge have been equally important in empirical research. The behaviouralist who argues for "objective" knowing as the sole source of scientific certitude omits a characteristic of his own experience— that in his own research, as in his everyday life, he is governed by a pragmatic motive, being content to fashion "reasonable" propositions and to make assumptions about the intentions of the Other.[36] A concentration on "objective"

---

[35] "The problems of objectification and verification cannot be resolved by appeals to technical skills in capturing or 'bottling' the phenomena invoked as observational sources of data. The sociologist must come to grips with the problem of making the background expectancies visible to the reader" (Cicourel, 1968, p. 15). This implies a further means of validation—if the background expectancies have been revealed, it should be possible to feed them back into the situation (by programming an untutored participant) and accomplish what the participants define as a "normal" performance (see Cicourel 1970a). The converse of this is to *remove* a background expectancy—that is, to "make trouble"—see pages 223–5 for further discussion.

[36] Blum similarly argues that "the social organization of knowledge is describable not in terms of the 'structural' properties of events-in-the-world which the knowledge is intended to formulate, but rather as a product of the informed understandings negotiated among members of an organized intellectual collectivity" (1970, pp. 320–1). I do not seek to deny that this also applies to ethnomethodology. All knowledge, it would seem, is ultimately commonsense knowledge (see Pollner, 1970) inasmuch as all inquiry presupposes an objective world whose existence is independent of the

knowledge alone typifies the research posture, criticized by Cicourel, which fails to bring to the surface the background expectancies of the actors and of the researcher. For, as Rogers points out, "objectivity" can only be concerned with objects, whether animate or inanimate—it transforms everything it studies into an object or perceives it only in its object aspects—that is, as acted upon but not acting. Furthermore, it depends upon a paradigm of the appropriate "scientific" method which necessarily changes as the universe of objects in the field is regularly challenged within the professional peer group.

VII

This paper began by offering "a rather simplified" critique of conventional views of the research process. I have attempted, however, to add to the polemic some discussion of alternative lines of action which, I believe, are currently proving more fruitful. I hope the time for polemic is passing and that we can proceed, in a rather less self-conscious way, about the business of building such alternatives.

SUGGESTIONS FOR FURTHER READING

Cicourel (1964) provides the basic text to deal with the critique of contemporary methodologies and to present an outline of some alternatives. Garfinkel (1967) is altogether harder but ultimately rewarding, while J. Douglas (1970b) offers a collection of papers which illustrate the potentialities of sociological research.

---

inquiry itself—that is, it seeks to remedy the indexicality of accounts. This ultimately produces what Cicourel calls a "self-validating circle" for in all accounts (including ethnomethodology) the gloss we use to describe the world confirms our view of it. The only obvious path away from the abyss is to treat the glossing activity itself as the object of study.

The work of Harold Garfinkel is of central importance to the understanding of pheno-menological sociology in general and of ethnomethodology in particular. Most important here are Garfinkel's discussions of the central concepts of ethnomethodology, namely "indexicality", "reflexivity" and "rational accountability". Filmer's chapter examines Garfinkel's characterization of ethnomethodology by a detailed explication of these concepts, and by a discussion of some problematic features of Garfinkel's own explications and application of them.

A particular problem identified in this review is that of the process by which rules, or formal structures, of everyday social interactions are generated. After explication of Garfinkel's ethnomethodological account of the manner in which this process is accomplished, the suggestion is made that it may be illuminated further by ideas drawn from Chomsky's rule-governed linguistics and the structuralist anthropology of Lévi-Strauss. Some of the concerns of their work, it is proposed, run closely parallel to some concerns of ethnomethodological analysis.

NINE

On Harold Garfinkel's
Ethnomethodology

PAUL FILMER

INTRODUCTION: THE INITIAL RELEVANCE OF
GARFINKEL'S ETHNOMETHODOLOGY

In their recent work, *The Social Construction of Reality*, Berger and Luckmann
(1966) claim to have attempted "a redefinition of the problems and tasks of the
sociology of knowledge" and a clarification of its theoretical perspectives, and
thereby to have produced "some general implications for sociological theory and
the sociological enterprise at large" (p. 207). Their conclusions, however, are
programmatic in espousing what they regard as an attainable ideal of a humanistic
sociology, the "proper object of inquiry" of which is "society as part of a human
world, made by men, inhabited by men, and, in turn, making men, in an ongoing
historical process" (p. 211).[1] Nevertheless, from their work there emerge certain
prerequisites and concomitants to the attainment of this ideal, any inventory
of which includes, as prerequisites:

1. A sociology of language (which a sociology of knowledge presupposes).
2. A sociology of religion (without which a sociology of knowledge is
   impossible).
3. A dialectical perspective, to be brought to bear upon the theoretical orientation of the social sciences, proceeding "to a specification of the dialectical
   processes in a conceptual framework that is congruent with the great traditions
   of sociological thought", in order to facilitate "an understanding of what

---

[1] The prerequisites and concomitants of Berger and Luckmann's reorientation which follow are
summarized by them (pp. 207–11) in a somewhat different order from the one in which I have given
them here.

Marcel Mauss called the 'total social fact' (which) will protect the sociologist against the distortive reifications of both sociologism and psychologism".

4. "Empirical research in the relation of institutions to legitimating symbolic universes" (on the grounds that this "will greatly enhance the sociological understanding of contemporary society").

And as concomitants:

1. A comprehensive theory of social action (to be developed from a combination of the theoretical positions of Weber and Durkheim—without losing the inner logic of either).
2. A sociological psychology (to be developed from the linkage made between the sociology of knowledge and the theoretical core of the thought of Mead and his school—that is, "a psychology that derives its fundamental perspectives from a sociological understanding of the human condition").
3. An "analysis of the role of knowledge in the dialectic of individual and society, of personal identity and social structure"—that is, "a systematic accounting of the dialectical relation between the structural realities and the human enterprise of constructing reality in history" ("a crucial complementary perspective for all areas of sociology").

In the existentialist/humanistic terms in which Berger and Luckmann conceive of him,[2] the sociologist is nothing if not a man of some kind of action; for example, at the very least professional, academic action, perhaps in the form of empirical research on the lines indicated in prerequisite (4). Indeed, the sociologist who, on reading their work, finds himself sympathetic towards it, cannot but be fired with enthusiasm to attempt implementation of the (albeit colossal) programme it proposes. Yet herein lies a problem: how to proceed? What are to be the logic and means of procedure of "humanistic sociology"? For Berger and Luckmann state only, and emphatically, that:

1. Their ideas posit neither an ahistorical "social system" nor an ahistorical "human nature".
2. Their approach is both non-sociologistic and non-psychologistic.
3. They "have no polemic interest in writing this book".
4. They "must consider the standard versions of functionalist explanations in the social sciences a theoretical legerdemain".
5. They are convinced "that a purely structural sociology is endemically in danger of reifying social phenomena".
6. Their "approach is non-positivistic, if positivism is understood as a philosophical position defining the object of the social sciences in such a way as to legislate away their most important problems". (Though they "do not underestimate the merit of 'positivism', broadly understood, in redefining the canons of empirical investigation for the social sciences"!)
7. They "have expressly refrained from following up the methodological implications of [their] conception of the society of knowledge".

---

[2] See especially Berger (1966, chapter 1, 2 and 8).

8. Their conception of sociology in general does *not* imply
   (*a*) that sociology is *not* a science;
   (*b*) that its methods should be *other* than empirical; or
   (*c*) that it *cannot* be "value-free".

More positively, they do say their conception of the subject implies not only that it is a humanistic discipline, but also that it "must be carried on in a continuous conversation with both history and philosophy or lose its proper object of inquiry" (Berger and Luckmann, 1966, pp. 207–11). Nevertheless, an unavoidable overall impression remains of equivocal negativism, and those sociologists who might have been moved to professional action by Berger and Luckmann's work may be forgiven deep reservations in the face of this.

I want to suggest, however, by discussing the work of Harold Garfinkel, that ethnomethodology provides a solution to the procedural dilemma (or stasis) of the sociologist who, accepting such a phenomenological critique of the implicit philosophy and methodological concepts of traditional sociology as that which Berger and Luckmann provide, wishes nevertheless to remain professionally active. For, in spite of their implicit assertions that sociology is, or can be, a science; that the use of empirical methods of study should not be denied it; and that it can, in some sense, be value-free, Berger and Luckmann postulate as highly problematic the devices and arguments that sociologists have used traditionally to resolve these issues. Yet nowhere is there to be found in Berger and Luckmann's work any attempt to deal with the crucial methodological implications of their critique—on the contrary, as they state quite explicitly, they "expressly refrained" from doing so, though, regrettably, they neglect to say why.

In his *Studies in Ethnomethodology* (1967) Garfinkel is concerned, it would seem, to establish the existence of a meaningful, ultimate and irreducible level of social reality for the purposes of sociological analysis, and this may be seen as a *constructive* response to the phenomenological critique of traditional sociology. The achievement of his ethnomethodology, then, lies in providing the basis for the substantive sociological study of everyday life. It should be stated at the outset of any attempt to argue for the attribution of such achievement to it, however, that to do so may be to proceed against an express caveat of Garfinkel himself, that

> Ethnomethodological studies are not directed to formulating or arguing correctives. . . . Although they are directed to the preparation of manuals on sociological methods, these are in *no way* supplements to "standard" procedures, but are distinct from them. They do not formulate a remedy for practical actions. . . . Nor are they in search of humanistic arguments, nor do they engage in or encourage permissive discussions of theory (1967, p. viii).

Nevertheless, proceeding in terms of D. H. Lawrence's dictum for literary critics, "Don't trust the writer, trust the tale", I want to examine what Garfinkel has written and how it might be used, rather than what *he* says he has written and how it ought *not* to be used.

WHAT IS ETHNOMETHODOLOGY?

In attempting to establish a reasonably firm answer to this question Garfinkel seems to be of little help, for he offers at least four definitions, plus at least one exegesis of ethnomethodology. All are fairly lengthy and are good examples of what have been referred to as the "dense and elephantine formulations" of ethnomethodologists (Gouldner, 1970, p. 394). However, since they provide a background to what I want to say, and since I shall be referring back to some of them, I want to begin by presenting them, as far as possible in Garfinkel's own words:[3]

Definition 1 :

> Ethnomethodological studies analyse everyday activities as members' methods for making those same activities visibly-rational-and-reportable-for-all-practical-purposes, i.e., "accountable", as organizations of commonplace everyday activities. The reflexivity of that phenomenon is a singular feature of practical actions, of practical circumstances, of commonsense knowledge of social structures, and of practical sociological reasoning. By permitting us to locate and examine their occurrence the reflexivity of that phenomenon establishes their study.
>
> Their study is directed to the tasks of learning how members' actual, ordinary activities consist of methods to make practical actions, practical circumstances, commonsense knowledge of social structures, and practical sociological reasoning analysable; and of discovering the formal properties of commonplace, practical commonsense actions, "from within" actual settings, as ongoing accomplishments of those settings. The formal properties obtain their guarantees from no other source, and in no other way (1967, pp. vii-viii)

Definition 2 :

> [Ethnomethodological studies] seek to treat practical activities, practical circumstances, and practical sociological reasoning as topics of empirical study and, by paying to the most commonplace activities of daily life the attention usually accorded extraordinary events, seek to learn about them as phenomena in their own right. Their central recommendation is that the activities whereby members produce and manage settings of organized everyday affairs are identical with members' procedures for making those settings "accountable". The "reflexive", or "incarnate" character of accounting practices and accounts makes up the crux of that recommendation (ibid., p. 1).

Definition 3 :

> . . . the term "ethnomethodology" . . . refer[s] to the investigation of the rational properties of indexical expressions and other practical actions as contingent accomplishments of organized artful practices of everyday life. [Ethnomethodological studies] treat that accomplishment as the phenomenon of interest. They seek to specify its problematic features, to recommend methods for its study, but above all to consider what we might learn definitely about it (ibid., p. 11).

---

[3] In some cases I have summarized Garfinkel's formulations in the interests of both brevity and clarity. The points at which this has occurred are noted.

Definition 4 :

... the term "ethnomethodology" ... refer[s] to the study of practical actions according to policies such as the following and to the phenomena, issues, findings and methods that accompany their use :[4]

[(a) The possibility that any aspect of every feature of any social occasion or event, performed by anyone in any context, may be a result of choice, makes that occasion or event worthy of study as the managed accomplishment of organized settings of practical actions.]

[(b) The differing structures of organization of] organized practices of everyday life are to be sought out and examined for the production, origins, recognition, and representations of rational practices. [However, these latter phenomena, being themselves] contingent achievements of organizations of common practices [and as such being] variously available to members as norms, tasks, troubles, [should not have their nature pre-empted in terms of some criterion of adequate rationality which is postulated as being universally valid. Since they are contingent achievements of the practices themselves, they must be considered, by definition, in context.]

[(c) Any social setting should be considered as self-organizing, to the degree that it] organizes its activities to make its properties as an organized environment of practical activities accountable [through their rational connections.]

[(d) The demonstrably rational properties of indexical expressions and indexical actions is an ongoing achievement of the organized activities of everyday life.]

At this point, it may be useful to summarize these four definitions and begin their explication. The first of them rests on the contention that the most apparently mundane and commonplace ("everyday") activities of social interaction have a highly systematic and organized character. Yet these are not so much endemic features of the activities, as features which are given to them when they are organized in order that they may be described, explained or summarized coherently (that is, made "visibly-rational-and-reportable-for-all-practical-purposes, i.e. 'accountable'"). This process of giving systematic features to inter-active behaviour in the process of making it accountable is described as its reflexivity since, presumably, the ordered requirements of coherent and articulate linguistic expression reflect upon, by organizing and making systematic, the apparently unordered character of everyday activities. This identifies the point at which order can be seen to be constructed by members out of the apparently disparate variety of everyday activities—that is, in the process of accounting for, or making sense of it—and so shows how the process of establishing order might be studied. The ways in which such study might be effected lie in attempting to learn the practices by which sense, or meaningfulness, is established in the process of describing and explaining interaction of an ordinary, everyday kind at an ordinary, everyday level (that is, by "discovering the formal properties of

---

[4] Ibid., pp. 31–4. The policies themselves are summarized in my own words, with constituent quotations from Garfinkel's formulations of them—except for number 4, which is Garfinkel's own final summary of policy number 5. I have also reduced the number of policies from 5 to 4, since policy 2 in the text (pp. 32–3) seems to me to be a prefatory explanation to policy 3 (p. 33), and not a policy in itself. In my summary, therefore, it has been incorporated into policy 2.

commonplace, practical commonsense actions"). Since the establishment of sense or meaningfulness is part of the process of everyday interaction itself (an "ongoing accomplishment"), it has to be studied by participation in ("from within") the interactions which make it up, because the meaningfulness of these interactions to their participants, or to observers of them, is the only way in which the everyday practices, according to which sense is made of everyday activities, can be shown as valid ("obtain their guarantees").

In definition 2, Garfinkel makes the same point more briefly, but he introduces it by stating that ethnomethodological studies commence from a rejection of the distinctions which are commonplaces of most sociological analyses, between "extraordinary", apparently important events and activities in social life on the one hand, and ordinary, so-called everyday ones on the other. *All* social events and activities, he implies, are of *equal* importance as subjects for ethnomethodological study.

Garfinkel's third definition is the briefest that he gives of the term ethnomethodology. It depends on a crucial distinction[5] between two kinds of expression —indexical and objective—necessarily employed in social interaction and in sociological analysis of it. Indexical expressions refer to the objects they describe in terms of their specificity and uniqueness, and are thus bound by the context in which they are used. Objective expressions, on the other hand, describe the general properties of their referent objects; that is, by those characteristics which establish the objects as typical, one of a type, and therefore as context-free—at least for the purposes at hand of whoever so describes them. Garfinkel's point in emphasizing the distinction between the two kinds of expressions is related to the distinction he draws in definition between commonplace and extraordinary activities. He implies that the very commonplace character of everyday activities is given to them, in part at least, by the kind of expressions which are used to describe them—that is, indexical expressions. Objective expressions are used, for the most part, in discourse which is usually termed formal or scientific—that is, which attempts to formulate propositions which are generally valid about *types* or *classes* of phenomena. In so far as sociology is to be considered as a science, it has to explain the commonplace, everyday social activities which are an important part of its subject matter, in the objective expressions required by formal discourse. Yet these activities, being commonplace and everyday, are also described adequately at a commonplace, everyday level, with indexical expressions, by the individuals who carry them out. Thus, sociology begins to explain them "scientifically" by substituting objective for indexical expressions in describing them; and Garfinkel suggests that such substitution may be unnecessary, on the grounds that indexical expressions can be shown to have rational properties through their ability to present the *ordered* character of everyday social activities in members' everyday accounts of those activities. The skills and techniques involved in the employment of the rational properties of indexical expressions in everyday life are the subject matter of

---

[5] The distinction is referred to here only briefly and will be discussed more fully below.

ethnomethodology. In particular, ethnomethodology seeks to ascertain what can definitely be known about the accomplishment of sense in the presentation of accounts of everyday activities in everyday life, by an examination of what is problematic about this accomplishment, and by developing methods for studying the processes by which it is achieved.

The fourth definition of ethnomethodology given by Garfinkel presents it as the study of practical actions and contains a summary of the points raised in the previous three definitions as examples of programmes ("policies") according to which this study should proceed. He adds, implicitly, that such a study is itself a reflexive activity, since it involves a study of the "phenomena, issues, findings and methods" that are involved in its constituent programmes.

In addition to these definitions, Garfinkel identifies the central topic of his studies (and, we must assume, of ethnomethodology also) as "the rational accountability of practical actions as ongoing, practical accomplishments". That is, rephrased as a question: How are practical, everyday interactions explicable in a reasoned fashion? Garfinkel justifies this as the central topic of ethnomethodology on five grounds, which may be summarized as follows:[6]

1. In giving accounts of actual situations, members will use terms which define or suspend the operation of factors which might typically be expected, by themselves and their audiences, to be contingent upon the situations they are explaining, in order to prevent the possibility of alternative explanations emerging to the ones that they will propose in their accounts.

2. The accounts will make sense to members' audiences because of the contextual knowledge they all assume that they share; and this knowledge will be a tacit feature of their interaction.

3. The accounts have a "wait-and-see" quality, in that not all of the knowledge which will be imparted in them to make sense of the actions they are accounting for, will be available simultaneously with the data being explained. Thus, parts of the account, during the process of its being given, will not make full sense until the whole account is completed.

4. The accounts are systematically and sequentially constructed.

5. The materials or parts of an account depend heavily upon context for their sense. Context can mean their sequence in the account, the biography of the member constructing the account, or the wider context in which the situation being accounted for has occurred.

Garfinkel further specifies the central topic of ethnomethodology by reviewing three of what he terms its

constituent, problematic phenomena. Wherever studies of practical reasoning are concerned, these consist of the following: (1) the unsatisfied programmatic distinction between and substitutability of objective (context-free) for indexical expressions;

---

[6] Ibid., pp. 3–4. In order to make a clearer explication of them than might be possible otherwise, the justifications have been rephrased and, in some cases, expanded from Garfinkel's text.

(2) the "uninteresting" essential reflexivity of accounts of practical actions; and (3) the analysability of actions-in-context as a practical accomplishment (ibid., p. 4).[7]

From the foregoing definitions and exegesis, two points emerge clearly: first that, according to ethnomethodology, sociology is the study of all aspects of everyday social life, however trivial they may seem, just as much as it is the study of extraordinary events; and second, that sociology is, in an important sense, itself an everyday activity. Garfinkel refers frequently in his writings to "practical sociological reasoning" and in doing so implies two parallel distinctions: (1) between what he calls professional and what may be termed "lay" sociology; and (2) between what he calls practical and what be termed "theoretical" or "formal" sociological reasoning. Garfinkel is arguing, it seems, that all men-in-society or what he calls all "collectivity members"[8] (this term is extremely important and will be discussed below) are sociologists in the sense that, by attributing meanings to, and claiming understanding of, one another's activities, they are all practical theorists. They are "doing sociology, lay and professional, making activities observable" (ibid., p. 2). So that practical sociological reasoning may be seen as the process which underwrites "the managed accomplishment of organized settings of practical actions" (ibid., p. 32); that is, as the basis of lay sociology. Garfinkel implies that there is no radical difference between professional sociologists and other men by what appears to be a deliberate blurring of any distinctions between them. For example, he adds the phrase *"professional sociologists included"* to the term "members" on one occasion; and on the same page exemplifies the investigator in a sociological inquiry as "a professional sociologist or a person undertaking an inquiry about social structures in the interests of managing his practical everyday affairs" (ibid., p. 77). Equally, though, the point of this emphasis would seem to be to encourage professional sociologists to behave more self-consciously, or ecstatically, as Berger would put it, than lay sociologists, in order that they should be able better to take account of their own involvement in the everyday world. The necessity for this is made crucial for Garfinkel precisely because the major, if not the only point of differentiation between the lay and professional sociologist is that the latter, at least, has both the ability and the obligation to reflect upon the structuring of sociological phenomena under investigation—which structuring may be a result of the very process of investigation itself.

It is at this point that the third of Garfinkel's definitions of ethnomethodology (given below) becomes illuminating—especially so, since it links up, in turn, with the first of the "three constituent problematic phenomena" of the central topic of ethnomethodology also referred to earlier, namely, "the unsatisfied programmatic distinction between and substitutability of objective for indexical expressions".

To amplify somewhat the distinctions made earlier: indexical expressions

---

[7] Each of these "constituent, problematic phenomena" are discussed by Garfinkel at length on pp. 4–10.

[8] See ibid., p. 57 and footnote, p. 76 and footnote.

refer to persons, places, objects, events and so on, in a way which represents them in the specific uniqueness of their particular and concrete manifestations. They are expressions, that is to say, which depend strictly upon context for their meaning—they are context-bound,[9] whereas objective expressions represent phenomena in terms of their general properties; ideally, they do not depend for their meaning upon the specific context of the particular manifestations of the phenomena they are used to describe, in the strict sense that their indexical counterparts do, and are thus intended by their users to be considered "context-free". Objective expressions are the only basis from which any study wishing to be considered a science in the archetypical terms of the natural sciences can proceed, for they make formal discourse possible—that is, they make possible the formulation of general statements about phenomena which are of near-universal validity under specifiable limiting conditions. They make possible the establishment of general categories or classes of phenomena, the constituent items of which are mutually substitutable for all practical purposes, in all situations wherein the conditions upon which their category or class membership depends are operative.

Garfinkel points out that, in spite of the "enormous utility" of indexical expressions, "they are 'awkward for formal discourse' " (1967, p. 5); and this can be seen as especially true for sociology. Indeed, the problem of substituting objective for indexical expressions may be seen as yet another formulation of the problem of the definition of social phenomena; for it is exactly the same problem which Durkheim (1938) attempted to solve in his methodological injunction to treat social phenomena as "things" (*"comme des choses"*). Typically, professional sociologists (even professional sociological theorists) will take this problem to have been solved; as Garfinkel points out:

> Areas in the social sciences where the promised distinction and promised substitutability occur are countless. The promised distinction and substitutability are supported by and themselves support immense resources directed to developing methods for the strong analysis of practical actions and practical reasoning. Promised applications and benefits are immense (1967, p. 6).

And it hardly needs reiterating that, without the possibility of such a distinction and substitutability, a so-called scientific or even, simply, systematic sociology would not be possible. The ways by which it is achieved, of course, are well known as positivism, functionalism and so on—the principal traditional "schools" of sociological theory and explanation. Yet it is at this point that Garfinkel raises the issue afresh, for he argues that

> *wherever practical actions are topics of study* the promised distinction and substitutability of objective for indexical expressions remains programmatic in every *particular* case and in every *actual* occasion in which the distinction must be demonstrated. In every

---

[9] For a detailed discussion of the philosophical and semiological importance of indexical expressions, see Bar-Hillel (1954). Garfinkel has further clarified his conceptualization of the importance of indexical expressions in ethnomethodological analysis: see Garfinkel and Sacks (1970, especially pp. 348–50).

actual case without exception, conditions will be cited that a competent investigator will be required to recognize, such that in that particular case the terms of the demonstration can be relaxed and nevertheless the demonstration be counted an adequate one (ibid., p. 6).

In other words, Garfinkel is contending that what we take to be the objective features of social reality are objective only because we express them in objective terms; that is, in terms of their common properties. Moreover, these common properties, it is implied, are not necessarily intrinsic to the objects and events themselves, but are given to them by the manner in which they are described; having no objective nature, they are, quite literally, given objective expression. So that traditional, established forms of sociological explanation may be seen as a set of mechanisms, a coding vocabulary, for the expression of certain phenomena in a way that accentuates their common properties rather than their specifically unique ones. That this is a feature of sociological explanation is not a startlingly new revelation—though Garfinkel puts it in a relatively original way. What is new, however, is Garfinkel's argument that it is a feature of all explanation. For this is to imply that at an everyday level the process of explanation is synonymous with the construction of social reality, of social life, itself. Thus, in accounting for their actions in a rational way, members are *making* those actions rational and thus making social life a coherent and comprehensible reality in a way that underlines the constructed nature of all reality.

An element occurring in each of the first two definitions of ethno-methodology, given earlier, now becomes relevant. It is identified most distinctly as the second of the three "constituent, problematic phenomena" of the central topic of ethnomethodology—"the 'uninteresting' essential reflexivity of accounts of practical actions". Garfinkel argues that all practical everyday accounts of all collectivity members, whether lay or professional sociologists, are reflexive at the commonsense levels (see ibid., p. 8). In other words, the very process of a member accounting for his unique and specific actions typifies them in terms of a framework of meaning which he shares with all other collectivity members; that is, commonsense. For, as Schutz has pointed out:

> Language as used in daily life . . . is primarily a language of named things and events. Now any name includes a typification. . . . By naming an experienced object, we are relating it by its typicality to pre-experienced things of similar typical structures, and we accept its open horizon referring to future experiences of the same type, which are therefore capable of being given the same name (1962, p. 285).

A member's expression of his experiences in the terms and concepts of common-sense involves their *typification*, while simultaneously depriving them of their specificity and uniqueness as his own *individual* experiences. Schutz expresses this paradox effectively when he says (following Husserl) that

> all forms of recognition and identification, even of real objects of the outer world, are based on a generalized knowledge of the *type* of these objects or of the *typical* style in which they manifest themselves. Strictly speaking, each experience is unique, and even the same experience that recurs is not the same, because it recurs. It is recurrent a

sameness, and as such it is experienced in a different context and with different adumbrations. . . . [Yet each type of object] has its typical style of being experienced, and the knowledge of this typical style is itself an element of our stock of knowledge at hand. The same holds good for the relations in which the objects stand to one another, for events and occurrences and their mutual relations, and so on (1964, pp. 284–5).

Thus, the *social* existence of a member's experiences, the fact that they are "known" in a sense which can be attested to and validated, is only established through their typification. And the process of their becoming known, through typificatory expression, is in itself the principle of organization of the experiences. Thus the accounting process is automatically or, as Garfinkel says, "essentially" reflexive upon the experiences themselves, depriving them of their uniqueness and specificity at the very moment, and by the very process, that they become known at all.

At this point, certain confusions seem to arise concerning Garfinkel's distinction between indexical and objective expressions. Since he first introduces objective expressions by describing them as "context-free", it seems reasonable to infer that indexical expressions, with which they are contrasted, are context-bound. Yet if this is the case, and if indexical expressions are a part of everyday language, and if, also—as Schutz's arguments suggest—the expressions of everyday language are meaningful, even as commonsense, only by virtue of their typifying properties in the description of experience, then do not these typifying properties of indexical expressions release them to some extent from the limitations of context? If this is so, then two further interrelated questions arise: first, how can there be any expressions that are context-bound to the extent of expressing the uniqueness and specificity of individual members' experiences, when their very existence as expressions depends upon their typifying properties? And second, what is the difference between objective and indexical expressions, if both of them are context-free by virtue of their existence as expressions?

The answer to the first question would appear to be in not inferring too strictly, from Garfinkel's description of objective expressions as "context-free", that indexical expressions are, by converse implication, context-bound. Thus, the second question is answered, presumably, by postulating a difference in degree, either of context-freedom between the two types of expressions, or of their ability to typify members' experiences when employed in accounting for them. Indexical expressions are thus characterized as adequate for the level of typification required in the accounting of so-called commonplace experiences; and objective expressions for that required by formal discourse.[10]

---

[10] It is interesting to note here that Schutz avoids possible confusion when drawing a similar distinction between commonsense and scientific explanation by differentiating between the kinds of "constructs of thought-objects" they produce for the interpretation of human action (1962, pp. 3–96, but especially pp. 7–47). This is not to imply a criticism of Garfinkel for persisting with the term indexical, however, since it carries connotations of reflexivity which are important to his arguments, as I have tried to indicate subsequently in the text. Moreover, other discussions of indexicality by ethnomethodologists have also, and similarly, revealed its highly problematic character; for example Garfinkel and Sacks (1970), also the papers by Cicourel, Douglas, Manning, Wilson in Douglas (1970b).

It is because members' uses of indexical expressions of everyday language in accounting for their everyday activities and experiences cannot help but typify them, that Garfinkel is able to demonstrate the "essential reflexivity of accounts of practical actions" and, more importantly, the phenomenon that this feature of accounts is "uninteresting" to practical social theorists. By referring to it as "uninteresting" Garfinkel clearly does not mean that it is unworthy of investigation, but that it remains typically and recurrently uninvestigated. That this should be the case for lay, practical social theorists in all their interactions is not surprising, since to investigate it (which would, of course, involve an acknowledgment of its existence) would be, at the least, a bewildering experience for the members concerned, for it would involve calling directly into question the sense of precisely that sense (that is, commonsense) which they take to be beyond question. For, as Garfinkel emphasizes,

> *recognizable* sense, or fact, or methodic character, or impersonality, or objectivity of accounts are not independent of the socially organized occasions of their use. Their rational features *consist* of what members do with, what they "make of" the accounts in the socially organized actual occasions of their use. Members' accounts are reflexively and essentially tied for their rational features to the socially organized occasions of their use for they are *features* of the socially organized occasions of their use (1967, pp. 3–4).

The reluctance of professional sociologists to investigate the essential reflexivity of accounts, however, especially in their professional sociology, is part of the problem to which ethnomethodology is addressed.

Professional sociologists present accounts of practical actions at a minimum of two levels: the first is the everyday level in making rational and accountable their own practical actions as men—in this sense there is *literally* no difference between sociologists and other men. The second level is the formal or professional sociological level, the level at which they are studying, as opposed to simply doing, sociology. And at this level they will be making rational and accountable the actions of other men—the subjects of their inquiring studies—in terms of a formal mode of sociological explanation, not in terms of everyday commonsense. Yet this second level of presenting accounts must be incorporated into the first, since it is part of the everyday practical actions of the professional sociologist. Thus, the latter, in his work and with his professional colleagues, accounts for practical actions in what is presumed to be a reasoned and coherent context of common meanings, or sense-in-common, which is yet not commonsense at all, but is the context or sense of formal sociological explanation. That is, in order to account for everyday interactions rationally, they are expressed in the rationally related, objective terms and concepts of formal sociological explanation. Thus, although they may not initially, or intrinsically, have rational properties, or be rationally accountable, they are given these properties reflexively in the very process of being accounted for in formal sociological terms. Garfinkel's main point would seem to be that, whilst this is obviously so in the professional accounts of sociologists, it is also—though less obviously—the case in the everyday accounts of all societal or collectivity members.

The implications of this for sociological methodologies are quite radical. For it implies that there is an implicitly formalized body of explanatory terms and concepts utilized by all social actors, whether or not they are professional sociologists, in making rational and coherent sense of their activities. This would have to be so, given the indexical properties of the terms of everyday language used to account for their activities by collectivity members, and given the process by which, despite these indexical properties of language, accounts of individual activities become *socially* (that is, collectively) known, in their verbal expression, as comparable to, and typifiable or generalizable in terms of, the activities of members other than the member to whom they were specific and unique as his very own activities. This is because the substitutability of objective for indexical expressions, which Garfinkel points to as an essential prerequisite for formal discourse, and thus for the development and transmission of scientific knowledge (and whose accomplishment is attested to by the existence of the methodology of any "science"), is also a practical accomplishment at the level of everyday social interaction. It is necessary for *any and all meaningful* discourse, whether or not such discourse be dubbed "formal" or "scientific". And its accomplishment is attested to, for Garfinkel, by the fact that all collectivity members, when accounting for their everyday practical actions, do not find it necessary to state even a tiny proportion of the limiting conditions—practical, conceptual, conversational and so on—which are nevertheless clearly implied by all members accounting their activities in order to provide a meaningful context within which their accounts can be made sense of by the other members who comprise the audiences at which the accounts are directed. Correlatively, members comprising the audiences must know of, and implicitly invoke, sufficient of these limiting conditions to make sense of the accounts.[11]

Thus is established the third constituent, problematic phenomenon identifying the central topic of ethnomethodology—what Garfinkel calls "the analysability of actions-in-context as a practical accomplishment". It emerges from the two previous constituent problematic phenomena and is indicated in most of the definitions given above. For the process of a collectivity member accounting for his experience is a process of making unique, specific and individual experiences commonly known, by organizing them in a coherent fashion— such organization (given the typifying properties of everyday language) being an endemic feature of their expression. The result of the expression of their experiences by members in all cases is to make the process of accounting-for an essentially (that is, inevitably, necessarily and unavoidably) reflexive one. It is their verbal expression that gives the experiences being accounted-for their rational, coherent and systematic properties. It puts them in a context, whether of commonsense or of formal sociological explanation, wherein they will seem rational and accountable to their audience. Thus it is that, according to Garfinkel,

In indefinitely many ways members' inquiries are constituent features of the settings

---

[11] See Garfinkel, (1967, pp. 24–31, 36–49) for demonstrations of how this process of implicit invocation subsequently may be made explicit.

H

they analyse. In the same ways, their inquiries are made recognizable to members as adequate-for-all-practical-purposes (1967, p. 8).

The task of professional sociologists in the terms of ethnomethodology thus becomes a matter of *not* taking for granted what is typically taken-for-granted at the level of everyday actions. They must make the accomplishment of adequacy in meaning (of sense) in everyday, commonsensical explanations, itself a topic of sociological inquiry. This seems, to Garfinkel, "unavoidably to require that they treat the rational properties of practical activities as 'anthropologically strange' " (ibid., p. 9). Thus sociological investigators are required to question the contexts of meaning in which members' everyday accounts of practical activities are set, in order to make them explicit as contexts which are, themselves, practical accomplishments. In other words, it is necessary for professional sociologists to show that commonsense is not sine qua non for social life in a metaphysical or metatheoretical sense—as "the natural order of things" or "human nature"— but in an operational sense, as a constructed social reality in terms of which progressive social interactions are possible because they are understandable; and understandable because they are being presented as being ordered systematically and rationally in commonsense terms.

The accomplishment of the everyday, taken-for-granted, commonsense social world as an ordered reality, though a commonplace phenomenon to collectivity members, is an "awesome" one to professional sociologists, according to Garfinkel, since it is accomplished in unknown ways. It is awesome, particularly, because it consists of two remarkable and interrelated properties: first, it consists "of members' uses of concerted everyday activities as methods with which to recognize and demonstrate . . . the rational properties of indexical actions"; secondly, it consists "of the analysability of actions-in-context given that not only does no concept of context-in-general exist, but every use of 'context' without exception is itself essentially indexical" (ibid., p. 10). The first property seems remarkable because the indexical expressions used by members accounting for their everyday practical activities are regarded typically by professional sociologists as inadequate for the purposes of formal discourse. This is because they do not facilitate description of the activities to which they refer in terms of the *general* properties of those activities. Since indexical expressions can have meaning only in the specific context in which they are employed by members to formulate everyday accounts, they provide no basis for generalization. Yet the context which binds the meaning of them to the unique occasions on which they are employed, and to the specific activities for which they are being used to account, establishes that indexical expressions are rational for all practical purposes *by its very existence*. For, as Garfinkel has shown, it remains largely unstated by the accounting members and their audiences—it exists as an *implicit* resource upon which all of them draw in accounting for all practical activities in order to make any coherent sense of those activities. The second property is seen as equally remarkable, then, because although members' accounts of their practical activities are made in a context which makes them understandable to their audiences, the context remains, nevertheless, quite specific to the experiences which are being accounted for, and of the indexical expressions being used to accomplish the accounts. They are not being made, that is, in terms of a set of generally and explicitly held principles of context—despite the premise, from which much professional sociology proceeds, that no general understandability can be accomplished without the use of such a set of principles. Indeed, the context of the practical activities accounted for by members is produced as a part of the accounts themselves, and is tied to the accounts because it is carried by the rational properties of the indexical expressions used to construct them. Indexical expressions are, thus, already accomplished resolutions of the paradox that much professional sociological activity is intended to solve by the development of objective expressions for the facilitation of formal sociological discourse. To learn, in detail, the practices by which this resolution is accomplished, then, becomes, for ethnomethodology, an imperative goal of sociological inquiry.

These remarkable properties of the commonsense world emphasize the dualistic nature of social phenomena. For while, as social phenomena, they are possessed of common, objective properties which define them as such and make them analysable and explicable in formal sociological terms, they also exist, as accounts of the activities, expectations, interrelations and so on of social actors, at a mundane, everyday level. As such, social phenomena are considered as situational, specific and unique. Meaning is attributed to them by a reconstruction of a similar kind, experienced by members who share or are experienced listeners to accounts of these activities, expectations, interrelations and so on. That is, they are objectified into quasi-classes[12] or quasi-categories in order that they may be given relatively objective expression and thus understood. Yet, typically, the expressions of these activities in members' accounts are still made in indexical terms, and thus remain so specific as to appear useless for the purposes of formal sociological discourse. For their general understandability extends only as far as members who have themselves experienced, or are experienced listeners to accounts of the things that are being reconstructed in the accounts.

Formal or traditional professional sociology can thus be seen, from this explication of Garfinkel's argument, to be a process of second-order objectification of the indexicality of everyday social experience. For it systematizes, according to the terms and concepts of its formal methodology, the accounts of members' experiences, which have themselves been already systematized in the accounting process. The proper subject-matter of ethnomethodological sociology then becomes the examination of the process of what might be called first-order objectification—that is, the everyday way in which members make rational and and accountable their everyday experiences. In other words, it is a sociology of everyday life. And the task of professional sociologists, in their ecstatic position

---

[12] The use of the prefix "quasi-" here is intended to follow that observed by Garfinkel (1967, pp. 2–3), and cited from Helmer and Rescher (1958).

of not taking for granted what their lay, fellow collectivity members do, is to lay bare the tacit, shared assumptions which are hypothesized as giving everyday life its ordered character. In doing so they will be admitting and discovering their own participation in the commonsense world, and in its construction as a reality. They will thus be presenting and analysing the experience of social interaction more meaningfully than can be achieved in the formal, abstracted terms of traditional sociology. Or, as Garfinkel phrases it in the first of his definitions of ethnomethodology cited above, they will be "discovering the formal properties of commonplace, practical commonsense actions from within actual settings, as ongoing accomplishments of those settings".

SOME PROBLEMATIC IMPLICATIONS OF GARFINKEL'S WORK

One of the central questions that all sociological analysis worthy of being so termed attempts to answer, is that concerning the basis of the systematic character of social life. Garfinkel appears less than definite, however, in his provision of an answer to this question on behalf of ethnomethodology. Instead, he offers two broad hints which, on examination, appear to be quite contradictory.

The first is given in his complete espousal of Parson's definition of the term which Garfinkel uses to define the individual, namely that of collectivity member.[13] Parsons defines the category of membership as "performing a role within a collectivity . . . i.e. the assumption of obligations of performance in [a] concrete interaction system". It should be noted here that the term role is defined by Parsons as "the structured, i.e. normatively regulated, participation of a person in a concrete process of social interaction with specified, concrete role-partners"; and the term collectivity as "the system of such interaction of a plurality of role-performers . . ., in so far as it is normatively regulated in terms of common values and of norms sanctioned by these common values".[14]

The second hint is given by Garfinkel's citation of the work of Schutz as "a magnificent exception" to the work of sociologists who, though they "take socially structured scenes of everyday life as a point of departure, they rarely see, as a task of sociological inquiry in its own right, the general question of how any such commonsense world is possible" (1967, p. 36).

Both Parsons and Schutz are referred to by Garfinkel on a number of occasions in his work, and in a way that establishes them both as of fundamental importance to it. Indeed, he speaks of Parsons's work particularly as "awesome for the penetrating depth and unfailing precision of its practical sociological reasoning on the constituent tasks of the problem of social order and its solutions" (ibid., p. ix). Yet in the context of Garfinkel's work, Parsons and Schutz make the strangest of bedfellows. For Parsons's work would appear to be in many ways

---

[13] I am grateful to Frank Pierce, of North-Western Polytechnic, London, for pointing out this problem to me. The espousal is made by Garfinkel in footnotes on pp. 57, 76 of *Studies in Ethnomethodology* (1967).

[14] Parsons etc. et al (1961, Vol. 1, p. 42). The reference is cited by Garfinkel in a footnote on p. 57 of *Studies in Ethnomethodology* (1967).

archetypical of precisely the neglect that Garfinkel bemoans in much sociology, of explaining how the commonsense world is possible; and to which neglect Schutz's work is dubbed such a "magnificent exception"! The Parsonian view of the individual collectivity member is of one whose freedom of interaction is limited considerably by his defining characteristics—that is, primarily, by his collectivity membership, by his "assumption of obligations of performance in [a] concrete interaction system . . . [which] is normatively regulated in terms of common values and of norms sanctioned by these common values" (Parsons, etc. et al, 1961, vol. 1, p. 42). Such an individual would be one who has deeply internalized, and whose actions are deeply determined by, principles of behaviour adumbrated in terms of an a priori systemic conceptualization of social organization. A sociology whose analysis proceeds in terms of such conceptualizations of its central phenomena could hardly be said, whatever its other merits, to be complying with Garfinkel's explicit injunction for ethnomethodology to regard even the most trivial everyday activities as consciously "organized" and "artful" practices.

Moreover, Parsons's view of the individual would seem to be very far from that of Schutz, which Garfinkel points to when enumerating what Schutz regards as background assumptions of persons engaged in everyday activities. "According to Schutz", says Garfinkel, "the person assumes, assumes that the other person assumes as well, and assumes that as he assumes it of the other person the other person assumes the same for him" a number of features of a common situation (1967, p. 55).[15] Among these features are the determinations of each event in the situation, and each of these determinations has two constituent aspects. First, they consist of what each person in the situation will hold them to be privately. Second (and simultaneously), they will consist of what each person, with the other person(s) in the situation will "have selected and interpreted [as] the actual and practical determinations of events in an empirically identical manner that is sufficient for all their practical purposes" (ibid., p. 56). Garfinkel, after Schutz, dubs this "a characteristic disparity between the publicly acknowledged determinations and the personal, withheld determinations of events" and claims that alterations of it "remain within the witness's autonomous control "(ibid., p. 56). Schutz, of course, explains this "characteristic disparity" by his thesis of the reciprocity of perspectives, according to which the different individual perspectives of the members of a social situation are overcome by two basic idealizations: of the interchangeability of standpoints; and of the congruency of the systems of relevances. The first states that two or more social actors are able to interact purposively in a common situation because each assumes that if he were to change places with any of the others he would, in each case, see the situation in the same way that they see it, and likewise, they would each see the situation as he does. The second idealization, which follows from the first, is that the biographical differences of each actor (that is, the specific and unique aspects of their per-

---

[15] Following this, on pp. 55–6, Garfinkel enumerates briefly eleven constituents which, he says, when compounded, make for Schutz "the feature of a scene 'known-in-common with others'."

sonality, character, individual historical experience, and so on) are considered by them to be irrelevant to their individual purposes at hand because, as Schutz puts it, they

> have selected actually or potentially common objects and their features in . . . an empirically isolated manner, i.e. one sufficient for all practical purposes (1962, p. 12).

Thus, the social situation which the actors share is defined by them in common, and in a form that is detached and different from that of each of them individually, or of anybody else. So that a concept of "knowledge held in common" about the situation by all its members becomes meaningful, regardless of the members' unique biographical circumstances and purposes at hand (ibid., pp. 11–15).

However, Garfinkel's citation of Schutz's work as a "magnificent exception to the work of sociologists" who rarely explain how a commonsense world is possible, need not be considered as the implied criticism of Parsons that it might seem, if it could be established that in Parsons's work could be found the basis of such an explanation. Now it might be possible to argue that the clear involvement of the member of the situation, in the self-conscious state that Schutz and Garfinkel clearly envisage him as being, is adequately conceptualized by Parsons when he is referred to as "assuming obligations of performance in [a] concrete interaction system". This would be despite the burden of Parsons's theory of socialization, however, since it relies so heavily on the concept of internalization;[16] and this would appear to imply that the process of defining action situations for members could hardly be characterized adequately as self-conscious. On the contrary, given that the "concrete interaction system" in which the Parsonian collectivity member assumes his "obligations of performance . . . is normatively regulated in terms of common values and of norms sanctioned by these common values", his definition of the situation is much better characterized as one typically determined and pre-empted by these common norms and values. Schutz and Garfinkel, on the other hand, would appear to require a theory of socialization based upon the concept of identification, in a sense which would enable collectivity members to be seen as able to exercise their "autonomous control" over the alteration of the knowledge held in common which defines their membership of interactive situations, as a means of controlling the conditions under which they pursue self-consciously defined goals. Even this, however, would not be totally incompatible with the implications of the Parsonian definition of collectivity member, if the definition of the common values and norms which regulate the concrete interaction system, in which the member assumes his obligations of performance, was itself a self-conscious process. But that, too, is surely a process whose nature is determined and pre-empted—in this case, by what Parsons regards as the necessary conditions for ordered social existence; that is, by the functional prerequisites of his social system.[17] Thus the stock of knowledge held in common by collectivity members, as far as Parsons is con-

---

[16] See Parsons (1964a). Parsons's theory of socialization is discussed at length by Baldwin (1961).
[17] See Parsons (1951, especially pp. 28–34). For an interesting discussion, see Sklair (1970).

cerned, would appear to be quite severely limited by these impersonal conditions —a conclusion which would appear to be validated by Parsons's adumbration of evolutionary universals as the most effective means of fulfilling the prerequisites under conditions of increasing social complexity.[18]

For Schutz, however, the origins of knowledge held in common are explained quite differently, through the interactive epistemological process of linguistic typification.

> The typifying medium par excellence . . . is the vocabulary and syntax of everyday language. The vernacular of everyday life is primarily a language of named things and events, and any name includes a typification and generalization referring to the relevance system prevailing in the linguistic in-groups which found the named thing significant enough to provide a separate term for it. The pre-scientific vernacular can be interpreted as a treasure-house of ready made preconstituted types and characteristics, all socially derived, carrying along an open horizon of unexplored content (1962, p. 14).

The emphasis here, in the use of terms and concepts like "relevance system", "linguistic in-group" whose members "found" some things "significant enough to *provide* a separate term for" them, is on the *activity* and *involvement* of collectivity members *themselves* defining their situation. And to characterize their vernacular as carrying along "an *open* horizon of unexplored content" is far from suggesting the determined, limiting conditions under which Parsons seems to imply knowledge is held in common.

But the crucially important theorist for present and future purposes is neither Schutz nor Parsons, but Garfinkel. And the problem is that Garfinkel would appear to be acknowledging an equally positive debt to both Schutz and Parsons, which adds up to an implied contradiction in his explanations of the ordered character of the everyday activities of collectivity members. For if members are defined in the relatively passive, deterministic fashion of Parsons, how can they act with the existential self-consciousness which Schutz necessarily attributes to them, as the basis for his explanation of social order which is being constructed by and for themselves in terms of the pursuit of their self-defined interests? The answer is, of course, that they cannot; and that, therefore, in Garfinkel's *work*, as opposed to his footnotes and *obiter dicta* about it, the Schutzian conception of member would appear to hold over the Parsonian. Indeed, Garfinkel appears to say as much when he points out that the "study tasks" of ethnomethodology "cannot be accomplished by free invention, constructive analytic theorizing, mock-ups or book reviews, and no special interest is paid to them aside from an interest in their varieties as organizationally situated methods of practical reasoning" (1967, p. viii). Parsons's work would presumably come into the category of "constructive analytic theorizing" (though some may feel it better placed amongst "free invention" or "mock-ups"). At any rate, according to this statement of Garfinkel, it would appear to be of interest to ethnomethodology only as part of the subject matter of its proper study—the

---

[18] See Parsons (1966). A shorter exposition will be found in Parsons (1964c).

ethnomethodology of formal sociology. Yet the circumstances of Garfinkel's citations of Parsons, as having completely satisfactorily defined the centrally important concept of collectivity member, would seem to belie this attribution to it of only epiphenomenal importance. A nagging doubt remains.[19]

For ethnomethodology, then, the basis of the systematic character of social life would appear to be found in Schutz's explanation of the origins of knowledge held in common by collectivity members; that is, in the linguistic typification of its constituent phenomena. Language is at the centre of all of Garfinkel's characterizations and definitions of ethnomethodology and of the constituent problematic phenomena of its central topic. Language is the principal mechanism by which members make their everyday activities "visibly-rational-and-reportable-for-all-practical-purposes, i.e. 'accountable', as organizations of commonplace everyday activities". It is through the common terms of language that unique or personal experiences are given what ostensibly is taken to be objective expressions in members' accounts of them. These accounts however, are

---

[19] In discussions with Garfinkel on an earlier draft of this paper, held at the Graduate Center of the City University of New York between 25 March and 2 April, 1971, he explained that at the time he was writing the paper in which these references to Parsons occur he had recently completed (Spring, 1959) a draft of a manuscript based on notes from his course, Sociology 251, at the University of California at Los Angeles, which was intended as a primer on Parsons. The manuscript remains unpublished; but Garfinkel claims, as I understand his account of it, that he was attempting in it a reconciliation of the works of Parsons and Schutz on social action. For he was confident, at that time, that the multiple realities which Schutz identifies in the structuring of attitudes of everyday life would prove fundamentally compatible with Parsons's use of the concept of collectivity as a specification of practical activity. (See here also Garfinkel's unpublished doctoral dissertation (1952) in which he attempts a detailed comparison of Parsons's and Schutz's ideas on social order.)

In other words, Garfinkel was attempting to use the concept of collectivity as an analytic "just-so story", borrowed from Parsons and applied to Schutz. Thus the concept of collectivity, as well as being an analytical construct of Parsons's formal, systemic sociology, might also be seen as a means, employed by collectivity members in an everyday fashion, to reproduce stable features of everyday activities in those recurrent everyday situations which Parsons refers to as sub-systems, for example "formal organizations", extended family and kinship networks, and so on. The collectivity, then, comes to be seen as a commonsense construct, in Schutz's sense, in terms of which members are able to account for any actual array of activities (occurring in what Parsons terms, a "sub-system") which purport to be, or require to be treated as, "facts of life" in so far as they appear to confront and to constrain members. Put yet another way, the collectivity would thus be seen as a self-organizing *set of activities*, providing, as it were from within itself, for the ways in which members are to identify it as a *system of social action*.

Garfinkel felt that it would follow from this presentation of the concept of collectivity as a *constructive* representation of normatively regulated action, that it might be eligible for close compatability in interpretation with the way in which Schutz attempts to explain the structuring of everyday life (that is, in terms of his theory of the reciprocity of perspectives), rather than the over-deterministic way in which Parsons does so by his theory of the reciprocity of expectations and sanctions. However, Parsons's subsequent work on socialization and on sociological systems theory (see above, footnotes 14 and 16) cleared up the initial ambiguities in his explanation of the structuring of everyday life, and in the meaning he intended to convey by his own use of the concepts of collectivity and collectivity member, in such a way that the bottom quite fell out of the alternative, more flexible, yet potentially compatible interpretation proposed by Garfinkel. It also rendered rather pointless the publication of Garfinkel's study of Parsons's work—at any rate, as a primer upon it.

In connection with Garfinkel's proposed interpretation of Parsons, outlined here, it is interesting to note that Schutz himself prepared a lengthy review of Parsons's *The Structure of Social Action*, which he decided against publishing after receiving comment upon it from Parsons (see Wagner, 1971, p. 3).

rational versions of members' experiences partly because of the requirements of linguistic sense, so that shared language is the source of the reflexivity between members' accounts of their experiences and the experiences themselves. And finally, it is in the shared language in which accounts are framed that the context, in terms of which the experiences are to be understood and analysed, is implied or explicitly stated. Language is used by Garfinkel, it should be stated here, in a much wider sense than the purely verbal, as comprised of common vocabulary, grammar and syntax, not only of words but of symbols, gestures, expressions, deportments and so on of all kinds—a point which becomes important in a part of the argument I want to develop subsequently.

The centrality of language to Garfinkel's ethnomethodology becomes particularly evident in the method by which ethnomethodological analysis proceeds, that of the *disruption* of ordered, stable, everyday social situations. The disruption is carried out on both physical and verbal features of interaction, by physical gesture as well as spoken expression—though normally only one feature is disturbed at a time. It consists of the experimenter or analyst, as a member of an everyday, social situation, refusing to interpret the accounts of the experiences, intentions, explanations, expectations and so on of fellow members in terms of the contextual knowledge assumed, on the basis of previous generalizable, inter-active experience, to be shared by all members of the situation. He expresses this refusal either by doubting accounts verbally, or by implying such doubt by his facial expressions and/or other physical gestures. Thus, these accounts are rendered non-rational, and the situation becomes disordered. Further *purposive* interaction becomes difficult, if not impossible, because much of the basis of common, everyday assumptions from which such interaction proceeds has been removed; the common stock of knowledge is denied, and the analyst's fellow collectivity members in the social situation are made to appear what Garfinkel calls "cultural" or "judgmental dopes".[20] An example may help to clarify this process.

Ten undergraduates were asked to participate in research being carried out by a university's department of psychiatry to explore alternative means of psychotherapy. Each was asked to discuss the background to a serious problem on which he wanted advice, and then to address to an experimenter—who had been falsely presented to him as a trainee student counsellor—a number of questions about it which would be amenable to monosyllabic "Yes" or "No" answers. The subject and the experimenter/counsellor were physically separated, and communicated by two-way radio. After the answer to each of his questions had been given, the subject was asked to tape-record his comments upon it,

---

[20] Garfinkel defines as a cultural dope, "the man-in-the-sociologist's-society who produces the stable features of the society by acting in compliance with pre-established and legitimate alternatives of action that the common culture provides." To be a judgmental dope, he clearly implies, is to treat as epiphenomenal rather than central, "courses of commonsense rationalities of judgment which involve the person's use of commonsense knowledge of social structures over the temporal 'succession' of here and now situations." (1967, p. 68). Garfinkel also shows himself to have been a judgmental dope in one case, in a striking way (ibid., Chapter 5 and app. to chapter 5, pp. 116–85, 285–8).

out of radio-hearing of the experimenter/counsellor. The subjects were told that it was usual to ask ten questions, and they were, of course, led to believe that they would be given bona fide answers to them. The experimenter/ counsellors, however, were given a list of monosyllabic answers, evenly divided between "Yes" and "No", but whose order had been predecided from a table of random numbers. Thus, in this experiment, certain crucial variables of everyday interaction situations had been neutralized: the shared language of subject and experimenter had been reduced to the verbal spoken dimension (intonation, in all probability, would also have been relatively unimportant as an agent of meaning, owing to the distortion of spoken sounds by radio); there was no chance of gestures or physical expressions intervening in the communication process because of the physical separation of subject and experimenter. Also, the possibility of the experimenter/counsellors' answers making any sense to the subjects depended entirely on their interpretations of them; indeed, the possibility of answers even being those anticipated by the subjects was reduced to a matter of chance. Garfinkel publishes two unedited transcripts of the exchanges and of the subjects' comments upon them, plus a detailed explication of his interpretive findings from them. The burden of these is that where the random answers to the carefully thought-out and phrased questions of the subjects appeared nonsensical, irrational or in some other way inappropriate or un-expected, then the subject reinterpreted them by reformulating what he assumed to be the context of meaning he held in common with the experimenter/ counsellor (and which he had attempted to communicate to the experimenter/ counsellor by the phrasing and content of his questions), in order that the latter's responses made sense after all. Even where a succession of plainly contradictory answers engendered the suspicion in the subject that he was being tricked, he appeared reluctant to proceed upon the assumption that this was so.[21]

Similarly disruptive experiments, of a more everyday kind, involved student-experimenters being required to engage friends or acquaintances in ordinary conversation whilst claiming not to know the import of ordinary, everyday con-versational expressions such as "How are you?". Or to return home to their families and attempt, for periods of up to one hour, to act as if they were boarders in their own homes. Or to engage someone in conversation and to behave as if they were assuming that their conversation partner was deliberately trying to mislead them. Or again, they were required to engage others in ordinary con-versation whilst performing the rather special gesture of bringing their faces so close to those of their partners that the tips of their respective noses almost touched. The reactions of subjects to these experiments were often extreme. Of forty-nine cases where students were asked to act as boarders in their own home, for example, nine "students either refused to do the assignment (five cases) or the try was 'unsuccessful' (four cases). Four of the 'no try' students said they were afraid to do it", a fifth said she preferred to avoid the risk of exciting her

---

[21] See Garfinkel (1967, pp. 79–94). The same experiment is written about in much greater detail by Peter McHugh, who assisted Garfinkel in conducting it (1968, pp. 59–126).

mother, who had a heart condition. In the remaining four-fifths of the cases, however, Garfinkel describes the reactions of the students' family members variously as "stupefied" or as exploding "with bewilderment and anger" (1967, p. 47). As Garfinkel points out, "the members' real perceived environment on losing its known-in-common background, should become 'specifically senseless'.[22] Ideally speaking, behaviours directed to such a senseless environment should be those of bewilderment, uncertainty, internal conflict, psycho-social isolation, acute, and nameless, anxiety along with various symptoms of acute depersonalization. Structures of interaction should be correspondingly disorganized" (ibid., p. 55).

The response to disorganization, however, in a number of the situations which Garfinkel analyses, is typically for members *not* to react with bewilderment, stupefaction or anger, but rather to attempt to intuit the principles according to which their situations can be reorganized, can be made rationally accountable once more. All members in everyday situations would thus seem to be interacting under the assumption that "persons' actual usages are rational usages in *some* language game" (ibid., p. 70). Thus the "programmatic" question that has to be answered, not only for members who wish to reorganize a disrupted situation, but also for sociologists of everyday life, is: What is *their* game? That is, by what rules, criteria or principles of this particular situation are the accounts of its members considered by one another as rational and coherent, as sensible for all practical purposes? Or, again, how can this situation be made analysable-in-context?

To attempt an answer to this programmatic question in the context of Garfinkel's work seems to be important, because it should reveal the basis of ethnomethodology as sociological analysis by revealing the principles according to which the accomplishment of organized settings of everyday social interaction is managed. Yet the revelation of these principles would nevertheless remain highly problematic in the context of traditional sociological analysis, for there is no suggestion to be found in Garfinkel's work that, once revealed, they would provide a basis for adumbration of the much more general explanation of everyday, practical social interactions that traditional sociology purports to offer. On the contrary, as I have attempted to show, Garfinkel explains at length and in detail just how and why it is that the principles he has revealed are a part of the organization of the settings of each of the particular, everyday actions whose accomplishment they help to manage. He has shown above all, that it is only because members' accounts of their practical everyday actions do make sense, are coherent and understandable to others beside themselves, that they can be known, attested to and validated as experience at all; and that this remarkable phenomenon is *not* accomplished by members making constant reference to such

---

[22] In a footnote to the use of this term, Garfinkel remarks that he has "borrowed" it from Weber and has "adapted its meaning". His adaptation of it, it is worth noting, amounts both conceptually and empirically to a negation of Weber's intended meaning. Garfinkel accounts for this on the grounds that, at the same time as considering potential compatibilities between the works of Parsons and Schutz, he was also considering them between the works of Schutz and Weber (see above, note 20).

formal "collections" of the principles of rationally explicable behaviour as those provided by the methodologies of traditional schools of sociological explanation, and frequently referred to in much of the literature of professional sociology under rubrics like "functional structuralism", "social actionism", etc., etc.[23]

It would seem to be for these reasons, then, that Garfinkel insists that ethnomethodological studies are "not directed to formulating or arguing correctives . . . do not formulate a remedy for practical actions"; and for much the same reasons that his work, where it is acknowledged by them at all, has attracted so much hostility from established and/or tradition-oriented sociologists.[24] Because it demonstrates so clearly the severe difficulties in formulating general sociological propositions which provide valid explanations for a wide range of social phenomena and events, it seems to constitute an intolerably radical challenge to sociologists whose work is carried out in terms of that traditional ideal of the process of sociological explanation which is derived from a version of the processes of explanation in the natural sciences, and customarily referred to as "scientific methods".[25] For this version of explanation, which is at the roots of the claims made for a scientific sociology, puts an enormous premium on the law-like character of the explanatory propositions of any science. It requires that its empirical generalizations be as near universally valid as possible, within the specified and specifiable limiting conditions which are said to operate in the particular occurrences, activities, events and so on that the propositions are employed to explain.

Hence, a typical response to Garfinkel's work is that of Gouldner, who claims that it seems

> to premise a social world resting on tacit understandings that, however important as a foundation for all else, are still fragile and rather easily eluded. The cultural foundation, in short, is precarious, and its security apparently rests in some part, on its sheer invisibility or taken-for-grantedness. Once made visible, however, it rather readily loses its hold. . . . His attention . . . is largely focused first, on demonstrating . . . [the] sheer existence [of these varying tacit rules] and, second, on demonstrating their role in providing a secure background for social interaction. . . . His emphasis leads to a conception of these rules as conventions, and thus to a view of society as dependent on the merely conventional—that is, on what are, in effect, rules of the game. . . . And all parts of society, including science (with its rigorous method), are seen to depend on these common sense, arbitrary rules and procedures (1970, p. 392).

---

[23] These rubrics are taken from Wallace (1969)—an interesting and explicit example of the kind of "collections" to which I am referring here.

[24] For example, A. F. C. Wallace (1968), Coleman (1968), Gouldner (1970, pp. 390–5), Dreitzel (1970, pp. xiv–xxi).

[25] An interesting extreme statement of that point of view from which sociology can be considered as a natural science may be found in Lundberg et. al. (1954). Less unequivocal, but still interesting discussions of this issue may be found, for example, in Rex (1961, Chapter 1, 2 and 9) or in Cohen (1968, Chapter 1). Recent work in the philosophy of science has, of course, cast considerable doubt on the concept of "scientific method" as a viable account of procedures of research and investigation, even in the natural sciences. See, for example, Popper (1962), Medawar (1969), Kuhn (1970a).

Despite his strange characterization of science as a "part of society", and the mysterious reverence which leads him to imply (apparently outraged at Garfinkel's suggestions to the contrary) that the "rigorous method" of science puts it beyond analysis as a practical social activity, Gouldner seems to be saying that although Garfinkel's ethnomethodological studies reveal the identity of the rules of social interactions, they do not reveal the origin of them; in other words, that Garfinkel has answered only the descriptive question: What are the rules of social interaction? but not the more important analytical one: Where do they come from? If this is what Gouldner means to say, then it reveals a fundamental misunderstanding of Garfinkel's arguments. For Garfinkel has demonstrated quite explicitly that the rules, or "the formal properties of commonplace, practical commonsense actions" are not only "features" of those actions, but that they "obtain their guarantees from no other source, and in no other way", and are thus only "analysable-in-context"—that is, "from within actual settings" of the "practical commonsense actions" which they help to "accomplish". The rules, then, are only established as such by their ability to organize the settings of practical, everyday, commonsense actions—an ability which is proven in so organizing these actions. Moreover, that the rules *have* organized them is evidenced by the coherence, rationality, sense and understandability of members' accounts of them. To answer the second question implied by Gouldner, then: the rules come from "the occasions of their use"; they are generated within the activities which they organize. This is the "reflexive" and "incarnate" character of the rules, which Garfinkel repeatedly emphasizes as an awesome and remarkable phenomenon. And it is just this emphasis in Garfinkel's work that Gouldner suggests, so disparagingly and misleadingly, "leads to a conception of these rules as conventions, and thus to a view of society as dependent on the merely conventional".[26]

It is their reflexive or incarnate character, above all, that makes the formal properties of everyday social interactions such recondite phenomena from the point of view of traditional sociological analysis. And that they are to an important degree inseparable from their specific context, makes them effectively inaccessible to positivistic professional sociologists. For, though they may indeed be what Durkheim has called "rules of the sociological method", they are rules of a method available to, and employed by, all social actors in every practical activity in which they are involved; they are not solely the license and legitimation of the *professional* activities of sociologists, and they defy extrication from their context and subsequent objectification as such. For these reasons, then, it is important to note that, despite the inclusion of the term in its very name, *ethnomethodology is not, nor should it be considered as, a methodology at all according to the terms of all existing, traditional sociological methodologies.*[27]

---

[26] This seems a particularly strange mode of disparagement for Gouldner to employ, since important parts of his own work seem surely to imply that, for him, there is nothing "mere" about social conventions of any kind! See, for example, Gouldner (1959).

[27] An interesting demonstration of this somewhat disconcerting proposition is to be found in the manner in which Garfinkel has chosen to set out his *Studies in Ethnomethodology*. It is presented somewhat in the format of a traditional sociological text, in so far as the substantive studies themselves

This does not mean, however, that ethnomethodological studies are not systematic, nor that they do not imply, themselves, certain rules of procedure.[28] In addition to the policies that Garfinkel outlines, according to which the study of practical actions proceeds, his work suggests at least two areas of existing sociological analysis which may be of importance to establishing the formal properties of them. They have already been discussed briefly in terms of the debts he acknowledges to Parsons and Schutz. In the case of Parsons, the answer would be quite unsatisfactory, since the rules of everyday social interaction would have to be found in the deeply internalized, fundamental, common norms and values embodying the deterministic, limiting conditions within which ordered social interaction is possible. Yet this explanation of the origin of the rules of ordered social interaction is surely implied on every occasion that Garfinkel states that he claims to mean by collectivity member exactly what Parsons means by it also. However, it must be discarded as misleading, on the grounds that it would render pointless the ability, frequently demonstrated in ethnomethodological experiments, to find new, sensible contexts and coherent organizational principles in terms of which disrupted situations can be reordered.

So that the more fruitful possible answer would appear to lie with Schutz— or, at least, in a direction pointed out by Schutz's remarks on "the vocabulary and syntax of everyday language" as "the typifying medium par excellence". This is the process by which the specific and unique experiences of members undergo first-order objectification. It is by their expression in language that any member's experiences are established as coherent and sensible, and it is in this process of accounting that the experiences are also made rational. It is, in effect, a presentation of the behaviour involved in the experience as ordered behaviour. Thus there would appear to be an order endemic in the process of typification itself—a point which Garfinkel emphasizes in his discussions of the reflexivity

---

[28] For example, some of the important principles according to which ethnomethodologists might conduct their studies would appear to reside in Garfinkel's injunctions to "treat the rational properties of practical activities as 'anthropologically strange' " (1967, p. 9); "by paying to the most commonplace activities of daily life the attention usually accorded extraordinary events, seek to learn about them as phenomena in their own right" (ibid., p. 1); to discover "the formal properties of commonplace practical commonsense actions 'from within' actual settings, as ongoing accomplishments of those settings" (ibid., p. viii).

(Chapters 2 to 7) are prefaced by an initial chapter purporting to answer the question "What is Ethnomethodology?" Yet, for the most part in the text of that chapter, Garfinkel is only able to set out any specific, constituent feature of ethnomethodology by citing detailed excerpts from the substantive analyses that demonstrate it in one or other of the succeeding chapters. For *the formal propositions of ethnomethodology, like those of practical actions (and because they represent practical actions) are productions of the organized occasions of their use.* They emerge, thus, out of the substantive ethnomethodological analyses presented in Chapters 2 to 7. So that a productive reading of Chapter 1 is better achieved *after* a reading of Chapters 2 to 7 than before, whereupon it may be seen as a carefully written conclusion to those studies. It may be useful, also, to preface reading it with a reading of Chapter 8, which raises a number of important questions about the nature of scientific rationality and the viability of its use as a basis for existing sociological explanations.

An instructive parallel with this feature of Garfinkel's work can be found by reference to another text on ethnomethodology—Cicourel (1964). Cicourel discusses the "Theoretical Presuppositions" of his work in a *concluding* chapter of that title (Chapter 7, pp. 189–224).

of members' accounts. It would seem reasonable to assume, therefore, that in the mechanism of that process may be studied the ways in which the rules that organize and structure the everyday interactive behaviour of collectivity members are constructed; for that same process is clearly their source.

CONCLUSION: WHERE MIGHT ETHNOMETHODOLOGY GO FROM HERE?

If Garfinkel's ethnomethodological analysis sought to remedy the defects of traditional sociological explanation, any attempt—such as this chapter—to explicate the general import of the analysis would be most easily concluded in the traditional professional fashion, by pointing out further areas of potentially fruitful research. However, perhaps the most remarkable achievement of ethnomethodology, as this chapter has attempted to show by examining Garfinkel's work, is the fundamental challenge it presents to three axiomatic features of traditional modes of sociological explanation, namely: the natural-scientific character of their rationality; their objectivity; and hence, the validity of their existing generalizations. It has produced, therefore, the compelling requirement that sociology should examine immediately and in detail its epistemological and philosophical roots, in order to present the dualistic, constructed and very tenuous character of its subject matter—social phenomena—as accurately as possible. This requirement, however compelling it may seem, has nevertheless been shown as an avoidable one for some sociologists in their response to Garfinkel's work;[29] yet there is already a mounting body of substantive work accumulating in response to it.[30]

By way of conclusion, then, I want to propose a contribution to the re-examination of some of the roots of sociology by suggesting, very briefly, that work in two disciplines closely related to sociology may be of relevance to the development of ethnomethodological studies. Their relevance would seem to stem from their apparent presentation of two directions in which the mechanisms of the process of linguistic typification may be found to be located. The two disciplines are social anthropology and linguistics; and the work of particular relevance here is, in each case, linked pre-eminently with the name of a particular thinker, Claude Lévi-Strauss[31] and Noam Chomsky[32] respectively. Both are important, I think, because their work suggests the existence of a corpus of

---

[29] See, for example, the works quoted in footnote 24.

[30] A recent collection of such work is J. Douglas (1970b), the bibliography of which (pp. 337–54) also cites a number of other works in this field. Further studies can also be found in Dreitzel (1970, papers by Cicourel, Emerson, McHugh) and in McKinney and Tiryakian (1970, papers by Blum, Garfinkel and Saks). In addition the works of Cicourel (1964, 1968) and McHugh (1968) are especially important.

[31] See, for example, Lévi-Strauss (1966, 1968, 1969). An extremely insightful discussion of Levi-Strauss's ideas may be found in Leach (1970).

[32] See, for example, Chomsky (1957, 1964, 1965, 1966a, 1966b). Chomsky's work is examined at length in Hockett (1968); and, less fully and less critically, in Lyons (1970).

autonomous, socio-cultural phenomena which is seen as both generative of interactive behaviour, and irreducible.

Both men argue that all men possess some process of conceptualization in common. Chomsky argues that this process is linguistic, on the grounds that men are able to establish that they know something by their ability to express or give utterance to it, primarily by verbal language. This is a property, he argues, of all men. Yet, virtually until the work of Chomsky himself (with the exception of a small number of seventeenth- and eighteenth-century European philosophers), the universal nature of this property has been disguised by the culturally specific orientation of linguistic studies. This has been a result of the realization and concern of late nineteenth- and early twentieth-century linguists and anthropologists, that a number of languages of structurally simple societies in the western hemisphere—particularly North American Indian societies—were in danger of dying out unrecorded. Thus, stringent attempts were made to record these languages in all their uniquenesses, and little comparative, analytical study between them and in relation to other languages was undertaken.[33] Yet Chomsky claims that comparative study should reveal significant common elements in all languages because, although language is a cultural phenomenon, yet it has distinct naturalistic properties. Principally, it is a production of the neurophysiology of man, which has, as it were, unquestionably objective facticity. The meanings of linguistic terms, obviously, are culturally related, if not entirely culture-specific; but the mechanisms of linguistic utterance are not so—they are a common property of all men. Now, if this point is linked with the proposition that men are able to establish that they know something by their ability to give it primarily linguistic utterance—that is, by making it "rational-and-accountable-for-all-practical-purposes"; and if the rules which govern everyday social interactions are, as they appear to be, endemic in the process of typification itself, and the medium par excellence of that process, as Schutz puts it, is language: then the idea of a common structure of linguistic expression possessed by all men in common would seem to be a line of inquiry well worthy of the interest, if not the pursuit, of ethnomethodologists interested in the processes by which the rules of everyday interaction are generated.[34]

There are, however, certain limitations for ethnomethodology in the Chomskyan approach to socio-linguistics. First, Chomsky argues that common linguistic structures are deep structures; and the relative ease with which the order of everyday interaction situations can be disrupted suggests that their rules are more superficial in location. And yet the extremes of behavioural disturbance which can be seen, according to some of Garfinkel's experiments, to follow upon disruption, would suggest that the rules may be more deeply anchored than might at first appear to be the case. Second, and more importantly, Chomskyan linguistics is still at a stage of theory construction, wherein its arguments are developed in terms of what Chomsky has called

[33] See Lyons (1970, Chapter 3).

[34] This direction has already yielded important work, for example by Cicourel (1964, especially Chapter 8, 1970b) and by Turner (1970).

an ideal speaker-listener, in a completely homogeneous speech-community, who knows its language perfectly and is unaffected by such grammatically irrelevant conditions as memory limitations, distractions, shifts of attention and interest, errors (random or characteristic) in applying his knowledge of the language in actual performance (1965, p. 3).

To carry out ethnomethodological analyses according to the terms of such an ideal-type construct would, of course, be the most certain way of all of being rendered a cultural or judgemental dope as a sociologist. As Garfinkel points out, the

> available theories [of the formal properties of signs and symbols] have many important things to say about such sign functions as marks and indications, but they are silent on such overwhelmingly more common functions as glosses, synecdoche, documented representation, euphemism, irony and double entendre. References to commonsense knowledge of ordinary affairs may be safely disregarded in detecting and analyzing marks and indications as sign functions *because* users disregard them as well. The analysis of irony, double entendre, glosses, and the like, however, imposes different requirements. Any attempt to consider the related character of utterances, meanings, perspectives, and orders necessarily requires reference to commonsense knowledge of ordinary affairs (1967, p. 71).

It is for this reason that I mentioned earlier that the interpretation of language in Garfinkel's work must be made in the widest possible sense, to take account, as he has done in his experiments and demonstrations, of factors affecting the meanings likely to be attributed to phenomena such as facial expressions, gestures, physical deportment, as well as the devices of verbal expression itself and the elements that Chomsky deliberately excludes from his construct of the ideal speaker-listener. Thus, whilst linguistics might provide a base from which the study of part of the processes of construction of rules of everyday interactions might proceed, the development itself would have to be in terms of semiology, the study of all, not only verbal and linguistic, signs and symbols. And in terms, moreover, of a semiology hitherto unknown; for, as Garfinkel has pointed out, available semiologies are concerned with the *formal* properties of signs and symbols, much as traditional modes of sociological analysis are concerned to formalize properties of social interaction in a way that disguises the rational features of their indexicality.

However, for ethnomethodology, the strongest reason for investigation, along modified Chomskyan lines, of the processes whereby rules of everyday interaction are constructed, lies in the notion of the generative grammar of language. For the rules of expression which are the grammar of a language are considered generative in the sense that they give rise to utterable sentences which may be treated, for all the practical purposes of a speaker, as infinite in number. So that any speaker is unlikely to say exactly the same thing twice— though the same meaning can reasonably be imputed to superficially dissimilar statements about the same phenomenon; or to superficially dissimilar accounts of similar experiences. And this latter, generative property of language vindicates

Schutz's characterization of it, upon which Garfinkel seems to rely so heavily, as "the typifying medium par excellence". Moreover, this process of generativeness in linguistic utterance would seem to provide a viable hypothetical model of the process by which rules of everyday interaction are constituted—that is, in their expression. If the process of expression is itself ordered according to certain principles of operation of naturalistic human phenomena, then this might provide a basis for the adumbration of systematic general principles which would account in part for the common organizational properties of everyday social life. It might provide, in other words, part of the basis of a general and substantive sociology of everyday life.

Chomskyan linguistics does not postulate a theory to explain how knowledge originates in and/or for man, though it may be claimed on its behalf that, since the existence of common knowledge is established socially through language, it may offer important insights into the ways by which this is achieved. Similarly, Lévi-Strauss argues that it is necessary to take the origination of knowledge in man for granted—in direct contradiction to a contention of Durkheim that it is explicable in terms of the internalization of natural and societal organizational distinctions,[35] on the grounds that these would make the process entirely culture-specific. He claims instead, on the basis of a comparative study of the mythologies of a wide range and variety of different cultures, that the human mind (*l'esprit humain*) has a common structure in all its manifestations—that is, in the expressions of all men. The mythology of any culture is, according to Lévi-Strauss, what defines consciousness, sense and meaning for that culture— hence his claim that even his own work, which he insists is both empirical and scientific, may be as well treated correctly as myth (1969, pp. 5–14). Detailed cross-cultural analysis reveals, he claims, that all myths are directly comparable, not in thematic terms, but in the ways in which they are structured for expression: all have in common a triadic structure, composed of two terms in binary opposition plus a third, mediating term. Every corpus of knowledge, all sets of meaningful symbols, according to Lévi-Strauss, are organized in this way, from the selection of colours from the colour spectrum for English traffic signals, to the Hidatsa Indians' myth of how they first learnt to hunt eagles.[36] And the existence of properties in common to such a remarkable degree cross-culturally, leads Lévi-Strauss to make the claim that all men organize their knowledge in a common way. The location of these common properties is the unconscious, which he insists is a naturalistic, species property of mankind. Its knowledge is given culturally specific expression in language. But the common organizational pattern of that knowledge suggests that all men, regardless of cultural differences, organize their knowledge in a common way. Indeed, the triadic scheme is even endemic (as, if it is valid, it should be) in the binary opposition between the natural and cultural properties of man that Lévi-Strauss

[35] See Lévi-Strauss (1945, pp. 515–29). For a statement of his arguments on this issue, see Durkheim (1961, pp. 21–33, 479–96).

[36] Both examples may be found in Leach (1970, pp. 21–7, 118–19).

is postulating, with language, as the mediating phenomenon (itself a naturalistic property of man), giving for each man or group of men, culturally specific expression to the perceptions of mankind's naturalistic unconscious. Indeed, the role of language in Lévi-Strauss's theory of social consciousness is that of a generative mechanism of expression similar in many respects to Chomsky's rule-governed linguistics.[37]

Now there may be strong reasons for remarking that the works of Chomsky and of Lévi-Strauss are not relevant to ethnomethodologists. For example, where Chomsky is concerned primarily with the universal neurophysiological basis of language, ethnomethodologists study its specific practical, social applications and the indexicality of linguistic expressions that accompanies this application— apparently a totally different area of interest. Similarly, Lévi-Strauss seems to be concerned to reveal a universal structure of the human mind as a formal determinant of all knowledge—a proposition which is itself, in a special sense, "mythical" according to the terms of his own arguments; whereas ethno-methodologists examine instead the practical processes by which members organize and account for concrete, practical actions as the substantive knowledge of commonsense.[38] Moreover, neither Chomskyan linguistics, nor Lévi-Strauss's structuralism would, of course, solve any specific problems or achieve any self-allocated research tasks of ethnomethodology: to claim that they could do so would be to imply the reduction of it to either or both of them; and all that is being suggested is the possible relevance to ethnomethodology of their respective examinations of the generative properties of, in the one case, language and in the other, conceptualization.

The phenomenological and ethnomethodological critiques of traditional sociology have pointed clearly to the dualistic nature of social phenomena: that, although they are the products of actions performed by men—who are, in some respects which are related to their activities, natural phenomena—social phenomena are nevertheless *constructed and reflexive*. Since part of their dualism, albeit for sociology the less important part, is to be found in their naturalistic features, then it may be that some knowledge of these features of social phenomena (if it can be provided by the work of, for example, Chomsky or Lévi-Strauss) may provide ethnomethodologists studying them with some insights. A possibility which, however, in no way reduces the radical theoretical and substantive reorientation of sociological analysis that has already been commenced by ethnomethodologists, and which depends so much on Garfinkel's work.[39]

---

[37] This similarity is pointed out by Leach (1970, p. 120, n. 3).

[38] That the pursuit of a detailed, comparative examination of Garfinkel's ethnomethodology and Lévi-Strauss's structuralism would be productive, in spite of the contrasts drawn in the text of this paper, might suggest itself to the reader if he should compare Lévi-Strauss's account of his "science of mythology" (1969, pp. 1–32) with Garfinkel's account of ethnomethodology (1967, pp. 1–34).

[39] I am extremely grateful to my fellow contributors to this volume, who were colleagues at Goldsmiths' College, and to Aaron Cicourel, Harold Garfinkel, Peter McHugh, Maurice Roche and Roy Turner. All of them made very helpful comments on an earlier draft of this paper. Whatever shortcomings remain are entirely my own responsibility.

SUGGESTIONS FOR FURTHER READING

On Ethnomethodology/Phenomenology

GARFINKEL, H. (1967) *Studies in Ethnomethodology*, Prentice-Hall, Englewood Cliffs, New Jersey.

CICOUREL, A. V. (1964) *Method and Measurement in Sociology*, Free Press, New York.

CICOUREL, A. V. (1968) *The Social Organization of Juvenile Justice*, John Wiley, New York.

McHUGH, P. (1968) *Defining the Situation*, Bobbs-Merrill, New York.

DOUGLAS, J. D. (ed.) (1970) *Understanding Everyday Life*, Aldine, Chicago.

McKINNEY, J. C., TIRYAKIAN, E. A. (eds.) (1970) *Theoretical Sociology*, Appleton Century Crofts, New York.

WAGNER, H. R. (ed.) (1970) *Alfred Schutz on Phenomenology and Social Relations*, University of Chicago Press, Chicago.

On Chomskyan Transformational Linguistics

CHOMSKY, N. (1965) *Aspects of the Theory of Syntax*, MIT Press, Cambridge, Mass.

CHOMSKY, N. (1966) *Topics in the Theory of Generative Grammar*, Mouton, The Hague.

LYONS, J. (1970) *Chomsky*, Fontana/Collins, London.

On Structuralism

LEVI-STRAUSS, C. (1968) *Structural Anthropology*, Allen Lane, London.

LEVI-STRAUSS, C. (1969) *The Raw and the Cooked*, Harper and Row, New York.

LEACH, E. (1970) *Levi-Strauss*, Fontana/Collins, London.

LANE, M. (1970) *Structuralism—A Reader*, Jonathan Cape, London.

PIAGET, J. (1970) *Structuralism*, Basic Books, New York.

General Bibliography

H. Alpert (1965) "Durkheim's Functional Theory of Ritual", in **Nisbet** (1965).

C. Argyris (1964) *Integrating the Individual and the Organization*, John Wiley, New York.

A. L. Baldwin (1961) "The Parsonian Theory of Personality", in **Black** (1961, pp. 153–90).

Y. Bar-Hillel (1954) "Indexical Expressions", *Mind*, vol. 63, pp. 359–79.

H. E. Barnes (ed.) (1948) *An Introduction to the History of Sociology* University of Chicago Press, Chicago.

H. Becker (1963) *Outsiders*, Free Press, New York.

P. Berger (1966) *Invitation to Sociology*, Penguin, Harmondsworth.

P. Berger and **S. Pullberg** (1966) "Reification and the Sociological Critique of Consciousness", *New Left Review*, no. 35.

P. Berger and **T. Luckmann** (1966) *The Social Construction of Reality*, Doubleday, New York (1967, Allen Lane The Penguin Press, London).

E. Bittner (1965) "The Concept of Organization", *Social Research*, vol. 31.

M. Black (ed.) (1961) *The Social Theories of Talcott Parsons*, Prentice-Hall, Englewood Cliffs, New Jersey.

H. and **B. Blalock** (1968) *Methodology in Social Research*, McGraw-Hill, New York.

P. Blau (1968) "Theories of Organizations", in *International Encyclopaedia of the Social Sciences*, Collier-Macmillan, New York.

R. Blauner (1964) *Alienation and Freedom*, Chicago University Press, Chicago.

A. Blum (1970) "The Corpus of Knowledge as a Normative Order", in **McKinney and Tiryakian** (1970, pp. 319–36).

A. Blum and **P. McHugh** (1971) "The Social Ascription of Motives", *American Sociological Review*, vol. 36, no. 1.

H. Blumer (1962) "Society as Symbolic Interaction", in **Rose** (1962).

H. Blumer (1967) "Sociological Analysis and the Variable", in **Manis and Meltzer** (1967).

H. Blumer (1969) *Symbolic Interactionism*, Prentice-Hall, Englewood Cliffs, New Jersey.

C. Bryant (1970) "In Defence of Sociology", *British Journal of Sociology*, vol. 21, no. 1.

S. Bruyn (1966) *The Human Perspective in Sociology*, Prentice-Hall, Englewood Cliffs, New Jersey.

W. Buckley (1967) *Sociology and Modern Systems Theory*, Prentice-Hall, Englewood Cliffs, New Jersey.

T. Burns (1961) "Micropolitics: Mechanisms of Institutional Change", *Administrative Science Quarterly*, vol. 6, no. 3.

W. Carson and **P. E. Wiles** (eds) (1971) *Crime and Delinquency in Britain*, Martin Robertson, London.

N. Chomsky (1957) *Syntactic Structures*, Mouton, The Hague.

N. **Chomsky** (1964) *Current Issues in Linguistic Theory*, Mouton, The Hague.

N. **Chomsky** (1965) *Aspects of the Theory of Syntax*, The M.I.T. Press, Cambridge, Mass.

N. **Chomsky** (1966a) *Topics in the Theory of Generative Grammar*, Mouton, The Hague.

N. **Chomsky** (1966b) *Cartesian Linguistics*, Harper & Row, New York.

N. **Chomsky** (1969) *American Power and The New Mandarins*, Penguin, Harmondsworth.

A. **Cicourel** (1964) *Method and Measurement in Sociology*, Free Press, New York.

A. **Cicourel** (1967) "Fertility, Family Planning and the Organization of Family Life", *Journal of Social Issues*, vol. 23, no. 4.

A. **Cicourel** (1968) *The Social Organization of Juvenile Justice*, John Wiley, New York.

A. **Cicourel** (1969) *Generative Semantics and The Structure of Social Interaction*, International Days of Sociolinguistics, Rome.

A. **Cicourel** (1970a) *The Negotiation of Status and Role*, in **Dreitzel** (1970).

A. **Cicourel** (1970b) "The Acquisition of Social Structure", in **J. Douglas** (1970b, pp. 136–68).

A. **Cicourel** (forthcoming) "Ethnomethodology", in **T. A. Sebeok** (forthcoming).

A. **Cicourel** and **J. Kitsuse** (1963a) *The Educational Decision-Makers*, Bobbs-Merrill, Indianapolis.

A. **Cicourel** and **J. Kitsuse** (1963b) "A Note on the Official Uses of Statistics", *Social Problems*, vol. 11.

A. **Cohen** (1966) *Deviance and Control*, Prentice-Hall, Englewood Cliffs, New Jersey.

P. **Cohen** (1968) *Modern Social Theory*, Heinemann, London.

J. S. **Coleman** (1968) *American Sociological Review*, vol. 33, no. 1, pp. 126–30.

D. **Cressey** and **D. Ward** (eds) (1969) *Delinquency, Crime and Social Process*, Harper & Row, New York.

M. **Dalton** (1959) *Men Who Manage*, John Wiley, New York.

J. **Douglas** (1967) *The Social Meanings of Suicide*, Princeton University Press, Princeton, New Jersey.

J. **Douglas** (1970a) "Deviance and Order in a Pluralistic Society" in **McKinney and Tiryakian** (1970, pp. 367–402).

J. **Douglas** (ed.) (1970b) *Understanding Everyday Life*, Aldine, Chicago (1971, Routledge & Kegan Paul, London).

J. W. B. **Douglas** (1969) *The Home and the School*, Penguin, Harmondsworth.

M. **Douglas** (1966) *Purity and Danger*, Routledge & Kegan Paul, London.

H. P. **Dreitzel** (ed.) (1970) *Recent Sociology No. 2*, Macmillan, New York.

É. **Durkheim** (1938) *The Rules of Sociological Method*, Chicago University Press, Chicago.

É. **Durkheim** (1952) *Suicide*, Routledge & Kegan Paul, London.

É. **Durkheim** (1956) *Education and Sociology*, Free Press, New York.

É. **Durkheim** (1961) *Moral Education*, Free Press, New York.

E. **Durkheim** (1961) *The Elementary Forms of Religious Life*, Collier Books, New York.

É. **Durkheim** and **M. Mauss** (1967) *Primitive Classification*, Chicago University Press, Chicago.

K. **Erikson** (1966) *Wayward Puritans*, John Wiley, New York.

M. **Farber** (1943) *The Foundations of Phenomenology*, State University of New York Press, Albany.

M. **Farber** (1966) *The Aims of Phenomenology*, Harper & Row, New York.

L. **Feuer** (ed.) (1969) *Karl Marx and Friedrich Engels: Basic Writings on Politics and Social Philosophy*, Anchor Doubleday, New York.

C. Frake (1966) "The Diagnosis of Disease Among The Subanun of Mindanao", in **Hymes** (1966).

H. Garfinkel (1952) "The Perception of the Other: A Study in Social Order". Unpublished doctoral dissertation, Harvard University.

H. Garfinkel (1967) *Studies in Ethnomethodology*, Prentice-Hall, Englewood Cliffs, New Jersey.

H. Garfinkel and **H. Sacks** (1970) "On Formal Structures of Practical Actions", in **McKinney** and **Tiryakian** (1970, pp. 337–66).

J. Galtung (1967) *Theory and Methods of Social Research*, Allen & Unwin, London.

B. Glaser and **A. Strauss** (1968) *The Discovery of Grounded Theory*, Weidenfeld & Nicolson, London.

E. Goffman (1968) *Asylums*, Penguin, Harmondsworth.

W. J. Goode (1963) *The Family and World Revolution*, Free Press, New York.

W. J. Goode and **P. Hatt** (1952) *Methods in Social Research*, McGraw-Hill, New York.

W. Goodenough (1966) "Cultural Anthropology and Linguistics", in **Hymes** (1966).

C. Gordon and **K. J. Gergen** (eds) (1968) *The Self in Social Interaction: Volume I. Classic and Contemporary Perspectives*, Wiley, New York.

D. A. Goslin (ed.) *Handbook of Socialization Theory and Research*, Rand McNally, New York.

A. Gouldner (1959) "Reciprocity and Autonomy in Functional Theory", in **Gross** (1959, pp. 241–70).

A. Gouldner (1970) *The Coming Crisis of Western Sociology*, Basic Books, New York.

A. Gouldner and **S. M. Miller** (eds) (1965) *Applied Sociology*, Free Press, New York.

L. Gross (ed.) (1959) *Symposium on Sociological Theory*, Harper & Row, New York.

G. Gurvitch and **W. E. Moore** (eds) (1945) *Twentieth Century Sociology*, Philosophical Library, New York.

G. Hawthorne (1968) "Explaining Human Fertility", *Sociology*, vol. II, no. 1 ; *Sociology of Fertility*, Collier-Macmillan, London.

O. Helmer and **N. Rescher** (1958) "On the Epistemology of The Exact Sciences", mimeographed.

C. F. Hockett (1968) *The State of the Art*, Monton, The Hague.

G. Homans (1961) *Social Behaviour*, Routledge & Kegan Paul, London.

E. Husserl (1965) *Phenomenology and the Crisis of Philosophy*, Harper Torchbooks, New York.

E. Husserl (1966) *The Phenomenology of Internal Time-consciousness*, Indiana University Press, Bloomington.

E. Husserl (1967) *Ideas*, Allen & Unwin, London.

E. Husserl (1970) *Cartesian Meditations*, Nijhoff, The Hague.

D. Hymes (ed..) (1966) *Language in Culture and Society*, Harper & Row, New York.

A. Inkeles (1969) "Social Structure and Socialization", in **Goslin** (1969).

E. Kaelin (1962) *An Existentialist Aesthetic*, University of Wisconsin.

A. Kaplan (1946) "Definition and Specification of Meaning", *Journal of Philosophy*, vol. 43. no. 11, p. 281.

A. Kaplan (1964) *The Conduct of Inquiry*, Chandler, San Francisco.

S. Kobrin (1959) "The Chicago Area Project", *Annals of the American Academy of Political & Social Science*, March 1959.

J. Kockelmans (ed.) (1967) *Phenomenology*, Anchor, New York.

T. Kuhn (1970a) *The Structure of Scientific Revolution*, Chicago University Press, Chicago.

T. Kuhn (1970b) "Logic of Discovery or Psychology of Research?" in **Lakatos** and **Musgrave** (1970).

R. Kwant (1967) "Merleau-Ponty and Phenomenology", in **Kockelmans** (1967).

Lakatos and **Musgrave** (eds) (1970) *Criticism and the Growth of Knowledge*, Cambridge University Press, London.

E. Leach (1964) "Anthropological Aspects of Language: Animal Categories and Verbal Abuse", in **Lenneberg** (1964).

E. Leach (1970) *Lévi-Strauss*, Collins, London.

H. Lefebvre (1970) *The Sociology of Marx*, Allen Lane, London.

E. Lemert (1967) *Human Deviance, Social Problems, and Social Control*, Prentice-Hall, Englewood Cliffs, New Jersey.

E. Lenneberg (ed.) (1964) *New Directions in the Study of Language*, The M.I.T. Press, Cambridge, Mass.

C. Lévi-Strauss (1945) "French Sociology", in **Garvitch und Moore** (1945, pp. 515–29).

C. Lévi-Strauss (1966) *The Savage Mind*, Weidenfeld & Nicolson, London.

C. Lévi-Strauss (1968) *Structural Anthropology*, Allen Lane, The Penguin Press, London.

C. Lévi-Strauss (1969) *The Raw and The Cooked*, Harper & Row, New York (1970, Jonathan Cape, London).

M. J. Levy (1952) *The Structure of Society*, Chicago University Press, Chicago.

D. Lockwood (1964) "Social Integration and System Integration", in **Zollschan and Hirsch** (1964, pp. 244–57).

G. Lundberg (1964) *Foundations of Sociology*, revised edition, David McKays, New York.

G. A. Lundberg, C. C. Shrag and **O. N. Larsen** (1954) *Sociology*, Harper & Row, New York.

J. Lyons (1970) *Chomsky*, Collins, London.

J. Manis and **B. Meltzer** (eds) (1967) *Symbolic Interaction*, Allyn & Bacon, New York.

H. Mannheim and **L. Wilkins** (1956) *Prediction Methods in Relation to Borstal Training*.

P. Marris and **M. Rein** (1967) *Dilemmas of Social Reform*, Routledge & Kegan Paul, London.

D. Matza (1969) *Becoming Deviant*, Prentice-Hall, Englewood Cliffs, New Jersey.

G. J. McCall and **J. L. Simmons** (1969) *Issues in Participant-Observation*, Addison-Wesley, Reading, Mass.

P. McHugh (1968) *Defining the Situation*, Bobbs-Merrill, Indianapolis.

P. McHugh (1970) "A Commonsense Definition of Deviance", in **Dreitzel** (1970).

R. M. McIver (1942) *Social Causation*, Ginn, New York.

J. McKinney and **E. Tiryakian** (eds) (1970) *Theoretical Sociology*, Appleton-Century-Crofts, New York.

G. H. Mead (1934) *Mind, Self and Society*, Chicago University Press, Chicago.

G. H. Mead (1959) *The Philosophy of the Present*, Open Court, Illinois.

G. H. Mead (1964) *Selected Writings*, Bobbs-Merrill, Indianapolis.

P. Medawar (1969) "Induction and Intuition in Scientific Thought", *American Philosophical Society*, Philadelphia.

M. Merleau-Ponty (1962) *The Phenomenology of Perception*, Routledge & Kegan Paul, London.

M. Merleau-Ponty (1964a) *Signs*, Northwestern University Press, Chicago.

M. Merleau-Ponty (1964b) *The Primacy of Perception*, Northwestern University Press, Chicago.

M. Merleau-Ponty (1967) "What is Phenomenology?" in **Kockelmans** (1967).

R. K. Merton (1957) *Social Theory and Social Structure*, Free Press, New York.

W. B. Miller (1962) "The Impact of a 'Total-Community' Delinquency Control Project", *Social Problems*, vol. 10, no. 2.

C. W. Mills (1943) "The Professional Ideology of Social Pathologists", *American Journal of Sociology*, vol. 49, no. 2, p. 165.

C. W. Mills (1959) *The Sociological Imagination*, Oxford University Press.

M. Natanson (1965) "On Alfred Schutz's Phenomenology", *Social Research*, vol. 32.

R. Nisbet (ed.) (1965) *Émile Durkheim*, Prentice-Hall, New Jersey.

E. Northrop (1947) *The Logic of the Sciences and Humanities*, Macmillan, New York.

T. Parsons (1937) *The Structure of Social Action*, Free Press, New York.

T. Parsons (1951) *The Social System*, Free Press, New York.

T. Parsons (1964a) *Social Structure and Personality*, Free Press, New York.

T. Parsons (1964b) "Durkheim's Contribution to the Theory of Integration of Social Systems", in **Wolff** (1964).

T. Parsons (1964c) "Evolutionary Universals in Society", *American Sociological Review*, vol. 29, no. 3, pp. 339–57.

T. Parsons (1966) *Societies: Evolutionary and Comparative Perspectives*, Prentice-Hall, Englewood Cliffs, New Jersey.

T. Parsons and **E. Shils** (1951) *Towards a General Theory of Action*, Free Press, New York.

T. Parsons et al. (1961) *Theories of Society*, Free Press, New York.

M. Phillipson (1971a) "Juvenile Delinquency and the School", in **Carson and Wiles** (1971).

M. Phillipson (1971b) *Sociological Aspects of Crime and Delinquency*, Routledge & Kegan Paul, London.

M. Phillipson and **M. Roche** (1971) "Phenomenological Sociology and the Study of Deviance", unpublished paper given at the B.S.A. Conference, Spring 1971.

E. Pivcevic (1970) *Husserl and Phenomenology*, Hutchinson, London.

M. Pollner (1970) *On The Foundations of Mundane Reasoning*, unpublished Ph.D. dissertation, University of California, Santa Barbara.

K. Popper (1959) *The Logic of Scientific Discovery*, Routledge & Kegan Paul, London.

K. Popper (1962) *Conjectures and Refutations*, Routledge & Kegan Paul, London.

G. Psathas (1968) "Ethnomethods and Phenomenology", *Social Research*, vol. 35, no. 3.

A. Rabil (1967) *Merleau-Ponty: Existentialist of the Social World*, Columbia University Press.

J. Rex (1961) *Key Problems of Sociological Theory*, Routledge & Kegan Paul, London.

C. Rogers (1965) "Towards a Science of the Person", in **Wann** (1965).

A. Rose (ed.) (1962) *Human Behaviour and Social Processes*, Routledge & Kegan Paul, London.

E. Rubington and **M. Weinberg** (eds.) (1968) *Deviance: An Interactionist Perspective*. Macmillan, New York.

R. S. Rudner (1966) *Philosophy of Social Science*, Prentice-Hall, Englewood Cliffs, New Jersey.

J. P. Sartre (1969) *Being and Nothingness*, Washington Square Press, New York.

T. Schroyer (1970) "Towards a Critical Theory for Advanced Industrial Society", in **Dreitzel** (1970).

A. Schutz (1962, 1964, 1966) *Collected Papers*, vols. 1–3, Nijhoff, The Hague.

A. Schutz (1967a) *The Phenomenology of the Social World*, Northwestern University Press, Chicago.

A. Schutz (1967b) "Phenomenology and the Social Sciences", in **Kockelmans** (1967).

A. Schutz (1968) "On Multiple Realities", in **Gordon and Gergen** (1968).

A. Schutz (1970) *Reflections on The Problem of Relevance*, Yale University Press, New Haven.

M. Scott (1968) *The Racing Game*, Aldine, Chicago.

M. Scott and **M. Lyman** (1968) "Accounts", *American Sociological Review*, vol. 33.

T. Sebeok (ed.) (forthcoming) *Current Trends in Linguistics, vol. 12*, Mouton, The Hague.

C. Selltiz, M. Jahoda, M. Deutsch and **S. Cook** (1965) *Research Methods in Social Relations*, Methuen, London.

D. Silverman (1970) *The Theory of Organizations*, Heinemann, London.

D. Silverman (forthcoming) "Accounts of Organizations: Organizational Structures and the Accounting Process", in **J. McKinlay** (ed.) *Processing People—Case Studies in Organization Behavior*, Holt, Rinehart and Winston, New York.

D. Silverman and **J. Jones** (forthcoming) "Getting In: The Managed Accomplishment of 'Correct' Selection Outcomes" in J. Child (ed.), *Man and Organization: The Search for Explanation and Social Relevance* (forthcoming), Allen and Unwin, London.

L. Sklair (1970) "The Fate of 'The Functional Prerequisites' in Parsonian Sociology", *British Journal of Sociology*, vol. 21, no. 1, pp. 30–42.

P. Sorokin (1956) *Fads and Foibles in Modern Sociology*, Free Press, New York.

H. Spiegelberg (1969) *The Phenomenological Movement*, vols. 1 and 2, Nijhoff, The Hague.

S. Strasser (1967) "Phenomenology and the Human Sciences", in **Kockelmans** (1967).

D. Sudnow (1968a) *Passing On*, Prentice-Hall, Englewood Cliffs, New Jersey.

D. Sudnow (1968b) "Normal Crimes", in **Rubington and Weinberg** (1968).

D. Sudnow (ed.) (forthcoming) *Papers in Interaction*, Free Press, New York.

A. Sutter (1969) "Worlds of Drug Use and The Street Scene", in **Cressey and Ward** (1969).

A. Turner and **P. Lawrence** (1965) *Industrial Jobs and the Worker*, Harvard University Press, Cambridge, Mass.

R. Turner (1970) "Words, Utterances, and Activities", in **J. Douglas** (1970b, pp. 169–87).

R. Turner (forthcoming) "Some Formal Properties of Therapy Talk", in **Sudnow** (forthcoming).

H. Wagner (1964) "The Displacement of Scope in Sociological Theory", *American Journal of Sociology*, vol. 70.

H. Wagner (ed.) (1971) *Alfred Schutz on Phenomenology and Social Relations*, Chicago University Press, Chicago.

A. F. C. Wallace (1968) *American Sociological Review*, vol. 33, no. 1, pp. 124–6.

W. L. Wallace (1969) *Sociological Theory*, Heinemann, London.

T. W. Wann (ed.) (1965) *Behaviourism and Phenomenology*, Chicago University Press, Chicago.

M. Weber (1949) *The Methodology of the Social Sciences*, Free Press, New York.

M. Weber (1964) *The Theory of Social and Economic Organization*, Free Press, New York.

W. F. Whyte (1943) "A Slum Sex Code", *American Journal of Sociology*, vol. 49.

W. F. Whyte (1966) *Street Corner Society*, Chicago University Press, Chicago.

G. Winter (1966) *Elements for a Social Ethic*, Macmillan, New York.

K. Wolff (ed.) (1964) *Essays on Sociology and Philosophy by Émile Durkheim et al*, Harper & Row, New York.

K. Wolff (1964) *Social Structure and Personality*, Free Press, New York.

P. Worsley (1956) "Émile Durkheim's Theory of Knowledge", *Sociological Review*, vol. 4, no. 1.

D. Wrong (1961) "The Oversocialized Conception of Man in Modern Sociology" *American Sociological Review*, vol. 26.

H. Zetterberg (1962) *Social Theory and Social Practice*, Bedminster, New York.

D. **Zimmerman** and **M. Pollner** (1971) "The Everyday World as a Phenomenon", in **Douglas** (ed.) (1971), op. cit 80–103.

D. **Zimmerman** (1971) "Record-keeping and the Intake Process in a Public Welfare Organization", in **S. Wheeler** (ed.) *On Record: Files and Dossiers in American Life*, Russell Sage Foundation, New York.

G. **Zollschan** and **W. Hirsch** (eds) (1964) *Explorations in Social Change*, Routledge & Kegan Paul, London.

SUBJECT INDEX

AUTHOR INDEX